1,000,000 Books

are available to read at

Forgotten Books

www.ForgottenBooks.com

Read online
Download PDF
Purchase in print

ISBN 978-0-259-27613-5
PIBN 10811981

This book is a reproduction of an important historical work. Forgotten Books uses state-of-the-art technology to digitally reconstruct the work, preserving the original format whilst repairing imperfections present in the aged copy. In rare cases, an imperfection in the original, such as a blemish or missing page, may be replicated in our edition. We do, however, repair the vast majority of imperfections successfully; any imperfections that remain are intentionally left to preserve the state of such historical works.

Forgotten Books is a registered trademark of FB &c Ltd.
Copyright © 2018 FB &c Ltd.
FB &c Ltd, Dalton House, 60 Windsor Avenue, London, SW19 2RR.
Company number 08720141. Registered in England and Wales.

For support please visit www.forgottenbooks.com

1 MONTH OF FREE READING

at

www.ForgottenBooks.com

By purchasing this book you are eligible for one month membership to ForgottenBooks.com, giving you unlimited access to our entire collection of over 1,000,000 titles via our web site and mobile apps.

To claim your free month visit:

www.forgottenbooks.com/free811981

* Offer is valid for 45 days from date of purchase. Terms and conditions apply.

English
Français
Deutsche
Italiano
Español
Português

www.forgottenbooks.com

Mythology Photography **Fiction**
Fishing Christianity **Art** Cooking
Essays Buddhism Freemasonry
Medicine **Biology** Music **Ancient Egypt** Evolution Carpentry Physics
Dance Geology **Mathematics** Fitness
Shakespeare **Folklore** Yoga Marketing
Confidence Immortality Biographies
Poetry **Psychology** Witchcraft
Electronics Chemistry History **Law**
Accounting **Philosophy** Anthropology
Alchemy Drama Quantum Mechanics
Atheism Sexual Health **Ancient History**
Entrepreneurship Languages Sport
Paleontology Needlework Islam
Metaphysics Investment Archaeology
Parenting Statistics Criminology
Motivational

LETTERS
TO
A YOUNG LADY,

IN WHICH

THE DUTIES AND CHARACTER OF WOMEN
ARE CONSIDERED,

CHIEFLY WITH

A REFERENCE TO PREVAILING OPINIONS.

BY MRS. WEST,

AUTHOR OF LETTERS TO A YOUNG MAN, &c.

Favour is deceitful, and beauty is vain; but a woman that fearest the Lord, she shall be praised.
Prov. xxxi. 30.

IN THREE VOLUMES.

VOL. I.

THE THIRD EDITION.

LONDON:
PRINTED FOR LONGMAN, HURST, REES, AND ORME,
PATERNOSTER-ROW.

1806.

T. Bensley, Printer,
Bolt Court, Fleet Street, London.

THESE LETTERS,

ON THE DUTIES AND CHARACTER OF WOMEN,

ARE,

(BY PERMISSION)

APPROPRIATELY AND SUBMISSIVELY

INSCRIBED TO

The Queen's Most Excellent Majesty;

WHOSE EXALTED CHARACTER
ENFORCES, BY AN EXAMPLE MORE POWERFUL
THAN PRECEPT,
THE STRICT PERFORMANCE
OF EVERY DOMESTIC, MORAL, AND
RELIGIOUS DUTY.
WITH THE DEEPEST SENSE OF THE HONOUR OF
THIS ILLUSTRIOUS PATRONAGE,
THE AUTHOR SUBSCRIBES HERSELF
HER MAJESTY'S
MOST DUTIFUL,
AND MOST GRATEFULLY
DEVOTED SERVANT,

JANE WEST.

PREFATORY ADDRESS.

Since the publication of the much favoured "Letters" referred to in the title-page, the author has been repeatedly advised to make the character and duties of her own sex the subject of a separate work, similar, and in some respects supplementary, to the former; yet still preserving those peculiar features which would render it more interesting and beneficial to women. It was urged on the one hand, that the late publication was in some parts adapted to females. This was admitted; but it was further observed, that, though all rational creatures are circumscribed within one general pale of moral and religious obligation, the peculiar path of each sex is marked by those nice shades of appropriation, which only an all-wise Being, intent on the general benefit of the whole human race, could impose: and this remark was exemplified by shewing, that any violation of this prescribed decorum exposed the offender to a degree of opprobrium by no means equal to the offence. To the remark, that of late women had been peculiarly fortunate in having had a number of admirable advisers, it was answered, that they had also been misled by many false lights, and were more exposed than at any former period to the artifices of seducers; who, intent to poison the minds of the unwary, had contrived to introduce their dangerous notions on manners, morals, and religion, into every

species

species of composition, and all forms of society; the sentiments and regulations of which had lately, as far as concerns women, undergone an alarming change. And with regard to the many really valuable moralists who have attempted to stem this torrent, the observation which the author formerly made respecting young men was equally true of women. The *extremes* of society were chiefly attended to; and if we judged by the style generally used by the instructor of the fair sex, we should think that the whole female world was divided into "high-lived company" and paupers*; that numerous and important body the middle classes of society, whose duties are most complicated, and consequently most difficult, being generally over-

* This observation must be taken with exceptions; among which, Dr. Gisborne's Tract on the Duties of Women holds a pre-eminent rank.

looked; and yet the change of manners and pursuits among these are so marked, that the most superficial observers must be alarmed at the prospect of what it portends. Something too was said of the advantage, as well as of the propriety, of intrusting female practitioners with the preparation of nostrums for the moral diseases of their own sisterhood; and a hint was given, that it would be patriotic to endeavour to restore the reputation of the fair college of pharmacopolists, which has been grievously tarnished by the practice of those quacks who had aggravated the diseases which they pretended to cure by stimulants or anodynes, till in many cases they were become too obstinate for any remedy. It was urged too, that a popular author was in conscience bound to employ the (perhaps) *transient* period of public approbation

approbation in using her most strenuous endeavour to repay the favour of generous protection, by endeavouring to give that turn to the taste and morals of society which would be most beneficial to its temporal and eternal interests. This solemn consideration, enforced by the dying injunctions of a much-respected friend, who, near the close of his valuable life, addressed an awful charge to the author, that she should "Pursue the course in which she then trod, and let all her future works tend not only to moral but religious edification," has determined her to conquer the timid, or perhaps prudential motives, which advised a timely retreat from the field of literature, before the sure indications of neglect should prevent her from doing so with honour. The present work is the consequence of this recovered bravery.

Aware that humble views are best suited to her abilities, she does not attempt to compose a correct and elaborate system of morals; nor will she examine the evidences and doctrines of religion with logical minuteness: able writers have preceded her in these departments. Her aim is, to present readers of her own sex, and station, with some admonitory reflections on those points which appeared to her of superior importance, either from their having been omitted or slightly discussed by other writers, or from the prevailing temper of the times requiring them to be recalled to general attention, and, if possible, placed in a novel, and therefore more attractive, point of view. To arrest the attention of those who are terrified by the uniform austerity of a melacholy censor, the sombre hue of precept will be relieved by such ornaments

ornaments as can be adopted without injury to the main design. Perhaps this last intimation is but a specious apology for a manner of writing, at first natural, and now so confirmed by habit, that a determination to avoid it would certainly give a disgusting stiffness to the following lucubrations.

The author is aware that there is a considerable resemblance between this and her preceding work on a similar subject. This was unavoidable, unless she had omitted what she judged the most important part of her undertaking, or referred her present readers to another publication: in either case, the present would be incomplete. She has endeavoured to give all the variety in her power, by varying her expressions, and the order of her reflections; by throwing in such new remarks as recent occurrences, or her own subsequent

quent reading, have supplied; by slightly passing over what she there attempted to explain in detail; and by supplying what an attentive review taught her to think deficient in her former work.

As these admonitions are chiefly designed for readers whose time is occupied in pursuits and duties which compel them to take up a book rather as an improving relaxation than a serious study, the epistolary style was adopted, as best suited to this purpose. It is, however, acknowledged, that these letters were *originally written* for the purpose of publication, although they are addressed to a young lady, the daughter of the dearest friend of the author's early life. By kindly permitting her name to be the vehicle for these reflections, Miss M—— has, in a considerable degree, beguiled the

fatigue

conveyed to the public, which only the sweetness of Miss M——'s disposition could excuse, or the unequivocal merit of her character counteract. Within the respectable circle which bounds her fame and her duties, it is well known, that, so far from wanting the advice of others, she teaches all who observe her conduct, by that noblest and most impressive mode of instruction, *example.*

LETTERS,

&c. &c. &c.

LETTER I.

Introductory Sketch of the Design.

MY DEAR MISS M ——,

TEN years have elapsed since the inevitable consequences of an excruciating and lingering decay deprived you of a mother, whose counsels and example would have been your best guide to all that was amiable and praise-worthy in your sex. It is not for us misjudging mortals, whose views are bounded by the narrow horizon of seventy years, to question the decrees of of that infinite Being, whose eye pervades the measureless ages of eternity; nor can we say how far the relations and advantages of that endless existence, on which Christianity allows us to believe the glorified spirit of your pious parent has now entered, depended upon the brief termination of her mortal course. Of this we are sure, that the merciful Father of the human race sees it expedient to perfect his creatures by sufferings, even as a child in a well-regulated family is trained to virtue and knowledge, by a system of discipline and restraint, of which it does not then discern the advantage. Thus, my dear Miss M——, your mother was doomed to pass through a rugged and painful passage in her early journey to eternity; and thus also, with respect to yourself, the young scion was left exposed just at that period when it seemed

seemed most to require shelter from the external violence of stormy winds, and from those diseases which arise from premature exposure, and often destroy the most promising vegetation.

 The same stroke which deprived you of a mother, separated me from the friend whom I best loved; whose partial approbation first stimulated me to break through opposing difficulties, and to bestow all the cultivation on my passion for literature which my situation in life allowed. Encouraged by her praises, guided by her taste, and (what was infinitely more important to me) corrected and improved in my moral judgment by the silent eloquence of her blameless manners, I started in the career of authorship, with the most sanguine expectations of full and immediate success. The premonitory cautions which she thought it right to bestow,

stow, were too gentle to repress the warm hopes of youthful inexperience; and it was only the successive disappointment of my first attempts which taught me that it was easier to please the candid and judicious, than to propitiate the multitude, when unsanctioned by the patronage of a mighty name, and unrecommended by a blameable sacrifice to false principle.

I shall not forget the tender solicitude with which my late friend exerted herself to obviate the effects of those mortifications of which her prudence had in vain forewarned me, and from which her energetic exertions could not protect an unknown or inexperienced writer. To the happy influence of her kindness, and her counsels, I may attribute my escape from the morbid pressure of despondency, and my still happier preservation from the

the torrent of false theories and disorganizing principles which was at that time poured into this country. As the effects of these subverting doctrines had not then appeared; and as, like their author Satan, they took the disguise of angels of light; a half-cultivated romantic mind, ignorant of men and manners, and enthusiastically attached to those visions of independence, philanthropy, energy, and perfection, which are so dear to the votaries of the muses, might have been seduced by the fair semblance in which these apostles of anarchy were then enveloped; especially as they affected respect for the palladium of religion. The mature and enlightened understanding of your excellent mother saw through the imposture, and taught her credulous friend to distinguish between pretences to superior virtue, and the

artless

artless unboastful reality. You, doubtless, recollect the apprehensions which she felt, lest the spirit of insubordination and discontent, though discountenanced by all wise and worthy Britons, should be diffused among the lower orders, who, being more inclined to feel the disadvantages of ignorance, than to acknowledge the comforts of obedience, would in consequence be betrayed to renounce the simple path in which their forefathers walked, and to follow those new lights which pretended to direct them to the tree of knowledge. She lived to see her apprehensions verified, nor has the evil yet ceased to work: may the Almighty, in his mercy, limit its progress!

Such were the obligations that I owed to your mother; and to which must be superadded, all the common offices of generous, active, affectionate friendship:

friendship: no wonder, then, that the lapse of years has not diminished my attachment to her memory. The solemn scenes which preceded her dissolution afforded an instructive example, to all around her, of the possibility of discharging the hard duty of consecrating affliction; and they taught us to mingle with our tears for her loss, the consolations which arise from a conviction of her beatitude.

Among the injunctions that I received from her dying lips, there is one to which I shall now more particularly refer: I mean her earnest desire that I would "write to *you*, and remind *you* of *our* friendship." My dear young friend, our correspondence has not suffered any long interruption since that period; yet I often feel as if I had not, in my private addresses to you, fully accomplished the wishes of your mother.

ther. It is a most inexpressible satisfaction to me, to perceive that you attain the age of majority with every fair promise of being the true representative of the revered deceased; nor can I point out any part of your conduct which my knowledge of her sentiments persuades me she would have wished to be altered. Yet I feel such an exquisite satisfaction in the idea of being employed in (I must not say her service, but in) shewing my attachment to what she best loved, that I cannot refrain from asking your permission to address to you some counsels and admonitions, which many young women of your age would find but too necessary in these portentous times. That "mystery of iniquity," whose course is marked on the continent of Europe by subverted empires, and desolated realms, has on this island been

at

at present busy in effecting those moral revolutions which are the forerunners of political ones. The manly sense and independent pride of Britons have (with few exceptions) nobly disdained to adopt the *political* example of a people to whom they have been accustomed to give laws in the field of arms; but it is much to be feared, that they have not with equal wariness resisted the blandishments of their vicious example, or braced up their minds to repel the consequences which result from luxury, dissipation, and every varied form of pleasurable indulgence. By these assailants the weaker sex are more particularly assaulted. Under the covert of continual amusement,—pride, levity, selfishness, disregard of punctuality, extravagance, and religious indifference, have stolen unsuspected upon our unguarded hearts,

hearts, and often have so far alienated us, as to occasion a total neglect of God's holy word and commandments. In this state, the mind is apt to weigh whatever is submitted to its judgment, rather by the loose scale of present expediency and convenience, than by the immutable standard of right, or the certain expectations of future consequences. Such is the process by which many are led to commit a crime, rather than make a breach in their politeness, and to injure their probity sooner than renounce an indulgence; and thus they lose, in the transient gratifications of the animal senses, the noblest distinctions and surest rewards of their intellectual being. But let us descend from general declamation, to particular instances of the change of public opinion as it relates to our sex.

The society, which young women who

who are devoted to a life of fashionable amusement frequently meet, creates a species of danger which in the present times is most truly alarming. The unblushing effrontery with which women of doubtful or lost character obtrude themselves upon public notice, is a marked characteristic of the age we live in, that was unknown to our ancestors (except, perhaps, in one profligate reign), and strongly demonstrative that the outposts of female honour are given up. What can more tend to debase the purity of virtue, and to enfeeble the stability of principle, than to find that a notorious courtezan retains all the distinctions due to unspotted chastity; nay, even to see her pointed out as a most engaging creature, with a truly benevolent heart; while all retrospect of her flagitious conduct is prevented, by the observation, that we have nothing to do with people's private character. Can we wonder, that, since the age is become so liberal, profligacy should not feel the necessity of being *guarded* in its transgressions?

If we turn from these flagrant violations of divine and human laws, which even the grossest depravity cannot justify, nor the most subtle sophistry palliate; may we not, in the licensed freedom of modern manners, trace many deviations from rectitude and delicacy? To what description of conduct must we refer that marked attention which married women permit from fashionable libertines? Is it compatible with any of the peculiar traits of the matronly character, prudence, decorum, and consistency? What is that mode of dress which they sanction by their example, the expense to which they

they devote their fortunes, or the amusements to which they sacrifice their time? A young woman who now adventures into the labyrinth of life, has more to fear from the seniors of her own sex, than from male artifices. The Lovelaces and Pollexfens have not indeed totally disappeared from the circle of fashion; but it is not youthful beauty and virgin innocence that *now* attract their pursuit. While the sprightly spinster waits till the coquetish wife dismisses her wearied Cecisbeo, to yawn out an unmeaning compliment to the immature attractions of nineteen, she must console her chagrin by resolving to take the first offer that she can meet with, provided the creature possesses the requisites of wealth and fashion to enable her to revenge her present wrongs on the *past* generation of beauties, and in her turn to triumph over the *succeeding*.

This reflection leads me to that passion for genteel appearance in dress, equipage, furniture, and every mode of expense, which is such a strong feature in the aspect of this luxurious age; and which really descends to every rank, even to those on whom poverty has stamped the marks of wretchedness. To outshine your equal in taste and smartness, is a rule which every understanding can comprehend, and which, requiring no great exertions of the mental or moral powers, becomes a marketable medium of fluctuating value in the commerce of life. Though the effects of this absurd propensity are most severely felt in the lower orders, its mischiefs are not unknown in those circles from which it was first derived. We females have had many monitors on this (to us) important topic; yet as the evil visibly gains ground, and even threatens to subvert all distinctions in society, all attempts to place in a clear point of view the absurdity of endeavouring to impose upon the world, by practising a cheat too familiar to deceive an idiot, deserve commendation.

Nor are the evils consequent on a life of dissipation the only dangers that young ladies may now dread. In retirement, they are haunted by another species of enemies, no less alarming to their understandings, to their morals, and to their repose. The species of reading, prepared to relieve the toils of dissipation, is faithful to its interests, and is either intended to mislead or to gratify. Under the former description may be ranked all those systems of ethics, and treatises on education, which are founded on the false doctrine of human perfectibility, and consequently reject the necessity of divine revelation and supernatural agency. Many elementary works on the sciences come under this description; and by these the young student may learn that she is a free independent being, endowed with energies which she may exert at will, and restrained by no considerations but those which her own judgment may think it *expedient* to obey. She is taught, that the nature she inherits was originally perfect; that its present disordered state did not arise from an hereditary taint, the consequence of original rebellion, but from wretched systems of worldly policy, ill-conceived laws, and illiberal restraints; which if happily removed, the human mind would at once start forth in a rapid pursuit of that perfection which it is fully able to attain. She will hear much praise bestowed on generosity, greatness

greatness of soul, liberality, benevolence, and this cast of virtues; but as their offices and properties would not be clearly defined, and as all reference to the preventing and assisting grace of God, or to the clear explanations which accompany Christian ethics, are systematically excluded from these compositions, it will not be wonderful if the bewildered reader should bestow these titles on the actions of pride, pertinacity, indiscretion, and extravagance. We have seen the effects of these theories on the vacant impetuous mind of uninstructed youth, sufficiently to determine, that, like the pagan corrupters of old times, who " changed the glory of the invisible God into an image made like unto corruptible man," they, while " professing themselves to be wise, have become fools."

But we will suppose a young woman happily free from the metaphysical mania, and influenced by no inordinate desire to distinguish herself among her companions by the disgusting affectation of superior knowledge; I mean by this a common character, who is willing to slide with the world; who reads to kill time; who adopts the opinions that she hears, and suffers the passing scene to flit by her without much anxiety, or much reflection. Unengaging as this character is, I confess that I greatly prefer it to the petticoat philosophist, who seeks for eminence and distinction in infidelity and scepticism, or in the equally monstrous extravagancies of German morality. Women of ordinary abilities were in former times confined to their samplers or their confectionary; and surely they were as well employed in
picking

picking out the seeds of currants, or in stitching the " tale of Troy divine," as now, when they are dependant on the circulating library for means to overcome the tediousness of a *disengaged* day. Novels, plays, and perhaps a little poetry, are the limits of their literary researches. Shall we inquire what impressions romantic adventures, high-wrought scenes of passion, and all the turmoil of intrigue, incident, extravagant attachment, and improbable vicissitudes of fortune, must make upon a vacant mind, whose judgment has not been exercised either by real information, or the conclusions of experience and observation? The inferences that we *must* draw are self-evident.

Let us introduce a third possibility, and suppose a young woman well-disposed, and possessed of such a superficial knowledge of religion as the fashion of the present day, and the time allotted to the acquisition of polite accomplishments, seem to permit. Such a one will, in her private studies, endeavour to improve her acquaintance with those eternal truths which will make her wise unto salvation. If she possess the consciousness of a sound understanding, and such pertinacity of temper as disposes her to independent thinking, is there not great danger of her adopting the leading dogmas of that indefatigable sect, which teaches us that reason is the paramount quality of the soul, and that it is our positive duty to *reject* whatever we do not wholly comprehend, notwithstanding any weight of testimony which supports the mysterious tenet, and maugre the experienced imbecility, or, (to use a more appropriate

priate term) *unripeness* of the human intellect? She will not find such assaults upon her faith confined to books of divinity, nor to tracts of devotion. Writers of this class are extremely numerous; I hope, and I believe, that they are *proportionably* more so than their converts; for this mode of thinking is intimately connected with a passion for literary reputation. Their rage for proselytism is not impeded by the fear of impropriety or absurdity: be their subject biography, history, geography, the belles lettres, or indeed any of the more abstruse sciences, the same persevering eagerness to thrust in an often-refuted objection to the established religion is apparent. Nothing, but a thorough investigation of the foundation on which that religion is built, can resist the undermining effects of these reiterated assaults.

If the character of the student lean to the Saturnine cast, if she be inclined to view the world through the jaundiced eyes of misanthropy and melancholy, to exaggerate human frailty, and to employ her attention rather in aggravating the errors of others, than in regulating the propensities of her own heart; if to this unhappy disposition to self-gratulation a love of mysticism, and an enthusiastic imagination, should be superadded, she is prepared for the assaults of disputants no less hostile to the religion in which I suppose her to be baptized and educated. By them she will be equally complimented with a liberty, which is ever most precious and desirable to those who have the least right to claim, or power to exercise it; I mean that of judging for themselves. She will be as much exonerated from respect to her

regular

regular pastor, as the before-mentioned disciple of reason; and she will imbibe a perhaps superior contempt for those forms and ordinances, with which I represent her as having complied more from habit, than from a just comprehension of their utility and efficacy. If her understanding or imagination be of that cast which can be warped by those soothing delusions of conversion, experience, and election, which are so inexplicably captivating to spiritual pride, she will enjoy in the reveries of Calvinism a degree of self-gratulation beyond what the sceptic can possibly feel; for the belief of being peculiarly favoured by our Creator must elevate the mind to a higher pitch, than the supposed liberty of questioning the verity of the revelations that he has made of his nature and his will can possibly effect. In either

ther case, the unhappy convert loses the light of that guiding star which would best direct her steps; I mean the assistance of a pure and holy religion.

I forbear to mention the dangers which young women are exposed to: from faithless confidants, indiscreet friends, artful parasites, needy dependants, and all that routine of interested servility so commonly appendant to beauty, birth, or fortune. These reptiles are not the spawn of modern times; I rather think, that as the world has grown less domestic, and more self-engrossed, sycophants of all descriptions have been less necessary, and consequently the trade is upon the decline. The best antidote to the enervating assiduities of these ear-ticklers is contained in those talismanic words which modern manners leave little leisure to observe, " Commune

mune with your own heart, and in your chamber, and be still."

We have hitherto considered the fair adventurer in the voyage of life as only exposed to external assailants; but it must be remembered that she carries with her a rebellious crew of passions and affections, which are extremely apt to mutiny, especially in times of extraordinary peril. The perishable commodity of female fame is embarked in a slight felucca, painted and gilded, indeed, and externally both convenient and beautiful; but by no means fitted for those distant voyages, and rough encounters with winds, seas, and enemies, which afford navigators of the other sex a welcome opportunity of showing their skill and magnanimity: yet the delicacy of the merchandise, joined to the fragility of these adorned vessels, imposes constant

stant anxiety and labour on their commanders; not only lest their precious cargo should lose either its polish or its purity, but from fear of falling into the hands of pirates, who are ever on the watch to pillage or destroy them. The risk is considerably increased, by knowing, that though the pilot often possesses many excellent and engaging qualities, the helm is seldom managed with adroitness, and the ship is rarely able to veer, to tack, and to scud before the wind, till very late in the voyage: I cannot, therefore, think it expedient that these fragile barks should venture to do more than sail *coastwise,* till they are taken in tow by some stouter vessel; especially as they are totally destitute of all materials to remedy the misfortunes incident to shipwreck. Whether it proceed from the false opinions, prejudices, or injustice of
men,

men, as some say; or, as I am inclined to think, from the wisdom of divine Providence imposing a greater degree of chariness on that sex which he designed to make the conservator of morals; so it happens, that women find a greater degree of difficulty than men in throwing off any species of reproach, whether it be deserved, or the false imputation of malignant slander.

We may inquire, how are women fitted to answer those severe demands which custom, and I may add reason, make upon their conduct? This investigation will lead us into an ample field; as it will not only require us to consider what education does in forming habits of watchfulness and self-controul, and in invigorating the discriminative and deliberative powers of the mind; but also, how far the present customs of society assist us in the proper

proper discharge of our required duties. In the course of this inquiry, we shall discover ample reason to bless our Creator, who originally intended us to " take our noiseless way along the cool sequestered vale of life," since we shall find every departure from this appointed path attended with danger, either to our peace, or to our renown.

What those duties are which the God of Nature requires us to fulfil; what resources he allows us under the sorrows incident to those duties; and what are the incidental as well as future rewards which we are authorized to expect, will form an agreeable exercise to the well-disposed mind, when it is wearied with viewing the labours and sorrows which result from fastidiousness, selfishness, vanity, irregular desires, and extravagant expectations. Think you, my dear Miss M——,

M——, that a discussion of such subjects will answer that idea of a correspondence, which occurred to your beloved mother at a most awful and mournful moment? What pleasure shall I feel, in addressing my sex through the daughter of that friend from whom I derived what is most valuable in my sentiments and principles! You were very young when you met with that severe misfortune which checked the gay career of fondly fostered childhood. Your age had not permitted you to reap the full profit of the attentions of your ever watchful parent. You felt that her sweet temper and serene cheerfulness made you happy; but you could not then justly appreciate the superiority of her understanding. You had learned to obey her injunctions, but you could not know the prudent and virtuous ends
which

which they were intended to produce. I lost her at a time when experience had taught me her full value. Though distance, and the intervention of nearer relations, and more imperious duties, rendered her life of less daily importance to me, those very circumstances combined to impress her observations and example deeper upon my memory. While my hands have been occupied in attending to the domestic calls of a rising family, my imagination has wandered to the scenes of early life, and to the beloved circle of which she was one of the brightest ornaments. The lively sally, the literary discussion, the perspicuous remark, have reflected pleasure on the sometimes tedious routine of daily avocation; and especially (such is the general effect of true friendship) did I feel the justness of her sentiments, and the validity

of

of her arguments, when "the wheel was broken at the cistern," and I could no more draw truth and knowledge from that fountain.

If my anxiety to discharge this hereditary obligation should make me deviate into the error of capricious testators, who like to bequeath their riches to their most *wealthy* connections, I can excuse myself by pleading, that the beneficial effects of moral reflections and prudential counsels are not confined to those to whom they are imparted. Like mercy, they have a chance of "being twice blessed;" the giver is amended, if not the receiver. If serious reflections on "our being's end and aim" are likely to produce a wholesome indifference to the transient measures of this world, methodizing and improving those reflections must deepen their impression on

the

the mind where they originated; and that heart must indeed be obdurate which can resist the energy of its own reproofs. Surely no common proficiency in hypocrisy is necessary to enable us to pen a sententious libel on our own conduct, or to fabricate a system contradictory to our lives.

I am aware, that the lively feelings of sentiment and affection which dictated my admonitory addresses to my eldest son, were the chief attraction which recommended that work to public favour. By permitting me to suppose your welfare connected with the present attempt, you will enable me to embark in it with the same sincerity, and nearly *equal* solicitude. Whatever the pretended cosmopolites may boast of the effects of universal philanthropy and general benevolence, we must embody those indefinite ideas,

and

and combine them with some strong tie of nature or of choice, before we can be really interested in the irregular compound. A work coldly written will be as frigidly perused; that on which the author's heart never engraved a discriminating token, cannot hope to stamp a lasting impression on the feelings of the reader.

You see, my dear Miss M——, how much of my literary reputation is in your power. Am I too presumptuous, if, building on our long friendship and your habitual kindness, I anticipate your acquiescence with my wishes? As soon as you announce it, I shall enter with spirit on my then pleasing task; and in the interim I remain

Your very affectionate friend, &c.

LETTER

LETTER II.

Original Destination of Women.

MY DEAR MISS M———,

THE assurance that I have not imposed too great a burden on your affectionate partiality, by your promise to receive my labours with pleasure, and to peruse them with attention, has enabled me to enter on my proposed undertaking with alacrity, to which the manner of your communicating this welcome intelligence has given a yet more powerful impetus. I shall now hurry you along without any ceremony, and immediately commence the proposed inquiry into the situation, duties, trials, and errors of our sex.

When we address Christian readers,

we presuppose their acquiescence in the facts that are recorded in holy writ. Without wasting our time in a philosophical analysis of the peculiar construction of our intellects, or the physical organization of our bodies, we may rest assured that we are endowed with powers adequate to the design of our creation; namely, to be the helpmate of man, to partake of his labours, to alleviate his distresses, to regulate his domestic concerns, to rear and instruct the subsequent generation; and, having finished our probationary course as accountable beings, to enter on another state of endless existence.

It would be foreign to our purpose, to pursue a minute investigation respecting the situation of women in other regions: a very few general observations shall suffice. The nearer the country is to what is called the state of nature (but which, in correct language, should be termed savage degeneracy), the more we find women depressed, servile, and miserable. The rude descendants of those wandering tribes, whom the miraculous interposition of the offended Deity at Babel dispersed through the distant quarters of the globe, amidst the degradation of mutual ignorance and mutual privation, have uniformly retained that superiority of the male species which it received at the creation, and which prevailed during the infant state of the world. It is impossible to account for the universal subjugation of women among savages, on the ground of their mental imbecility or bodily disadvantages; for it is a well-known fact, that exertion invigorates both the intellectual and corporeal faculties; and as these wretched victims of

male

male tyranny execute the tasks of intense and continual labour, while their more indolent lords engross all the sensual indulgencies which a state of barbarism affords, the general laws of even-hauded Providence must repay their hard services with more athletic vigour and acute intelligence. In consequence, travellers remark, that the women belonging to the wandering tribes of barbarians, whenever the restraints of jealousy have permitted them to hold intercourse with strangers, have generally displayed more quickness and reflection than the males, as well as a superior share of those virtues of compassion and benevolence, which are the sure indications that the mind has expanded beyond the merely selfish pursuits of animal life. This observation has little reference to our present inquiry; but every incidental

remark

remark that corroborates the testimony of holy writ is conducive to the main design of this correspondence.

The progress of any people toward civilization is uniformly marked by allotting an increased degree of importance to the fair sex; but this is not always done with benevolent regard to their happiness. The violent passions and capricious humours of men intervene; and in the eastern and southern regions of the earth, where those passions are most impetuous, women are ever considered rather as a precarious and valuable property, than as rational creatures, possessing a claim to self-enjoyment. Those restraints of barbarous policy under which Mahometan and Gentoo women labour, are still more injurious to our genuine character, than the dangerous exertions of Patagonian divers, or the agricultural

toil

toil of female Africans. When women are only taught "to dance, to dress, "to troll the tongue and roll the eye," voluptuous passions, frivolous pursuits, low artifices, and all that envy, revenge, jealousy, fear, and disguised hatred, can dictate to the doubtful favourite of an hour, must agitate the female breast; alternately solicitous to repair the ruins of time in her own person, and to counteract the attractions of a rival. In the secluded harem, where polygamy immures the victims of its passions and the disturbers of its repose, we must not look for the friend or helpmate of man.

In Europe, and its numerous colonies, the blessed influence of divine revelation has fixed our sex in a more happy situation. Our equal claim to immortality, which the gospel recognised, removed many prejudices against us. The abolition of polygamy raised us, from mere objects of sensual desire, to friends and companions; and wherever the institution of marriage is formally acknowledged, women become a branch of the body politic, amenable to the laws of their country, and also to public opinion, which alike takes cognizance of their conduct, and protects their persons. To the solemn obligation of this heaven-ordained bond, this sacred source of all domestic relations and charities, all polished nations superadd that general sense of courtesy and refined attention which chivalry introduced; to whose enthusiastical and romantic, yet salutary modification of the rough martial manners of the middle ages, society is more deeply indebted than this sceptical age is willing to allow. Its effects on the situation of our sex must

not

not be limited to those times, when the mistress of the tournament awarded the prize among contending assertors of her charms; we feel them in every act of complacence and politeness which we continue to receive from the lords of creation, in the high importance affixed to female virtue, in the assiduities of love, and in the decorums of society.

Our country has long been eminently distinguished as the seat of pure religion and enlightened laws. It cannot, therefore, excite surprise that travellers should admire the enviable state of our countrywomen, who appear to move in their natural sphere, and are neither treated with the phlegmatic neglect visible among our northern neighbours, nor with the ostentatious obsequiousness which the more polished nations of the continent practise to a degree of farcical affectation. The effect of this judicious treatment has been equally conspicuous in the mild chaste attractions of the British fair; their simple elegance, domestic habits, and all the graces of discretion, delicacy, and ingenuous attachment, have been as loudly praised, as the valour, magnanimity, and sound sense of their heroic partners.

I know, my dear Miss M——, your bosom possesses that share of patriotic virtue, which teaches you to exult with the proud feelings of conscious participation in the rank which Britain *now* holds among the nations of the earth. In every clime that the sun visits is her ingenuity admired, and her valour revered. But can this pre-eminence be long supported, if female virtue, degraded and abashed, shrinks from investigation, and resigns,
with

with her claim to superiority, all her pretensions to *reward* the present race of heroes, and to *model* the future? The triumph of the red-cross knight ceased, when lovely Una no longer rode beside him attired in the panoply of vestal innocence.

Before we wander through the mazes of fashion, or review the changes which wealth and luxury have produced in our characters, let us consider our sex as fulfilling the designs of our Creator in this highly-favoured country; where the laws of God and man were till lately assisted by the habits of society, and all united to make us become what we ought to be. It is not only in the conjugal state that we are designed to be the helpmates of our co-heirs of immortality; as daughters, sisters, mothers, mistresses of families, neighbours, and friends, the active duties of female usefulness may be happily exerted. Even the insulated spinster has no right to consider herself exempt from the general obligation; the want of nearer claims leaves her *more* at liberty to pursue the wide range of benevolence; nor can she be justified in resigning her mind to the waywardness of self-indulgence, while there is a human being within her sphere of action whom she could benefit or relieve by the kind offices of humanity.

In our progress from the cradle to the grave, successive duties adapted to our different powers crowd upon our attention. The first tasks which filial duty requires are affection and obedience; which often compel us to participate in the sorrows and labours of our parents, before we feel, from our own particular distresses, "that man is born to woe." While attending on the sick bed

bed to which fraternal affection has chained us, or while watching the languid couch of the source of our life with all the anxious observance of ready diligence, we gather that experience, and imbibe those habits of tenderness and patience, which in riper years we are required to exercise in our own families. During the short reign of beauty (or, to adopt a language more universally just, while courtship gives a seeming pre-eminence), discretion teaches us a cautious use of power, especially over him whom we propose to select as the *arbiter* of our future lot. And when the awful marriage contract removes us from acting a subordinate part in the family of our parents, and fixes us as vicegerents of our husband's household, we enter upon the most extended circle in which (generally speaking) Providence

dence designed us to move. Nor is that circle so circumscribed as to give cause to the most active mind to complain of want of employment; the duties that it requires are of such hourly, such momentary recurrence, that the impropriety of our engaging in public concerns becomes evident, from the consequent unavoidable neglect of our immediate affairs. A man, in most situations of life, may so arrange his private business, as to be able to attend the important calls of patriotism or public spirit; but the presence of a woman in her own family is always so salutary, that she is not justified in withdrawing her attention from home, except in some call of plain positive duty. The management of that part of her husband's fortune which is committed to her trust; the comfortable arrangement of domestic affairs;
the

the attention which the bodily wants of a rising family require; the still greater vigilance which should be bestowed on the formation of their minds and the regulation of their tempers; the superintendence of servants, which, as the establishment increases in number, becomes more important and more perplexing, and among whom a mistress ought in some sense to perform the part of a vigilant observer, a magistrate, and a protecting friend; when, I repeat, it is considered that we owe these perpetual obligations to all those who are resident under our roof, those ranks of life which are exempt from the necessity of bodily labour seem supplied with ample occupation, by diligently observing the apostolical injunction, "of keeping at home, and guiding their own houses with discretion." But this is not all: by becoming

coming wives, we do not cease to be daughters, sisters, or friends; and the demands which arise out of these relationships are certainly of the number of those *plain positive* duties which justify a temporary dereliction of our own immediate charge. Society has also a claim upon us: they who entirely limit their attention to their own households, and will neither open their purses nor their hearts at the call of benevolence, nor bestow their time and their attention on the demands of good neighbourhood, must expect to live disliked or despised: they are indeed punished for their rebellion to general laws, by growing morose, narrow-minded, or whimsical, and by contracting such *peculiar* habits as are the forerunners of spleen and misanthropy. Home should be made pleasant to our husbands; and men are never more pleased with

with it, than when it affords them the agreeable change of pleasant society. The interest and welfare of our children require that we should introduce them to proper connections. These prudential considerations are enforced by the positive duties which we owe to our superiors, equals, and inferiors: thence follow the obligations of respect, complaisance, and benevolence; whoever needs our services, presents a claim to them which can only be obviated by some stronger obligation; and here discretion is to act as umpire.

But we have duties still more important than what we owe to kindred and society: I mean those of a creature to its Creator; and surely a married woman, whose sensibilities are multiplied in so many dear connections, has the least excuse for neglecting this most important obligation. Can she forget the

the morning and evening sacrifice, whose tender feelings are so peculiarly susceptible of injury from every quarter by which sin or sorrow can assail the human mind?

With the duties of a responsible dependant being, those of a rational creature are necessarily blended. What is that which is to survive the ruins of this clay-built tenement, and to exist to all eternity? Certainly it is our intellectual part; and shall we, while in this probationary state, neglect its cultivation? Talents, we know, are not bestowed to rust in inactivity; and our desire for useful and improving knowledge, should only be bounded by our opportunity for acquiring it. This restraint makes it incumbent upon us, not to suffer our literary propensities to supersede the active duties which our situation and relative connections

peremptorily

peremptorily require; and as these claims will in most cases leave us but little leisure, it behoves us to husband that little by applying it well. The knowledge that will be most useful claims the precedence; that which may be most easily acquired seems to be entitled to the second preference. Though something should be granted to peculiar taste, especially when it appears to be the strong propensity of genius, and not the craving of caprice, it is in general advisable, that women should not (especially after they have embarked in the active duties of married life) devote their attention to any difficult study, or abstruse science. Uninviting as their aspect is to strangers, it is well known, that mathematical problems, and metaphysical deductions, afford such gratification to those who have made some

progress

progress in those branches of learning, that they often entirely absorb the faculties, and render the common duties of life tasteless and disgusting.

From the wide range of occupations which call upon us in middle age, let us extend our researches to the decline of life; and here, as long as the power of usefulness is intrusted to us, we find objects to claim its exertion. If we are deprived of our wedded partners, the sole management of our fortunes, or perhaps the active superintendance of the business which supports our families, devolves upon us. We should provide for this in early life, by gaining such knowledge of money transactions as will preserve us from imposition: few acquirements are more useful to females; and the increasing intricacy of public imposts and legal securities, renders it daily
more

more requisite. Here, too, that knowledge of the world which occasional intercourse with society affords becomes of high importance, as it enables us to guard against the blandishments of art and the snares of villany, to which I believe our sex is more peculiarly exposed. When we have lost the advantage of a counsellor and friend, whose interest was inseparably connected with our own, we become doubly bound to recur to the stores which recollection furnishes, and to exert our most wary vigilance, lest we should be made the dupes of knaves, or the tools of parasites.

Our children, probably, at this period, will not require our continual attention; but numerous occasions will arise to exercise our care and love, and to convince us that we do not live for ourselves alone. A third generation,

tion, too, generally steps forth, in whom the active calls of earlier life again revive. Much of the comfort of our old age depends upon our discharging the claims of renewed maternity with propriety. The season of life is now apt to suggest the love of ease, and at the same time confines our views to present objects and local pursuits. It now, therefore, becomes more than ever our duty to prevent the increasing influence of selfishness, by encouraging those benevolent affections which at this season of life are seldom so lively as to mislead us, unless we suffer them to wander into devious and crooked paths. It is now in our power to be highly beneficial to our fellow-creatures, without those active exertions which our infirmities would probably render painful. Yet let it be remembered, that it is by kind assistance,

assistance, or cautious interposition, not by officious interference, that age is enabled to reflect the light of its own experience on youth. As increasing pains and debilities warn us of the speedy termination of our earthly journey, it becomes *indispensably* necessary, that cheerfulness, patience, and fortitude should be our constant companions; for unless they are inmates in our bosom, we can only hope for the cold services of reluctant duty, or interested assiduities, instead of the grateful attentions of attachment and esteem. It not unfrequently happens, that, added to our own infirmities, we are still required to lend our aid to relieve those of our wedded partner. Generally speaking, the pains and privations of advanced life affect men more than women; for their happiness mostly consists in active exertions;

their

their enjoyments are less domestic; they are not so accustomed to endure and to submit; and they often have it in their power to *controul* or to *escape* from unpleasant sensations. To sympathize in the anguish, and endure the irritability of a beloved object, and at the same time to struggle against the burden of our own infirmities is a task which is often imposed upon our declining years.

To these domestic duties and obligations, may be added what belongs to our whole sex, as the refiners of manners, and the conservators of morals; and in these cases every judicious statesman readily allows our relative importance. No nation has preserved its political independence for any long period after its women became dissipated and licentious. When the hallowed graces of the chaste matron have

have given place to the bold allurements of the courtezan, the rising generation always proclaims its base origin. Luxurious self-indulgence; frivolous or abandoned pursuits; indifference to every generous motive; mean attachment to interest; disdain of lawful authority, yet credulous subservience to artful demagogues; the blended vices of the savage, the sybarite, and the slave, proclaim a people ripe for ruin, and inviting the chains of a conqueror. As far as the records of past ages permit us to judge, female depravity preceded the downfal of those mighty states of Greece and Italy which once gave law to the world. We have inspired testimony, that the licentiousness, pride, and extravagance of "the daughters of Sion," during the latter part of her first monarchy, hastened the divine judgments, and

and unsheathed the sword of the Babylonish destroyer*. The events that we have witnessed in our own times confirm this position: in most of the realms that have been overcome by the arms of France, a notorious dereliction of female principle prevailed; and the state of manners in France itself, as far as related to our sex, had obtained such dreadful publicity, as allows us to ascribe the fall of that country in a great measure to the dissipated indelicate behaviour and loose morals of its women. Thus, though we are not entitled to a place in the senate, we become *legislators* in the most important sense of the word, by impressing on the minds of all around us the obligation which gives force to

* See various passages in the prophetical parts of Scripture; especially Isaiah.

the statute. Were we but steadily united in resisting the corruption of the times, the boastful libertine, the professed man of gallantry, the vapid coxcomb, the prophane scoffer, the indecent jester, and all the reptile swarm which perverted pride and false wit produce, would disappear. It is us that they seek to please, or rather to astonish; and if we were but steadily resolved to repay their vanity with contempt, and to bestow our smiles only on what was meritorious, or really brilliant, the habits of the gay world would undergo a most happy transformation.

Women are generally considered as the arbiters of taste in a great degree; nor is this a trivial distinction: taste is influenced by the moral qualities; the quick perception of what is grotesque or absurd, even in what are termed the fine arts, is rarely confined to mere mechanical proportion or effect. Undefined ideas of "perfect, fair, and good" associate with the rules by which we judge the merits of the performance. As these arts are designed to be the lively representations of nature, to decide on the fidelity of the imitation, our souls must be alive to the sublimest feelings, capable of investigating the beauties of creation; and of deciding on the genuine expressions and gestures of heroical virtue; and thus exalted *moral* perceptions become requisite to the connoisseur, as well as to the artist. But the fine arts are capable of a yet superior exaltation: we do not merely admire the nice touches of Flaxman's chissel, nor the happy adjustment of parts which are so visible in his designs; we see in them the Christian as well

well as the statuary. While devotion kindles at the paintings of Peters; while we contemplate with the rapture of anxious emulation the pious family bursting from the dark dungeon of the grave, or, with the spirit of the beatified child, avert our eyes from the distant blaze of rainbow-tinctured glory, the reflections of critical vertu are suspended; and we confess that these artists (like our divine bard) have derived their inspiration from

> " Siloa's sacred brook that flow'd
> Fast by the oracle of God."

Let us turn from these inanimate productions of genius, to public amusements, and those species of literature which are allowed to be influenced by female decision. What ample improvements are here offered to our reforming taste! Surely it is in our power to banish from the stage, not only what is offensive to decency, but what is seductive to principle. I even think that we might extend our proscription to what is grossly unnatural and absurdly improbable; at least we might only leave a sufficient quantity of these latter qualities to exhilarate the spirits, and relieve the sombre effect of graver scenes. I have no *austere* design of banishing wit, or even broad humour, from our theatres. The laughable equivoque, and all the extravagance of low character and absurd situation, shall retain their place: they are truly English, and may be so managed as to be perfectly innocent; I only declare my hostility to practical jokes, extravagant grimace, irreverent allusions to sacred subjects, and, above all, to that inexhaustible fund of profane swearing, which liberal actors always keep

at

at hand to supply the mental poverty of *necessitous* authors. I enter my strongest protest against the *wit* of an oath; and, maugre the authority of Sterne, I even doubt its *benevolence.* Surely, the ancient expletives of a cough, or an application to the cambric handkerchief, were better substitutes for the barrenness of the author's brains, or the inattention of the prompter. The vocabulary of blasphemy is too limited to permit the lover of novelty to enjoy his darling gratification; and, as Acres humourously observes, " nothing but their antiquity renders common oaths respectable." The most that can be done by the brightest imagination is, to ring changes upon a few worn-out curses, by way of proving its supreme contempt for the institutions and religion of its country, and of instruct-our strict attention It is a subject which we must hereafter resume; I will, therefore, only observe in this place, that among those heathen nations whom we now profess to imitate, the vicious and the virtuous parts of the sex were as much distinguished by their apparel as by their manners. The chaste propriety of matronly and virgin attraction was prohibited from adopting the incentives allowed to the courtezan, who avowed her aim by sacrificing modesty to allurement. It is true, the figures of these unhappy women, lightly shaded with loose drapery, supplied the statuary and the painter with those wanton graces which they consecrated as the attributes of the deity of licentious pleasures; yet, with a decorum which marked the prevailing sentiments of the times, they constantly adopted a very different

ent paraphernalia when they formed a representation of the goddesses of marriage and wisdom. When we consider, also, that this costume of Grecian impurity, this marked characteristic of the shameless idol of Paphos, has been yet further debased by being adopted by Parisian fiends, during the most bloody and most voluptuous scenes of a revolution which elevated poissardes into leading fashionables; English ladies, distinguished for modesty, elevated by birth, and enlightened by Christianity, should certainly reject the degrading imitation with the most *lively disdain.*

This enumeration of the offices and duties of our sex naturally leads us to consider, by what peculiar trials our heavenly father exercises our virtues, and prepares us for a happier world. They seem to result chiefly from the tempers, dispositions, infirmities, and misfortunes of our near connexions; for we are far less able than men to be the carvers of our own fortunes, and must generally consult *more* than our own inclinations in order to be happy. The colour of our lives is so influenced by the propensities of our wedded partners, that in very many (perhaps in the majority of) marriages, the business of the wife is to controul her own inclinations, instead of projecting how she may gratify them. This subservience is not solely confined to the conjugal tie, nor does it only revert backward to the consecrated claims of paternity; our brothers, nay even our sons, will demand the privilege of Adam; and whenever we fix with them in a domestic residence, we must conform to their humours, anticipate their wishes, and alleviate their misfortunes, or else forfeit their affections and forego their society.

Observe, then, what numerous infelicities, from ill-managed tempers, corrupt inclinations, criminal pursuits, capricious whims, imprudent determinations, and obstinate vices, threaten our repose on the one side; while, on the other, how frequently must we be summoned to attend the couch of restless agony, to minister all the few comforts which finite humanity can afford to lingering sickness, or even to sustain the dying head on the bosom of faithful sympathizing love. Our office of help-mate is not limited to the gay season of life. Like Prior's Emma, we are not only required to embark "on the smooth surface of a summer's sea:" we are not permitted

"To quit the ship and seek the shore,
"When the winds rattle and the surges roar."

Our services are most valuable, and consequently most requisite, in the dreary season of distress; whether it be occasioned by adversity or disease; whether the storm proceed from false friends or secret enemies, or from the imprudence or guilt of the sufferer; whether it affect the fortune, the reputation, or the person of him with whom our fate is interwoven; the faithful wife, the tender mother, the dutiful daughter, or the affectionate sister, must still be the guardian angel to bring the cup of consolation; and though the world renounce or condemn the sufferer, her arms must (except in cases of very extraordinary wickedness) afford the wretched outcast a secure asylum.

Of all the sorrows that threaten our sex, none seem to me so exquisitely painful, as those which result from the vicious conduct of our near connections. Indeed, these are so excruciating, as to be insupportable without the

the aid of religion. Yet, in this case, even her golden shield cannot entirely blunt the shafts of adversity; since the views that she presents of the future state of unrepentant sinners, must excite awful apprehensions. Let us here stop to inquire, how far it is in our power to avoid a misfortune which it is so difficult to sustain; and I trust it will be found, that it is in our power to escape the sharpest of its many pangs, by so regulating our conduct, that we may never have cause to reproach ourselves with deserving such heavy affliction. Let us endeavour to lead a libertine brother or a deistical father to the safe paths of piety and virtue; showing them, by our own deportment, that they really are the paths of pleasantness. Let us resolve, that no charm of person and manner, no attraction of rank or fortune, shall prevail upon us to take for the partners of our lives men whose vices will either corrupt our principles, or wring our hearts with most poignant misery. Give not your unborn offspring a father whose example you must teach them to avoid. Choose not for your companion on earth, one from whom, as often as you reflect, you must hope to be eternally separated*. If you are offered one who will assist you in your heaven-ward journey, and aid you in the highly important duty of leading your young ones to their heavenly home, give him a *decided* preference, however inferior he may be in worldly advantages to his profligate rival. And here we will observe, that though a wife rarely has power to reclaim her dissolute spouse, a sedulous attention to the duties of a mother in the important points of moral and religious instruction, will most probably preserve her from the

* See Letter 12.

severest of maternal pains: I am sorry to say only *most probably*; for, alas! we have seen many instances in which the best instruction has been found ineffectual. "Education," said one of the soundest divines of our church, "is "not grace;" and he felt the force of that melancholy concession. One point, however, will be secured; we shall then know that we shall not be called to account for the loss of an *uninstructed* soul; besides, while the offender lives, we shall never renounce the hope of his reformation. "We "cast the seed upon the waters," observes an eminent professor of the science of education *, "and we ex- "pect not to find it till after many "days." The temptations of the world, the ebullitions of youthful passions, the seductions of bad example, may retard

* Dr Vincent. See his Defence of Public Edu-

its germination; but if it has once been sown in early youth by a careful hand, while the mind was vacant and the memory vigorous, it will not be totally destroyed. Even at the eleventh hour the labourer may recollect his neglected vineyard; and, if he were early initiated in the method, he may still anxiously work during the small portion of time that remains, and receive a limited reward.

The perplexities which pursue us in the management of our households, belong to that species of vexations which for a time occupy the whole mind, and afterwards appear in so trivial a light that we wonder how we could suffer them to tease us. In weak frivolous dispositions they are apt to gain such an ascendancy, as to form that very disgusting character a fretful scold; and sometimes, as the Lilliputians contrived to bind down Gulliver, a numerous

rous combination of diminutive inconveniencies will shackle superior faculties. Nothing gives us so mean an opinion of human nature, as the consideration of what petty circumstances are necessary to our comfort, and how much the best and wisest of our species owe even the blessing of self-possession to the success of mechanical contrivances, and the regularity of servile occupations. An ill-dressed dinner shall not only cloud the temper, but also retard the plans of a statesman; the negligence of a valet may interrupt the formalities of law, or violate the decorums of parliament; the inattention of a clerk or subaltern may suspend the most important naval or military operations. No wonder, then, if women, whose daily round of domestic inspection exposes them to a continual recurrence of domestic vexations,

tions, and who must, if properly influenced by a sense of duty, feel anxious to preserve the decorums of family regularity, should often find their minds unhinged by the inconveniences arising from the carelessness, ignorance, or depravity of those from whom they require diligence, ability, and fidelity. This species of trial often makes severe inroads upon our tempers, and not unfrequently contributes much to alienate the affections of our husbands; who, being less exposed to these provocations in trivial concerns, are apt to under-rate their power of irritating the mind.

In most situations of life, the personal offices of the mistress of a family are occasionally requisite; in all, her *superintendence* is indispensable. It is our duty to avoid leading others into temptation; and we unquestionably do so, so, when, by a total intermission of observation, we teach mercenary people that they may be negligent or profligate with impunity. To superintend and conduct a household with regularity, propriety, elegance, and good humour, is a happy art. The more important business in which men are mostly engaged, often wearies their faculties and discomposes their minds; yet, without considering that their little monarchies at home are liable to commotions, they think themselves entitled to find them at all times a pleasant retreat from perplexity and contradiction. This expectation may be unreasonable. I do not pretend to justify men from the charge of being selfish; but, as they certainly do expect that the smile of complacency should always illumine the countenances of their female companions, whenever it is is not suspended by sympathy for them, it is both politic and praise-worthy in our sex to endeavour at that self-command, which certainly, when acquired, is our best title to superiority in the scale of moral excellence.

The care of children, especially in their earlier stages of existence, is a demand upon the patience and firmness of the mother, which, if she come only *poetically* prepared for the undertaking, she will find exceeds her ability. Sleepless nights, and anxious days, fall to the lot of those who steadily resolve to discharge every duty which the tender scion of humanity requires to raise it to maturity. Nor is the task of teaching the "young idea how to shoot" always delightful. The fertile soil will produce weeds, and the vigorous plant will often shoot with an unhappy bend, which only constant

constant attention can reform. "Line "upon line, precept upon precept," must be supplied; and, like the prophets of old, the maternal instructress must throw in "here a little and there a little." And while we are thus employed in correcting others, we must also remember to watch ourselves with a special care. The observation of children, like their other faculties, is more acute than discriminating; they can readily discern when Mamma is peevish or passionate; but they do not understand that her troubles are more important than the dirtying of a doll, or the breaking of a favourite toy.

The slighter construction of our bodily organs, or sedentary habits, and the inconveniences and sufferings attached to us as mothers, exercise our patience in a species of trials, to which men are by nature less exposed; though in in a state of society the dangers incident to war, navigation, and hazardous occupations, not to mention more frequent exposure to inclement seasons, or the diseases which spring from intemperance, prevent the comparison of length of days from preponderating in their favour. Yet if we consider, that the calamities of war, or sudden accidents generally remove their victims by an *instantaneous* stroke, we must allow that women are oftenest called to endure lingering decay and protracted suffering. Less equal to fatigue, less capable of exertion, we feel more of the evils incident to debility and lassitude. I am here speaking of English women in their natural state, not in the artificial character which fashion compels them to assume; for, certainly, were we to enumerate the toils which a fine lady *voluntarily* endures,

endures, we must allow that a porter is a less robust animal.

After reviewing the evils which beset us from without, let us revert to those bosom traitors which internally assault us: I mean the passions. I can by no means allow, that ours are naturally so violent as those of men; but I fear they are often less subjected to their lawful sovereign reason, and more under the domination of the usurper fancy. Precluded by our situation from an early or intimate acquaintance with the world, we are more exposed to the misrepresentations of interested reporters; and if our graver friends should fall into the common error of exhibiting their description of life in the dark shade of the phantasmagoria, the buoyant spirits of youth will determine us to consider the magic lanthorn with which

our

our chamber-maids, our romantic acquaintance, and novel writers, amuse us, as a more faithful delineation of *living* manners. Hence arises the eternal expectation of splendid conquests, faultless adorers, wonderful events, and extraordinary conflicts, all ending in perfect and uninterrupted felicity, which haunt the mind of youth. To this cause we must attribute the fluctuations of vanity, the dreams of expectation, the fretfulness of competition, and the gloom of disappointment. Hence the humble duties of social life are rendered disgusting, and its simple pleasures vapid. Public places are thus converted into a field for knight-errantry; and the prudent friends who endeavour to confine us within the sphere that our narrow fortunes render necessary, assume the part of those giants of old, who

who kept *princesses* immured in *castles*. In this situation of our minds, every tolerably agreeable man that we meet is in danger of becoming a conquering Paladin. If our acquaintance be extensive, and our tempers lively, coquetry is apt to steal upon the unpractised, yet designing female; a more limited circle, and greater susceptibility of disposition give birth to some fixed attachment; and as we persuade ourselves, that an union with the preferred object is all that is wanting to our happiness, every obstacle that occurs is considered, not as a trial incident to our mortal being, but as a wicked or inhuman contrivance against our repose. Hence arise envy and jealousy of real or imaginary rivals; resentment or dislike of friendly interference; and hence we become the inevitable prey of disappointment, either by the frustration or by the possession of our desires. For let no woman, who surrenders her mind to all the extravagance of romantic expectation, think that it is even *possible* she should ever know the bliss of full fruition. If, while she is exempt from the immediate pressure of pain or distress, she see nothing in the present scene which can call forth the amiable sympathies of her heart, let her rest assured that the gaily decorated future, which she paints in such vivid colours, is but the vision of fancy. It is like a distant landscape illuminated by the beams of the rising sun, all lovely, glowing, and splendid; but when she comes to travel over it, she will find the same inequalities of road, and all the difficulties which require that watchfulness, and cause that lassitude, of which she now complains.

The

The humours of a husband will seem as intolerable as those of a parent; and "the rose distilled" will be annoyed by the same enemies which vexed it "while it grew on the virgin thorn."

Our internal trials, however, do not always proceed from the errors of vanity or the fictions of romance. Our sex generally possesses a most acute sensibility, which sometimes proceeds from the susceptibility of our bodily organs; often from the weakness of our judgment; occasionally from badness of temper, and frequently from real tenderness of heart. Since this latter must be acknowledged to be the only justifiable source of impassioned feeling, it behoves us, from our earliest years, to consider the irritation that proceeds from any other cause, as an infirmity, which we must endeavour to subdue. Corporeal weakness seems to belong to the medical department; yet, as nervous cases are allowed to be the opprobrium of the healing art, and as they are alike irregular and obstinate, it behoves us to inquire, whether there are any *preventive* medicines. Innocent cheerfulness, a constant habit of varied occupations, exercise, and, above all,

"Genial air, kind Nature's genuine gift,"

happily often

"Annihilate the train of nervous ills."

Persons who are a prey to these disorders are unquestionably real objects of pity; but they usually deal so liberally in *self-compassion*, that they require to be but sparingly indulged with the *commiseration* of others. They would probably start at being told, that while they consider themselves as the most unhappy of the human species, they resemble tyrants in more than that miserable

miserable distinction. A nervous lady is a complete despot, who rules, if not with a rod of iron, at least with a sceptre that is infinitely more formidable to a generous mind. Happiness flies her approach, and even humble comfort cannot resist her assaults. These victims to imaginary ills and evils often possess a great share of real goodness of heart; and a powerful appeal from benevolence, or affection, generally acts as an invincible stimulant to rouse the patient from the languor of hypochondria, and effects a local cure, though the disease seldom fails to return, when the relaxed mind has lost its accidental energy. Does not this testify, that the malady is not wholly organic, and that, at least in its commencement, selfishness and indulgence contribute to its violence? That it is attended with real suffering, is granted; but it is equally certain, that the human mind is armed with power sufficient to resist the attack of pain; because the same person who often sinks into the extremes of nervous depression, at other times may be produced as an instance of fortitude, by enduring extreme agony with cheerfulness. It is thus in the common affairs of life, we frequently see that mind irritated by " trifles light as air," which has sustained real affliction with unyielding heroism. The state of the case seems to be, that when by bad habits and excessive dissipation, or through long confinement, over-watchfulness, great anxiety, or severe misfortune, the spirits become broken and the body debilitated, every little addition of pain or inconvenience alarms us; self predominates in all our thoughts; we no longer

longer compare ourselves with others, and judge from a fair-drawn parallel; but we accumulate upon our own heads every calamity and every disease, hereditary or contagious, which we can carry to our own mountain of misery, by any extravagant stretch of fancy. The natural consequence is, that we sink under its pressure. I have bestowed the more time on this subject, from a conviction that this malady often assaults most amiable women, who would shrink from themselves with horror, could they foresee the uneasiness that they cause, or the lamentable *transformation* which they suffer, while they are under the influence of this "foul fiend;" whom, though it is almost impossible to *vanquish*, it is easy to *avoid*. As the champion of my sex, I here enter my protest against the forced construction, that I suppose hypochondria to be merely a feminine infirmity. As it either originates in, or is aggravated by the patients permitting the imagination to revolve on the narrow pivot of self, the lords of the creation are indebted to their more athletic frames and active occupations, if (which is certainly questionable) they are more exempt than we from the assaults of nervous irritability..

Susceptibility, proceeding from weakness of judgment, and badness of temper, takes a variety of forms. Sometimes it teases ourselves and our connexions in the shape of bodily complaint; but it often assumes the colour of an injured character, suffering from an ungrateful, perfidious, undiscerning world. It sharpens supposed neglects, creates imaginary afflictions, and delivers us over a prey

to

to fastidiousness, resentment, and spleen; or perhaps it assumes the aspect of excessive tenderness and tremulous philanthropy. In this disguise, it is so admirably delineated, by the pencil of an *unknown* master in the school of poetry, that I must recal these well-known lines to your recollection:

" Taught by nice scale to mete her feelings strong,
" False by degrees and exquisitely wrong,
" For the crush'd beetle first, the widow'd dove,
" And all the warbled sorrows of the grove,
" Next for poor suffering guilt, and last of all
" For parents, friends, a king's and country's fall.
" Mark her fair votaries, prodigal of grief,
" With cureless pangs, and woes that mock relief,
" Droop in soft sorrow o'er a faded flower,
" O'er a dead jackass pour the pearly shower *."

It is most true, my dear Miss M——, that this pseudo humanity always seats herself upon an inverted pyramid,

---

* New Morality, in the Poetry of the Anti-Jacobin.

which totters under her. The poor fly that is eaten by the spider, and the dear dog that *would* die of old age, form the basis of an ample superstructure; and her pity always increases in violence with her consciousness of its being utterly unavailing. She is most admirably described in a deservedly popular allegory *, as gazing through a telescope in search of distant distress, and overthrowing the petitioner who was at her elbow soliciting her hospitality.

The trials which arise from real sensibility governed by good sense, are of that improving kind which immediately proceed from the will of Divine providence, and bring with them present complacency and future reward. Some severe sects of Christians seem desirous, by their too rigid interpreta-

* Progress of the Pilgrim Good Intent.

tion

tion of particular texts of scripture, to deprive us of all the consolation arising from conscious well doing. It is true, if we compare our finite virtues with the purity and goodness of our Creator, the largest accumulation of mortal excellence must become as dust upon the balance. It is also acknowledged, that when our whole lives are referred to the test of his holy laws, they must fall so infinitely below the prescribed standard, as to compel us to trust for mercy on a surer foundation than our own righteousness. We grant that in many things we offend, and that our best deeds are tainted by infirmity. Yet virtue, circumscribed, imperfect, backsliding yet sincere virtue, still exists in the human heart. Her identity is acknowledged by every precept which requires her exertion; nay, she is even authorized to expect and to claim a *reward* * from that God by whom she is exercised and sanctified.

Amid those qualities which will entitle their blessed possessors to shine like stars in the kingdom of their heavenly Father, genuine benevolence claims pre-eminence. Let us not, then, consider the tenderness of heart which leads our sex to exert this glorious quality, as one of our trials, but as our noblest distinction; a distinction which the concurrent voice of travellers determines to be limited to no climate, enfeebled by no external circumstances, but as active amid the privations and ignorance of savage life, as in the refinement and opulence of civilized society. In every age and nation, women are alike distinguished by their promptitude to assist the miserable, and to sympathise with the unfortunate,

---

* Matt. xxv. 21 and 23.

nate, even at the expense of their own enjoyments.

But this world presents a mixed scene, in which artifice and fraud are constantly endeavouring to ensnare unsuspicious generosity; and hence arises the duty of placing our hearts under the guidance of our understanding, and of enlightening our judgments by the united radiance of knowledge and experience. The unavoidable trials of real sensibility chiefly arise from the difficulty of striking a due balance between the promptitude of a generous temper, and the caution of an intelligent mind. Only general rules can be prescribed for our direction in this instance; and as it is much easier to lay them down, than to apply them to individual cases, we must act for ourselves after all, and can seldom aspire to higher praise than purity of intention.

I forbear to mention the trials that proceed from change of fortune, from false friends, artful enemies, and opposite interests; from disappointed ambition and defeated enterprize; from accidental adventures, mysterious intrigue, and intricate business. To these troubles we are less exposed than men; and, speaking collectively, we only feel them in their rebound. Providence has withdrawn us from the turmoil of worldly contention; and it is only some peculiar circumstances, or the improper encouragement of a busy disposition, which removes us from our proper sphere, domestic retirement.

Instead of presuming, with culpable hardihood, to question the wisdom or the justice of that dispensation which has determined our lot in life, let us direct our attention, from what we might have been, to what we are; and if we find, by the general constitution of our bodies, and the frame of our minds, that we are rightly placed; if we discover, too, that our relative situation in society has many real advantages, let dissatisfaction and disobedience yield to acquiescence and gratitude.

Our weaker strength and more delicately organized frame evidently point out our unfitness for those laborious and dangerous exertions, which the common wants of civilized life demand from man. The necessity for our being thus exempted is further apparent, because the future generation would immaturely perish, or languish in the miseries incident to neglected infancy, if at one period we were exposed to severe fatigue and alarming perils, and at another were compelled by extreme toil to desert our feeble offspring, who, unlike the brute creation, plead by their

their helplessness for indulgence to their mothers. The laborious and hazardous undertakings to which women are compelled to submit in savage countries, are considered as the preventive of such an increase of inhabitants as would prove too redundant for their scanty supply of provisions. And if these physical causes present insurmountable obstacles to our engaging in athletic or dangerous employments, there seems to be no less substantial moral reasons for our withdrawing from that species of public business in which the labours of the head are principally required. An eccentric writer, who thought audacity a proof of genius, and mistook insubordination for independence and greatness of soul, seemed to suppose that the professions of a lawyer, a physician, and a merchant, were no ways incompatible with women. Little ingenuity is necessary to

disprove a theory which puzzled for an hour, and then sunk into oblivion, overwhelmed by the weight of its own absurdity, till it was fished up again by some second-hand dealers in paradox and innovation. That we can neither gain happiness nor advantage, from renouncing the habits which nature communicated and custom has ratified, is evident, by considering the qualities for which we have been most valued, and how far they would accord with an alteration in our relative situation. Could modesty endure the stare of public attention; could meekness preserve her olive wand unbroken amid the noisy contention of the bar; could delicacy escape uninjured through the initiatory studies of medicine; could cautious discretion venture upon those hazardous experiments which private as well as public utility often require;
could

could melting compassion be the proper agent of impartial justice; or, would gentleness dictate those severe but wholesome restraints, which often preserve a nation from ruin? Though I am inclined to think highly of my own sex (so highly, that I fear all my claims in their behalf will not be readily allowed), I confess that I can see nothing in the Utopian scheme of an Amazonian republic, which is not in the highest degree absurd and laughable. My conviction that we should make wretched generals, patriots, politicians, legislators, and advocates, proceeds from my never having yet seen a private family well conducted, that has been subjected to female usurpation. Notwithstanding any degree of science or talent which may have illuminated the fair vicegerent, the awkward situation of the *good man* in the *corner* has always excited

excited risibility, and awakened such prying scrutiny into interior arrangements, as has never failed to discover "something rotten in the state of Den-"mark." For, alas! my dear Miss M——, it is not only the temperament of our virtues which indicates the necessity of our being shielded from the broad glare of observation; there is, generally speaking, (and, you know, Providence acts by general rules both in the natural and moral world) too much impetuosity of feeling, quickness of determination, and locality of observation, in women, to enable us to discharge public trusts or extensive duties with propriety. The warmth of our hearts overpowers the ductility of our judgments; and in our extreme desire to act *very* right, we want forbearance and accommodation, which makes our best designs often terminate

exactly

exactly opposite to what we proposed. The qualities that we possess are admirably fitted to enable us to perform a second part in life's concert; but when we attempt to lead the band, our soft notes become scrannel and discordant by being strained beyond their pitch; and our tremulous melodies cause a disgusting dissonance, if they attempt to overpower the bold full tones of manly harmony, instead of agreeably filling up its pauses.

Experience, which enables men to penetrate into the designs of others, and to develope specious characters, is the result of such intimate knowledge of the world as must by us be very dearly bought. Fertility of resource and boldness of invention, which in the comprehensive mind of man become the parents of stupendous efforts, when modified by female passions, are apt

apt to degenerate into petty craft. More energetic and sanguine, but less endowed with courage and perseverance, we should, I doubt not, make well-intentioned and active, but rash and hasty reformers. Soon roused and soon intimidated; eager to adopt or to reject; unwilling to doubt, to temporize, or to examine; distracted by a multiplicity of cares, yet engrossed by one, how could we successfully manage the jarring interests and contending passions of the instruments that we should find it necessary to employ? Those nice susceptibilities of character, and that acuteness of moral feeling, which induce us to attend even to "the grace, the manner, and the decorum" of virtue, would never permit us to connive at a smaller evil in order to escape a greater; nor could we, consistently with our ingenuousness,

nuousness, act upon the politic principle of "divide and conquer." Our compassion and tenderness would never authorize us to exert that necessary severity, which is often obliged to devote a part to save the whole; yet both public and private affairs must often be conducted upon these principles. Our impatience of calumny would, on the one hand, urge us to that hasty vindication of our motives and actions, which would cause a premature disclosure of our designs; while, on the other, our strong perception of impropriety, and horror of reproach, would restrain us from adopting such measures as did not carry on their face their own justification. In fine we have too little of the "serpent's worldly wisdom" to indemnify us for bringing the "harmless dove" from its rural nest. Our adminis-

administration, whether of public or private affairs, would want the great desiderata of vigour, consistency, and extension; and we should ourselves be mere visionary perfectionists, the dupes of the specious, and the prey of the ambitious. Would this change in our destination promote general happiness? Should we ourselves have cause to rejoice in it?

It is possible, I allow, to produce many illustrious examples of female heroism and capacity; but *singular* occurrences do not overthrow the general conclusions of experience. The reigns of some of our British Queens may be fairly urged in proof of women being capable of discharging the most arduous and complicated duties of government with ability and perseverance. My observations are not designed to recommend the expediency

diency of a Salique law of exclusion from *hereditary* rank; but to strengthen the principles which consolidate *domestic* harmony. Besides, the sceptre's being ostensibly grasped by a female hand does not reverse the general order of government. The representative of authority is then indeed changed in gender; but power is lodged in the same sex which was wont to exercise it; men still execute the measures which men advise; and the sovereign is but an heiress, whose conduct is restricted and influenced by those laws which are virtually her guardians. But, to relieve the tedium of a discussion which I fear you will think dry and unnecessary, suppose we indulge in a slight historical digression. Will you deem me very hardy, if I attempt to strengthen my argument by

by some observations on the instances which our own island has afforded us of female supremacy? I will not derive them from the *supposed* influence of royal consorts or mistresses, but from the reigns of our actual queens.

The history of the first Mary is directly in point. She was, indeed, destitute of those amiable qualities of mercy and gentleness, which are considered as our best and most natural endowments; but in lieu of these, she was possessed of tremendous perseverance and sanguinary consistency. Good intentions, or at least sincerity of purpose, was never denied her; she aimed at what she thought reformation; she unquestionably wished her people to become " wise unto sal- " vation " in her own way; and her narrow mind presented no better expedients to make them so, than the faggot gallantry. If we compare her latter years with those of our first Edward,—whom in her public actions she much resembled, our sex must feel humbled at the parallel.

The miseries of the unhappy Queen of Scotland, so evidently ascribable to the graces, the virtues, and the failings of her sex, must, while they still draw the tear of pity for her fate, excite our lively sympathy for every woman who is called to the dangerous estate of sovereign power; especially in a realm where the fundamental rights of the constitution and the bounds of prerogative are not *decidedly* settled. How beautiful was the picture which she exhibited in early life of conjugal virtue and domestic felicity! how must we regret the death of Francis, which banished her from " Fair France," and sent her to a kingdom barren of social delights,

diency of a Salique law of exclusion from *hereditary* rank; but to strengthen the principles which consolidate *domestic* harmony. Besides, the sceptre's being ostensibly grasped by a female hand does not reverse the general order of government. The representative of authority is then indeed changed in gender; but power is lodged in the same sex which was wont to exercise it; men still execute the measures which men advise; and the sovereign is but an heiress, whose conduct is restricted and influenced by those laws which are virtually her guardians. But, to relieve the tedium of a discussion which I fear you will think dry and unnecessary, suppose we indulge in a slight historical digression. Will you deem me very hardy, if I attempt to strengthen my argument by

by some observations on the instances which our own island has afforded us of female supremacy? I will not derive them from the *supposed* influence of royal consorts or mistresses, but from the reigns of our actual queens.

The history of the first Mary is directly in point. She was, indeed, destitute of those amiable qualities of mercy and gentleness, which are considered as our best and most natural endowments; but in lieu of these, she was possessed of tremendous perseverance and sanguinary consistency. Good intentions, or at least sincerity of purpose, was never denied her; she aimed at what she thought reformation; she unquestionably wished her people to become " wise unto sal- " vation " in her own way; and her narrow mind presented no better expedients to make them so, than the faggot and the block. In her eagerness to obtain the desired end, she overlooked impossibilities: hence her marriage, in the decline of life, with a young foreign prince; hence her mal-administration of the domestic concerns of the state, and of its continental alliances. Her reign is a melancholy expansion of the passions of a weak woman, driven to cruelty and self-disgust by the opposition of her subjects, the bigotry of her advisers, and her own ignorance, rashness, and obstinacy.

I shall not be driven from the tenets that 1 have defended by the bright splendour of the Elizabethian æra; for no writers, except the parasites of her own court, ever ascribed *feminine* virtues to that *renowned* princess. Her education, conformably to the general taste of that age, was

learned

learned and comprehensive; and her understanding possessed the rare advantage of being alike solid and penetrating. The difficulties of her early life taught her discretion, and may I not also add dissimulation? while her long prospect of the throne which she was one day to ascend, induced her to study the science of government before she was called to wield the sceptre. In all but vanity, her mind was masculine. This vice certainly led her into a perfidious, though perhaps political sacrifice of a lovely competitor; and induced her, when past her grand climacteric, to court the praise of beauty, which even in youth she never possessed; and, unmindful of the deathless laurels which crowned her vigorous and successful administration, to decorate her withered brows with the myrtle of affected gallantry.

gallantry. If we compare her latter years with those of our first **Edward**, whom in her public actions she much resembled, our sex must feel humbled at the parallel.

The miseries of the unhappy **Queen** of Scotland, so evidently ascribable to the graces, the virtues, and the failings of her sex, must, while they still draw the tear of pity for her fate, excite our lively sympathy for every woman who is called to the dangerous estate of sovereign power; especially in a realm where the fundamental rights of the constitution and the bounds of prerogative are not *decidedly* settled. How beautiful was the picture which she exhibited in early life of conjugal virtue and domestic felicity! how must we regret the death of Francis, which banished her from " Fair France," and sent her to a kingdom barren of social delights,

delights, the haunt of ambition, and the den of morose fanaticism! How do we participate in her reluctance to relinquish the charms of elegance and refinement; in her endeavours to soften the harsh character of her subjects, and to conciliate the alarmed suspicion of Elizabeth, to whose superior and more wisely cultivated understanding, she could only oppose graces and accomplishments, which were to her not only useless, but actually hastened her fall! We see the weak precipitation of her sex in her rash assumption of her rival's title, and her hasty marriage with Darnley; and we discover the unrestrained feelings of wounded sensibility, in her avowed contempt of him after her discovery of his ingratitude and meanness. The events immediately following are so perplexed by contradictory statements, that though

gallantry. If we compare her latter years with those of our first Edward, whom in her public actions she much resembled, our sex must feel humbled at the parallel.

The miseries of the unhappy Queen of Scotland, so evidently ascribable to the graces, the virtues, and the failings of her sex, must, while they still draw the tear of pity for her fate, excite our lively sympathy for every woman who is called to the dangerous estate of sovereign power; especially in a realm where the fundamental rights of the constitution and the bounds of prerogative are not *decidedly* settled. How beautiful was the picture which she exhibited in early life of conjugal virtue and domestic felicity! how must we regret the death of Francis, which banished her from " Fair France," and sent her to a kingdom barren of social
delights,

delights, the haunt of ambition, and the den of morose fanaticism! How do we participate in her reluctance to relinquish the charms of elegance and refinement; in her endeavours to soften the harsh character of her subjects, and to conciliate the alarmed suspicion of Elizabeth, to whose superior and more wisely cultivated understanding, she could only oppose graces and accomplishments, which were to her not only useless, but actually hastened her fall! We see the weak precipitation of her sex in her rash assumption of her rival's title, and her hasty marriage with Darnley; and we discover the unrestrained feelings of wounded sensibility, in her avowed contempt of him after her discovery of his ingratitude and meanness. The events immediately following are so perplexed by contradictory statements, that

though

though general opinion now seems inclined to consider her conduct rather as imprudent than wicked, I will pass them, and hasten to the last scenes of her life; when, sinking with fatigue, destitute of friends, abandoned, helpless, and forlorn, the lovely fugitive threw herself upon the mercy of a sister queen; and, through eighteen years of tedious confinement, saw the sun only rise

" To mark how fierce her angry guardians frown'd,
" To mark how fast her waning beauty flew."

To the last period of her mournful days, she felt no other effect of her royal birth, than from its elevating her to be the alternate mark of jealousy and ambition. The symmetry of her person, the susceptibility of her temper, the graces of her manner, the elegance of her accomplishments, the warmth of her attachments, all that
made

made the woman amiable, destroyed the queen.

Our second Mary only occasionally held a delegated sceptre; and as her tuneful panegyrist * justly observes, was " instructed to command," by obeying the hero William. Her regencies may be produced as the brightest example of female administration, combining all those qualities of firmness, promptitude, vigour, prudence, and clemency, which constitute the definition of a well-ordered state. Yet this wise and amiable Princess certainly knew that the passive virtues were best suited to her sex. " Never," says a cotemporary author, "were the reins of government " more reluctantly assumed, more " wisely managed, nor more willingly " resigned." Her conjugal deportment

* Prior.

to a husband whom she eclipsed in amiable qualities, is a shining example of discreet acquiescence in general laws. Her positive refusal to accept a *solitary* sceptre, was not affectation, but wisdom. Her political interference was always marked by beneficial effects, because it was never unnecessarily obtrusive. The revered character of this exemplary lady, the sacred theme of Prior's chaster muse, adorned by every public and every private excellence, still call the muses to weep over her early tomb. Should her imperial robes be destined to array another English queen, may they, like the mantle of Elijah, convey a portion of her hallowed spirit; and may the inheretrix of her regalia resemble the blessed spouse of William, in all but her premature exchange of an earthly for a heavenly diadem!

The

The royal sister of this illustrious princess ascended the throne with equally good intentions, but with inferior abilities. The splendid successes that attended her public administration are confessedly attributable to the wisdom of her statesmen, and the heroism of her naval and military commanders. Her private infelicities, and the distractions of her latter years, are a proof of the unfitness of women to manage the intricate perplexities that arise from contending parties, or to struggle against those gentler sympathies of nature which in elevated situations must give place to the sterner virtues that extensive responsibility imposes. Her subservience to those violent tempers whom her station authorized her to overawe; her desire to accomplish ends which were utterly incompatible, and to reconcile characters essentially discordant;

discordant; her attachment to her exiled disinherited brother, and to many ungrateful favourites who had recommended themselves to her esteem by specious qualities, rendered her dignity a crown of thorns, which pressed hard on the aching brows of inbecile sickness. Yet, considered as a woman, what can we censure in Queen Anne? Pious and sincere as a Christian, anxious for peace, compassionate to the afflicted, affectionate to her kindred, an excellent wife, disposed to friendship, sincere, placable, and compliant.

I allow, that the reigns of many of our kings present as many, or I will say more enormous errors than the worst of those which I have specified; but let it be remembered, that their maladministration arose from what, it must be acknowledged, were their errors or their

their vices. In most cases, it was from the predominance of some amiable *female* quality, that our queens erred in their public duties. You well know, that it is not my aim to affirm our absolute unfitness to take the lead, whenever peculiar circumstances enforce the necessity of our so doing; for we may then, equally with the other sex, hope for that supply of preventing and restraining grace which will enable us to do our duty in the state of life to which we are *called*; and whenever the exaltation of a woman to a highly responsible situation can be foreseen, a particular regard to her education and early habits may enable her to blend the authoritative, magnanimous, and discriminating qualities that her station will require with the milder virtues of her sex. These assistances we cannot hope to possess, if we rush madly from our sphere, and resolve, uncalled, to venture on untried and forbidden paths. Cheerful acquiescence in the will of him who disposes of the lot, and steady application to the improvement of the talents with which we are intrusted, is our duty; we have already proved, that it is also our interest.

The propriety of our seclusion from public affairs is necessarily interwoven with domestic subjection. The humour of the present age leans so strongly to the aspiring qualities, independence and self-controul have such attraction in their magical sound, that I must prudently shelter my opposition to their delusive enchantment under the protection of mighty names, when I pronounce the dependant situation of our sex *advantageous.* "One very "common error," says Dr. Paley,
"misleads

" misleads the opinions of mankind on
" this head; viz. that, universally, au-
" thority is pleasant, and submission
" painful. In the general course of
" human affairs, the very reverse of
" this is nearer the truth : command
" is anxiety, obedience ease." While
applying this admirable observation to
ourselves, as dependant upon the wills
of our near connexions, I shall not
become the advocate of male tyranny.
Referring to the origin of authority
and submission, we may be assured,
that they were imposed for mutual
benefit. " Men do not," as another
great divine observes, "claim the su-
" premacy for any inherent superio-
" rity, nor for their own individual
" solace; but rather, that domestic
" peace may not be violated by per-
" petual competition. The right of
" command must be placed some-
                              " where,

" where, or how could the little re-
" public be regularly ordered; where
" then shall it be properly bestowed?
" Shall it be confided to strength and
" courage, enterprize and activity; or
" shall these qualities be made subser-
" vient to weakness, apprehension,
" gentleness, and a love of repose?
" Would not this be to constitute a
" state of perpetual warfare, as the
" qualities of the governor and go-
" verned would be diametrically op-
" posite to what their respective duties
" required?"

No portrait can be more truly amia- ble, than that of a well-disposed well-informed woman ordering her domestic affairs with propriety, and guided in the more important concerns of life by the judgment of a worthy intelligent husband; and if we meant also to draw a picture of human felicity, we
could

could not do better than copy from the same original. A well-disposed mind, conscious of its own imperfections (and no mind which is well disposed can avoid feeling them), shrinks from the burden of unnecessary responsibility. It can make allowances for the errors and failings of others; it cannot so lightly pardon its own. By committing our affairs to the disposal of one in whom we can confide, we always propose to ourselves quiet and self-enjoyment; but in a voluntary choice every degree of mismanagement subjects us to the reproach of misplaced confidence; where the choice is made for us, acquiescence is at least entitled to the solace of conscious rectitude: the authority of the agent will not prevent the effects of his weakness or mismanagement, but our submission is then justifiable.

Domestic

Domestic retirement is not only the scene where the passive virtues display their heavenly energies; it is also their secure asylum. From how many temptations is our sex preserved, by being placed in this enviable shade! We are so hedged in, and separated from the contagion of many vices by general opinion, established customs, and even by the natural repugnance of our own minds, that we must use violence before we can burst through the sacred enclosure, and solicit, or rather seize, contamination. We will mention, as instances, intemperance, profaneness, treachery, and cruelty. Even in the eyes of debauchees, a female bonvivant is contemptible; and indecorum of expression startles the most profligate, when it proceeds from that sex, whose presence is acknowledged to be such a restraint upon the boldest blasphemer,

blasphemer, as only ignorance and ill manners can surmount. Well might the inspired writer observe, that "there "is no wickedness like the wicked- "ness of a woman;" for the effrontery which enables her to brave infamy, ascertains the annihilation of those -lively sensibilities which might have led her back to commiseration and contrition. It is observed in the lower walks of vice, that when a woman is concerned in a robbery, murder generally follows; this is a probable consequence, for cowards are always cruel; and those small remains of generosity, which even a course of rapine cannot always eradicate, are foreign to a heart which has only conquered the restraints, but not the selfishness of fear. In men we have often seen ambition united with many excellent qualities; it has even been styled the error of

great

great minds. Conscious of ability, and insatiate of renown, conquerors and statesmen have generally been solicitous to do that "holily which they "would do highly;" but when woman has delivered herself up to unlawful cravings, her lively passions, and her eager desire to attain her purpose, combating with the sense of her weakness, has generally driven her upon the most detestable means of accomplishing a bad design. Macbeth, in the very act of murder, retains somewhat of the "milk of human kindness;" but "his fiend-like queen" has no other thought than self-security. Do not object that we contemplate these historical characters through the medium of fiction; their portraits are delineated with the most perfect resemblance to human nature. That of Lady Macbeth presents what, I believe,

believe, is rather rare in the annals of vice, a woman *genuinely* ambitious; for in our sex ambition is commonly a subaltern quality, stimulated by love, hatred, revenge, fear, or vanity. Like Kenrida in Shenstone's elegies, the aspiring female mostly anticipates. " How sweet are slumbers on a couch of state," or else wishes "To crown at " once the lover and the love." But the same baleful effects proceed from the mixed as from the primary passion; whenever an Athaliah covets undue pre-eminence, she arises with a determination "to cut off all the seed-royal." These observations, my dear Miss M——, are not wholly irrelative to the million. Ambition presents other temptations beside crowns, and has less bloody, though equally destructive consequences as those to which we have just alluded. I am

persuaded

persuaded that we must refer to this passion, when, under the guidance of vanity, many of those extravagancies which we shall be called upon to lament in the course of our correspondence, as ruinous to domestic peace, and derogatory to female character.

I do not think that women have less temptation to anger than men; because in the routine of family affairs they generally meet with perpetual, though trivial, trials of meekness; and we know, that the solid rock is more likely to be fretted by continual droppings, than broken by the rushing of a hasty cataract; but the present forms of society, and I grieve to add, its seemingly irresistible propensities, may make us enumerate as one of our advantages, that anger is not likely to involve *us* in very serious consequences. While the only sinful part of chivalry is is preserved from that oblivion which has involved its high-souled chastity, integrity, and generosity, we must congratulate ourselves that we are not likely to be *called out* for an unguarded expression, perhaps uttered unconsciously in a moment of temporary delirium. You will smile at my enumerating this security amongst our advantages; but the bloody register of false honour is become so voluminous, that it really is a consolation to reflect, that the whizzing ball or gliding steel are not likely to be classed in the list of *our* mortal diseases.

The customs of society give us advantages not highly valuable of themselves, but capable of being converted to real benefit. The attentions that we receive as women may certainly be, as Mary Wolstonecraft terms them, " engines of refined voluptuousness," when they minister to our caprice, our vanity, and our frivolity; but they are capable of a higher direction, and may be so received, and so directed, as to reform the morals of those from whom we require them. Gallantry (I here use that term in its *inoffensive* signification) has been so modified and curtailed by prevailing manners, that it is to be hoped women will not join in a conspiracy to annihilate the small degree of knightly courtesy which yet exists, by themselves assuming the deportment of amazonian boldness, or affecting amazonian independence. By indelicacy of habit, by unblushing confidence in conversation, and by the discovery of a vindictive disposition, we forfeit the respect to which the passive virtues, our natural endowments, are entitled, and must receive from all but brutes or monsters.

The passive virtues, my dear young friend, are not mean, servile, or cowardly. Dr. Paley places them in such a point of view, as may excite the emulation of the most aspiring mind. His definition is, "passive virtues are "of all others the severest, the most "sublime, and perhaps the most ac- "ceptable to the Deity." The foundation on which they stand is fortitude, magnanimity, and disinterestedness; and their sure reward is self-possession, and that peace of God which passeth understanding. The overstrained softness of affected refinement is as inimical to these heavenly qualities, as the fury of a virago; a life of uselessness and indulgence can never be a life of happiness. Whoever erects herself into the golden idol of self-importance will be perpetually harassed, by seeing inflexible integrity refuse to fall prostrate before her. Whatever painted gauds may pass upon the world as the trappings of happiness, it can only reside in the bosoms of those who are exercised in good works. The offices which are daily required of women, enable us to lay claim to this enviable distinction. Our relative situation in life preserves us from many temptations; we are more guarded by our natural propensities from some vices; and from others, we are more secured by habit and general opinion. We are in less danger of having our integrity censured by the allurements of fraud, ambition, or contending interests; but these are not our best advantages: our most glorious distinction is, that we are better fitted for receiving the tenets and obeying the precepts of that faith which will make us wise unto salvation; for, however infidels may misrepresent and cavil at lowliness and singleness of heart, these are the dispositions which fit us for the reception of the stupendous plan of redemption, and prepare us for evangelical holiness. Credulity and terror may make us superstitious, and obstinacy and ignorance may beget bigotry; but bigotry and superstition are mere opprobrious appellations when applied to true religion, and only reflect odium on the bestower. Here, then, our peculiar qualities give us advantages, which strength, courage, and wisdom, when unsanctioned by piety, cannot impart. A consciousness of infirmity is the admonition of nature, bidding us look up to " the rock from whence " we were hewn," and depend upon the power that has promised "to save " all who trust in him." Our general habits of submission and constraint tend to subdue our stormy passions, and to eradicate our corrupt desires; the humble offices of life in which most of us are engaged, make us acquainted

quainted with the wants of our fellow-creatures, and also dispose us to relieve the sorrows in which we have such full participation; while all the emotions of hope, fear, joy, grief, affection, and gratitude, to which our susceptible hearts are so peculiarly alive, form the very basis for a pure but animated devotion. Surely, then, my dear Miss M——, contemplating these inestimable privileges, these securities from vice, these incentives to virtue, these helps of grace and hopes of glory, we may adopt the language of a nervous, though now neglected instructor * of our sex, and "thank God that we were born women." Leaving you to improve these reflections as your piety will best suggest, I remain, &c.

* The Author of the Ladies' Calling.

LETTER

LETTER III.

Change of Manners in the Middle Classes.

MY DEAR MISS M——,

From the consideration of what we are designed to be by Providence, the proposed series of our correspondence leads us to inquire, what we become when we renounce the obligation of duty, and submit to be new-modelled by caprice or affectation. Though the woman of fashion boasts of having emancipated herself from those restraints which fetter the inclination of the woman of propriety, we shall discover that she really is in a state -of bondage, and has voluntarily submitted to injunctions no less numerous, and far more servile, than those which she has rejected. She has her trials too; for the wisdom of Divine Providence never suffers any glaring violation of its laws to brave its authority, without being reproved, or at least feeling the internal consequences of its pertinacity. We need not extend our researches to the comforts and advantages of a life of voluptuous dissipation, or indolent self-indulgence; they possess none. The punishments of the wicked do not, like the corrections of the faithful, heal the heart they are intended to probe.

Moralists are always censured for giving an exaggerated caricature of their own times. I am ready to admit, that in some respects we have improved upon our ancestors; that vice ceases to be gross, and manners are no longer stiff or pedantic; that society is governed by more agreeable and
convenient

convenient laws, and that dress, when it does not outrage modesty, is regulated by a purer taste, than that which ordained long waists, long ruffles, high pokes, and farthingales. It is also acknowledged, that our comforts are materially increased by mechanical and mathematical discoveries, and that knowledge is more generally diffused. I believe the learned are agreed, that in profound studies, which do not depend upon experimental philosophy, mechanical contrivance, or natural history, this age cannot sustain a comparison with those which laid the foundation of our church, and perfected our civil constitution. If the most proper study of mankind is man, our ancestors had the advantage of us in knowledge. Nor can we claim uncontested pre-eminence in charity; because donations from those ample stores which internal peace and commerce have diffused over this nation, must not be rated in arithmetical proportion with the *pittance* that could be spared from the urgent necessities of individuals, at a period when agriculture was ill understood, and often interrupted by civil wars, and when arts and manufactures were unknown. The benevolence, public spirit, and magnificent liberality of those perilous and needy times, are proved by the irrefragable testimony of many religious and charitable foundations, by stately edifices devoted to the advancement of learning, by splendid asylums for infancy and sickness, and by comfortable habitations for age and penury.

Charity is therefore only, what it ever has been, a striking feature in our national character. It is, indeed, so predominant a distinction, that even selfish-

selfishness, languishing in the dissipation and luxury of what is called high life, cannot avoid imparting some of its superflux to the poor and needy. Justice should be always done even to the least deserving; and it is to be lamented, that the author of a very spirited and well-principled satire*, while describing the "barren and dreary de-" sert of the fashionable world," has neglected to mark out the green Oasis† of charity. Perhaps it would have been false candour to have applied the name of this sublime Christian grace to the liberality of philanthropy; however, as even that indicates some remnant of moral feeling, some interrup-

---

* The Fashionable World Displayed.

† This term is used by modern travellers in North Africa, to signify those spots of cultivation which occasionally diversify the immense deserts that lie between Barbary and Negro-land.

tion of the frigid cold of a life of pleasure, it should not be passed over without commendation, though its motives do not entitle it to the praise of religious obedience.

It is no new observation, that the extremes of society are unfavourable to virtue. Wise Agur formed a wish upon this head three thousand years ago *, which for piety and prudence is alike entitled to everlasting remembrance. The levity and dissipation of the middle ranks are the singular and alarming characteristics of the present times. A dissolute sensual nobility is no novelty. It is also upon record, that the lower orders in these kingdoms have been dissatisfied, clamorous, negligent of their proper duties, and inclined to assume political

* Prov. xxx. 8.

supremacy. But the middle classes, where temperance, diligence, and propriety used to reside, the favourite abode of rectitude, good sense, and sound piety, have undergone a change within the last fifty years which must startle every considerate mind; so far as it relates to women, either as to the cause or the cure, it presents a topic demanding our close attention.

Though the effects of commercial prosperity are in some degree generally diffused over the nation, it has principally affected the intermediate orders. Successful adventure, professional skill, patient diligence, or laborious industry, often bring a rapid increase of wealth to families that have not, either by habit or education, been taught the proper use of it. The first blessing which fortune seems to offer to an ill-regulated or ill-informed mind is self-enjoyment, the second is distinction; hence arise luxurious modes of living, and absurd exhibitions of grandeur. It would be well, if the consequences of these errors were limited to what inevitably follows extreme indulgence, I mean disease and contempt; but the effects are rarely confined to the faulty individual. The gains of successful adventure are soon lost by a reverse of fortune; the savings of diligence and industry cannot supply the waste of carelessness and indolence; the profits of the professional man die with him, and nothing remains to his family but the hoard which frugality reserved in the hour of prosperity. Yet if people so circumstanced will vie in expense with hereditary wealth, what must be the consequence? what indeed, but that which we hourly see, in bankruptcies, suicides, helpless widows and destitute orphans, in every species of nefarious fraud, extortion, and swindling imposition; we must also add, that the ruin caused by this rage for luxury and show is visible in the madness of gaming-houses, and in the licentious haunts of prostitution.

Would to heaven our sex could be vindicated from the heavy censure that must fall upon those who, to purchase the *eclat* of a few years, not the *happiness* of an hour, involve themselves and families in destruction! An impartial review of living manners compels me to confess, that we are in this point often more culpable than our weakly indulgent partners. It is Eve who again intreats Adam to eat the forbidden fruit: he takes it, and is undone. Men in this rank of life have generally less *taste* than women; they are amused by their business through the day, and at its weary close they would generally be contented with the relaxation which their own families afforded, if those families were social, domestic, cheerful, and desirous to promote their amusement. But since the potent decree of fashion determined it to be unfit for the wife of a man in reputable circumstances to employ herself in domestic arrangements, or useful needle-work, time has proved a severe burden to people who are destitute of inclination for literature. To relieve themselves from a load, the weight of which they are too proud to acknowledge, they have felt obliged to mingle with what is called the world. Did any of these adventurous dames consider the heavy services which this association requires, did they fairly rate the fatigue, the perplexity, the slavery of being *very genteel* upon a *limited* scale, they would think it better to prefer a plain system of social comfort, even at the expense of that ridicule

ridicule which, I lament to say, such a deviation from refinement would incur. Yet, when there is no housekeeper in the spice-room, nor butler at the sideboard, an elegant entertainment occasions more labour and perplexity to the mistress of the house, than she would undergo by a regular performance of services highly beneficial and praiseworthy. What anxiety is there that every part of the splendid repast should be properly selected, well dressed, and served in style! What care to keep the every-day garb of family economics out of sight, and to convince the guests that this is the usual style of living; though, if they credit the report, it must only confirm their suspicion that their hostess is actually insane. What blushing confusion do these *demi*-fashionists discover, if detected in any employment that seems to indicate a little re-maining regard for prudence and œconomy! What irregularity and inconvenience must the family experience during the days immediately preceding the gala! what irritation of temper, what neglect of children, what disregard of religious and social offices! And for what is all this sacrifice? to procure the honour of being talked of; for happiness, or even comfort, are rarely expected at such entertainments. Notwithstanding all due preparation, something goes wrong, either in the dinner or the company. The face of the inviter displays mortification, instead of exultation; and the invited disguise the sneer of ridicule under the fixed simper of affected politeness. Nor let the giver of the feast complain of disappointment. She aimed not to please, but to dazzle; not to gratify her guests by the cheerful hilarity of her table, but to announce her

her own superiority in taste or in expense. When the hospitable hostess spreads her plain but plentiful board for friendship and kindred, for those whom she loves or respects, those whom she seeks to oblige, or those to whom she wishes to acknowledge obligation, where vanity and self are kept out of sight, and real generosity seeks no higher praise than that of giving a sufficient and comfortable repast with a pleasant welcome, a fastitidious observance of any accidental mistake, or trivial error, might be justly called ill-nature and ingratitude; but when ostentation summons her myrmidons to behold the triumph, let ridicule join the party, and proclaim the defeat.

But this insatiable monster, a rage for distinction, is not content with spoiling the comforts of the cheerful regale; luxury has invented a prodigious number of accommodations in the department of moveables; and the mistress of a tiny villa at Hackney, or a still more tiny drawing-room in Crutched Friars, only waits to know if her Grace has placed them in her baronial residence, to pronounce that they are comforts without which no soul can exist. Hence it becomes an undertaking of no little skill, to conduct one's person through an apartment twelve feet square, furnished in *style* by a lady of *taste*, without any injury to ourselves, or to the fauteuils, candelabras, consoletables, jardiniers, chiffoniers, &c. Should we, at entering the apartment, escape the workboxes, foot-stools, and cushions for lapdogs, our debut may still be celebrated by the overthrow of half a dozen top-gallant screens, as many perfume jars, or even by the total demolition of a glass cabinet stuck full of stuffed monsters. By an inadvertent remove of our chair backwards, we may thrust it through the paper frame of the book-stand, or the pyramidal flower-basket; and our nearer approach to the fire is barricadoed by nodding mandarines and branching lustres. It is well, if the height of the apartment permits us to glide secure under the impending danger of crystal lamps, chandeliers, and gilt bird-cages inhabited by screaming canaries. An attempt to walk would be too presumptuous, amidst the opposition of a host of working-tables, sofas, rout chairs, and ottomans. To return from a visit of this description without having *committed* or *suffered* any depredation, is an event almost similar to the famous expedition of the Argonauts. The fair mistress, indeed, generally officiates as pilot; and by observing how she folds

or

or unfurls her redundant train, and enlarges or contracts the waving of her plumes, one may practise the dilating or diminishing graces according to the most exact rules of geometrical proportion; happy if we can steal a moment from the circumspection that our arduous situation requires, to admire the quantity of pretty things which are collected together, and inquire if they are really of any use.

Dress is such an important subject to women, that I must claim permission to refer to it frequently. Two chief ends seem to be pursued by those who imitate the great in this particular; namely, that it should show their wealth, and proclaim their uselessness. When the cost of a gown excels the countess's, which it resembles in shape, the wearer feels an immense satisfaction, no matter though her dress be
but

but a publication of her vulgar manners; elegance is, in her opinion, a saleable commodity; she has the draper's bill in her pocket (I hope with a receipt to it), and she knows that she is better dressed than her ladyship by fifteen shillings a yard. It may, however, happen, that deficiency in cash or credit may limit the taste of the fashionist to the meer vamping up and remodelling her old wardrobe; but, as an exact copy would argue a very little soul, it now becomes necessary to caricature the mode, and to exhibit in full extravagance that which, when really modified by taste and worn with propriety, was graceful and becoming. Either way the wearer announces her intention of not being mistaken for the drudge of patient utility. The flow of her drapery, the slight texture of her attire, the tasteful arrangement of her tresses,

tresses, and the studiously inconvenient situation of her ornaments, proclaim an airy sylph, a Grecian nymph, a "mincing mammet," or, to speak in her own language, a very fine lady: they cannot possibly denote the industrious housewife, or the help-mate of man.

The pursuits of this *lusus naturæ*, this creature formed to feed on the toils of industry, consist of laborious idleness. As, after all her exertions, her situation in life does not allow of her being genteel in *every* thing, parsimonious œconomy and heedless expense take their turn. To be as smart, not as her equals, but as her superiors, it becomes necessary that she should excel in contrivance; I do not mean in that prudent forethought, which enables a good wife to proportion the family expenditure by the regular order

der of necessities, comforts, conveniences, and superfluities: this gradation must be reversed, and superfluities take the lead. French wines may be introduced on great occasions, by a daily retrenchment of small beer; and wax-lights may be had for routs, by limiting the number of kitchen candles. If her husband and children dine on hashed mutton, she can provide ices in the evening; and by leaving their bed-chambers comfortless and inconvenient, she can afford more drapery for the drawing-room. Even white morning dresses will not be so very expensive, provided you are expert in haggling with the washer-woman, and do not dislike being dirty when you are invisible; and if you know cheap shops, and the art of driving bargains, you may even save money by making *useless* purchases. New

modelling

modelling your household and personal ornaments is, I grant, an indispensable duty; for no one can appear three times in the same gown, or have six parties without one additional vandyke or festoon to the window-curtains. These employments will therefore occupy your mornings till the hour of visiting arrives; then you must take care to dismiss the bed-gown and work-bag, and, having crammed every thing ungenteel out of sight, assume the airs of that happy creature who has nothing in the world to do, and nothing to think of but killing time. Fashions are now to be discussed, public places criticised, shopping schemes adjusted, and evening parties fixed. After your morning ramble, you will just get time to treat your own family with a little of that spleen and chagrin which have been excited by your having seen an
acquaintance

acquaintance in her carriage while you were still compelled to be on foot, or by having met one better dressed than yourself, whose husband cannot *half* so well afford it. You must, in compliance with the pressure of time, hurry over the business of the toilette; and if during the remainder of the evening, you are not quite in so great a crowd as a duchess, you may at least console yourself with the consideration that you are as useless to your family.

My dear young friend will smile when I add, that our second-rate ladies plead that they undergo all this from motives of *conjugal duty* and *maternal affection*. It is necessary, they say to keep up connections; their husband's credit depends upon their appearance; nobody notices them if they do not live like other people; or
perhaps

perhaps the good man himself insists upon their being very smart and living in style. When this latter excuse happens to be the fact, we certainly mus seem to sail with the stream; but th plans of expense which we dare no openly oppose, a regard to our children and indeed self-love, should induce to counteract gradually. Vanity i rarely a prevailing feature in a man' character; men sometimes, indeed choose that their wives should be gail adorned, and hurried through a roun of amusements, because they are their property; but much oftener they do this out of gallantry, with a view to gratify them, and by way of showing them their attachment. In the latter case, it is very possible to decline, with affection and steadiness, every expensive attention which prudence disapproves; and in the former, this mania of unconjugal *ostentation* may be checked, by appearing rather to *endure* than to *enjoy* the exhibition. Men are far more sensual than vain; they are less influenced by general opinion, and less affected by petty detraction. The passion of self-indulgence leads them into expensive habits. Disdaining the fictitious happiness which depends upon the breath of others, dissipated men pursue what they call *substantial* bliss. They know that the club will at least for an hour exclude sorrow and ensure gaiety. The circulating glass has with them the united properties of Lethe and Helicon. To a man of this cast, the society of his wife and children is vapid, or at least not sufficiently poignant to be long entertaining. If his tavern-engagements can be counteracted by a well-dressed dinner, and a few a few cheerful friends at home, a woman is justified in resorting to these measures, by way of weaning him from his more dangerous propensities; even though she should be obliged to sacrifice those pure domestic pleasures, which happy wedlock affords those people whose fortunes are equal to their wants;

" An elegant sufficiency, content,
" Retirement, rural quiet, friendship, books,
" Ease and alternate labour, useful life,
" Progressive virtue, and approving heaven."

I cannot admit the generally-received excuse, that convivial meetings and tavern associations are promoters of business; because I have known men transact a great deal, and even rise from low life to opulence, by means of an established character for probity, integrity, and sobriety. The general habits of the superior part of the mercantile

cantile world confirm my opinion. But, granting that the convenience of driving a bargain, or forcing trade, may withdraw the husband from the domestic circle, the dissipation of the wife is left without excuse. The craft of deceiving by false appearances is followed by too many, to be a profitable *speculation* any longer; and wealthy people, whom it is desirable to make dupes, are much sooner induced to trust a man by the appearance of order and œconomy in his family, than by hearing that it is the gayest in the street; which cautious traders often think is the surest omen of approaching bankruptcy. Nor is the wisdom of the mother more apparent than that of the wife, in thus cultivating taste at the expense of propriety; from a design of procuring respectable connexions for her daughter;

which intention is almost sure to be frustrated by one circumstance: every body is embarking in the same traffic; and the market is so full of well-dressed spinsters, who are adepts in the art of spending money, that if our laws permitted the same plurality of wives to men of fortune as the Koran sanctions, still many an elegant belle would be in want of a good *establish-ment.* The nymphs of modern times, who spend their days in music and dancing, differ much from the ancient heroines of pastoral and romance; for these latter, if they fed at all, subsisted upon the wild productions of groves and meads, quaffed the limpid stream, and reposed under umbrageous trees; so that they really were very *cheap* companions. But now, ornaments are no longer composed of natural flowers, unless, like Lady Teazle, the fair one

pur-

purchases roses at Christmas. Penelope (except we seek for her in the circle of royalty) cannot fabricate a vest for her son or sire; and even " white-handed Phyllis " disdains "to " dress herbs and other country messes " for Corydon and Thyrsis;" and indeed I much fear that those gentlemen would no longer find them " savoury." The rich gudgeon, for whom *portionless* elegance drops such numerous baits, often possesses that most ungallant acquirement, arithmetic; and, having discovered that a dowerless wife will have the same conjugal anxiety to support his pecuniary reputation, seems inclined to ally himself to a gold-fish. Compassionating the claims of those numerous young women, who found their expectation of being supported on their total inability of helping themselves, I would advise,

advise, by way of experiment, that some few mothers would show a wish of furnishing the next generation with *wives,* by cultivating those qualities in their daughters which will prevent them from being converted into *mistresses.* Diffidence, frugality, and industry, are indeed quite out; but, for that very reason they will certainly be stared at, and may give their possessor that notoriety, which those who only herd with a crowd never can obtain; and it is even possible that some whimsical humourist may take a fancy to such vulgarity, and, remembering his old grandmother's proverb, may overlook the want of fortune with a wife, when there appears to be something in her which promises to wear well. I grant that such a man must be a quiz; yet quizzes have made good husbands; at least, it is better to be

the

the wife of such a one, than to be eternally transforming an old tambour muslin into fresh nets to entangle a Titus or a Brutus, who, being himself upon his preferment, perfectly understands the mystery of *entrapment.*

I can no longer support a strain of irony. My soul is moved to the liveliest indignation, and keenest sorrow, at the wilful degradation of my sex. With what propriety do we complain of the state of dependence in which God and the laws of our country have placed us, when we render ourselves infinitely more helpless, more destitute (shall we not say more servile and despicable?) by deserting our proper sphere, by neglecting the useful duties that we might perform, by sacrificing the interest and the affections of our families, not to be even an object of admiration, distinguished for elegant

gant frivolity and expensive nothingness; but for the sake of starting in a crowd to run the race of folly, of echoing a forged tale of happiness and splendor, which has been too often told to be even specious? For let me once again repeat the often-urged fact, dissipation, finery, and extravagance, are *too frequent to attract attention.* Even if you strain the bursting nerves of credit, and not only squander every shilling of your children's property, but ruin every one whom you can ensnare, some rival, equally unprincipled, but better situated, will outshine you. Could these poor slaves of vanity, who judge by the supposed opinion of the world, hear the contemptuous sarcasms which this unsuitable parade and expense excite from those whom they attempt to propitiate, it is possible that the dread of ridicule might
prove

prove a more powerful restraint, than the reproachful tears of their ruined offspring, and the curses of their creditors. In the higher circles, a more costly dress than the occasion requires is considered as an indelible proof of vulgarity; the grandeur of the lady's paraphernalia is contrasted with the pettiness of her attendant lacquey, the shabbiness of her buggy, or the leanness of her laborious Rozinante; and the suitability of the *tout ensemble* must be arranged with no common skill, if it escapes the prying glance of piqued superiority. An uncommon assemblage of feathers, a treble accumulation of train, a double row of plaited Valenciennes, or a sleeve decorated till it reminds one of Petruchio's whimsical description[*], as in-

---

[*] "What! up and down, carv'd like an apple-tart,
"With snip, and nip, and cut."
SHAKSPEARE.

disputably announce the entry of some would-be fine lady to a well-bred assembly, as a copper complexion does a native American to the Canadian settlers; and the company wait, with the *nonchalance* of good breeding, till some cockney misapplication of the W, or provincial inversion of the aspirate, determines the stranger's tribe and latitude. For let it not be supposed, that the propensity to appear what we are not is limited to crowded cities: few retirements are so sequestered, as to prevent their being explored by the visitations of this ostentatious passion for *saleable* refinement. The village madam hopes her showy array, and fastidious scrupulosity, will convince you that her husband cannot be a farmer; and, at the peril of a brisk retort, you must forbear to insinuate to the market-town *elegante*, that she may be wanted in the shop.

They

They suppose that it is very vulgar to be thought useful; and the acknowledgment of an honest avocation is to them a reproach. Yet, though wealth and commerce have rendered the *externals* of the gentlewoman so attainable, that she is no longer to be distinguished by her habit; it is left to more patient and less prosperous times to transcribe the complaisance, affability, condescending attention to the claims of others, love of propriety, and regard for decorum, which are the *essentials* of this desired distinction: the adoption of these latter qualities is too arduous an undertaking, and requires too many privations. Rudeness of habit is soon cast aside, rudeness of manner is more adhesive. The country lass doffs the former at the dress maker's, where she leaves her red cloak and her humility; but she is infinitely too much delighted with her transformation, to suppose respect to superiors, or civility to equals, can be necessary, now that the Miss Stitchwells have pronounced her *quite another thing.* Is there, my dear Miss M——, a more disgustin produce than insolence engrafted o awkwardness? or are any airs so ridi culous, as those which are assumed b purse-proud ignorance?

Your excellent mother filled a si tuation in life too decidedly respect- able to derive any real elevation from attempting to outstep the modesty of nature. Her good sense taught her both to perceive and preserve its ad- vantages. I enjoy a soothing grati- fication from reflecting, that as, by avoiding the extremes of parsimony and extravagance, she gave an exam- ple of prudence to people of her own rank;

rank; so the wisdom of the maxims by which she governed her conduct was *generally* useful. When the pressure of the times presented those claims to which country gentlemen are especially exposed, she did not plead public-exigency as a reason for restraining private benevolence; nor did she make her domestics miserable by penurious restrictions. " The " world," she observed, " will always " allow you to spare from yourself. " If you never attempt to outshine " your neighbours, they will pardon " your old gown, and permit you to " stay at home unquestioned." By limiting our wardrobe, or giving up an excursion, it is possible to avoid the censure of being mean, and the pain of knowing that we embarrass our husband's affairs.

It is worth considering, at how much

much less expense of time, fortune, and comfort you may purchase the reputation of solid, than you can of brilliant qualities, provided you are contented with being a good *plain* character; for few are inclined to contest the right of a claimant to that distinction. I do not advise you to gain it by struggling against the torrent, but by getting out of its way, and suffering it to glide quietly by you. If the attention of your superiors be the object at which you aim, this is the surest way to obtain it; for, to return to the observations of my deceased monitor, "though every rank
" in life has pressed into the station
" immediately preceding, none seem
" conscious of their own advancement,
" while all are piqued at the exalta-
"tion of their inferiors." The clergyman's daughters will express much
indigna-

indignation that the Misses Flamborough have imitated their Sunday hat, at the very moment that they are fabricating a head-dress resembling what the baronet's lady wore at the last county assembly. It is in vain, therefore, to rush forward with precipitation; our superiors will only suffer us to overtake them for one moment; and then, with a smile of contempt, they will vault on a higher eminence, where you must try to perch beside them, or else be thrown down by the crowd of jostling inferiors, who are pressing hard upon you. To step aside is the only wise method; and, to be convinced of the absolute necessity for our so doing, let us for a moment turn our eyes on the lower orders of society. Our attention shall be first directed to that with which we are most connected, domestic servants.

vants. What is their appearance; what are their pursuits; what, generally speaking, is their moral character? The propensity to appear what they are not, has operated so strongly in this class, that few mistresses, however besotted themselves, can refrain from complaining of its ill effects; and it is impossible to go into a mixed company, without being assailed with narratives of the extravagance, ignorance, folly, and finery of maid-servants. Yet, to say that they only faithfully copy the examples which are set before them, would not (generally speaking) be too severe an answer. But this subject must be reserved for future discussion*.

We have seen, that no speculative advantages can accrue either to our husbands, or our daughters, by our

* See Letter XIVth.

extravagance. Suppose we now estimate the pleasure really enjoyed by a woman who devotes herself to expensive gratifications, who wears the most elegant dress, gives the most sumptuous entertainments, goes every where, and sees all that is to be seen. I allow that the being thus occupied must be too much devoted to self-enjoyment to feel anxious about her deserted family; to care whether her children are brutes, idiots, or cripples, further than as they affect herself; to be solicitous how her husband amuses himself in her absence; to shrink at the apprehension of the carelessness or the dishonesty of her servants; or to mind having her morning slumbers broken by a levee of clamorous duns. We may deny that she ever attains what she pursues, pleasure; and our proof of this assertion is derived from the

the palling effect of satiety on the physical constitution of our bodies; and from the certain fact, that pleasure ever flies away the fastest when it is most eagerly pursued. The rational dame, who spares one evening in the week from domestic occupations, will enjoy a lively party, a well-acted play, a concert, or a ball. She will feel the force of contrast; and every agreeable incident will be engraven on her memory, for the purpose of amusing the beloved group, who will crowd around her next morning, to inquire the history of the gay evening. She has a still greater chance of being gratified, as she will enter the festal scene with spirits undepressed by that load of bodily debility which sleepless nights and listless days must occasion; beside, amusement is not the business of her life; and if what she enters into

into falls short of her expectation, it is but a petty disappointment, and she has other resources.

"The sleep of the labouring man " is sweet," says the inspired penman; and surely nothing is so delightful, as, after a day spent in the peaceful exercise of some honest calling, to sink upon our pillows, conscious of well-meant endeavours, and confiding in that God who has promised to accept them. Fatigue of this kind never injures the animal frame; it is repaired by rest and refreshment; and the morning, which renews the *demand* for exertion, revives the *power* of compliance. The fatigue which arises from excessive dissipation is of another description. The exhausted body has lost the ability of revivification; the clamour of music, the clashing of carriages, assail its feverish slumbers;

the

the mazes of the dance, and the glare of theatrical scenery, still flit before the frequently unclosed eyes; the passions are not yet calm in the throbbing bosom; envy enumerates the ornaments of a rival, and chagrin dwells upon the slight curtsey of an opulent acquaintance. The votary of pleasure rises unrefreshed, and a listless yawning morning is the penalty which she must pay to nature for having forced her beyond her ability. These are the moments that engender spleen; the dissatisfaction that she feels is averted from herself, on whom it ought to fall; but, as she really is unhappy, it must fix somewhere. Very probably, she will discover that her evening's chagrin was owing to her husband, who either *looked* as if he did not wish her to go out, or *prevented* her making a more pleasant party, or
restrained

restrained her expenses, or *dropped* some harsh expression which broke her spirits, always meek and tenderly sensitive. Perhaps the children are troublesome, cross, humoursome, and want more attention than she has leisure to give them; or perhaps the French governess may be negligent, the abigail impertinent, or the cook tipsey. It is happy when the disease fixes in some remote part, and only prompts the sufferer to treat her family with a detail of the cruel usage that she has undergone; and a pathetic explanation of the extreme hardship, that she, who has such a relish for pleasure, should never be permitted to taste it. Mistaken creature! who told thee that this world was made for butterflies? Call me not too severe, nor suppose that I overcharge the portrait. I know the depravity

pravity of the human heart too well (shall I own too experimentally?) not to be convinced that they who have no time for self-consideration, and religious communing, may be esteemed fortunate if they do not fall into still grosser faults and misfortunes.

To descend a little from the line of society that we have been considering: I have often contemplated the good city pair, who set out for their box in the country on Saturday night, and return time enough to open shop on Monday morning. We rustics might suppose, that after the fatigue of six days they would look forward to the sabbatical rest with ecstacy; and that their purpose for going into the country was to enjoy the heavenly blessings of reflection and devotion in retirement. Quite the reverse; their intention is to have a party of friends. The

travelling

travelling vehicle is laden with provisions; and though the mistress of the "snug retreat" arrives at it late and weary, she must unpack her plate, dust her china, and arrange her dessert that evening. A little indulgence next morning would be excusable, provided the family were in readiness to perform the appropriate duties of the Sabbath; but, unhappily, there is a multiplicity of reasons to prevent this observance. The church is a long way off; it is cold and damp; the pew is in an obscure corner; the weather is suspicious, and a shower would destroy the patent net mantle; or perhaps (which is a still more insurmountable difficulty) the patent net mantle was left in London. The kitchen too now begins to give " dreadful note of preparation;" not from " armourers accomplishing the knights,"

knights," but from the shop-maid's chopping force-meat, the apprentice's cleaning knives, and the journeyman's receiving a *practical* lesson in the art of waiting at table. For, do not suppose that the entertainment is to be merely comfortable and social. No; it is to be a display, a set out, and as much intended to elevate and surprise as a Grosvenor-square gala. Certainly it is fortunate, that the legislature still prohibits opening shop of a Sunday; as but for this remission of worldly toil, many people would be obliged to leave the garden of taste quite uncultivated. The company at length arrive; they admire the furniture, praise the garden, and declare their intention of *coming very often;* for it is so delightful to be out of the smoke of London. Dinner is now served; and then "they eat, they drink," but probably

bably not "in communion sweet;" nor do they "quaff immortality and joy," because they neglect to visit the fount where those blessings are dispensed. Surely, if it were not for being a *little* in the fashion, a quiet domestic religious Sunday would be quite as comfortable. But I betray my ignorance in using this term: comfort is abjured by all who enlist in the ranks of vanity; and as, among the high ton, the eclat of the fête depends upon the violence of the squeeze; so, among second ton, the prodigiousness of the preceding fuss determines the pleasure that your visitors are to give you. One morning's trouble would be enough for a common-councilman's wife; but who would mind being perplexed in the extreme for a whole week, provided one could say that we gave a dinner to *Alderman* Marrowfat, and *all* his family.

Permit me to attend to an apology which is often made for this style of gentility; I mean, that it is patriotic; though, in refuting this pretence, I may deviate a little from the prescribed bounds of female authorship. It is allowed, that fine ladies of all descriptions are *nuisances* in their own families; but then it is said they are *public* benefits; they force trade, promote the circulation of cash, and reward the ingenuity of manufacturers. To preserve the metaphor, whatever is forced must be proportionably delicate and hazardous. If luxury, by becoming universal, increases the wealth of the community, the artificial wants of each individual are also multiplied; and though the merchant receives more for his commodities, the demands of his family, and the frequent insolvency of his connexions, leave him in a worse situation, than when frugality and moral honesty were more prevalent. Those, indeed, are the solid pillars upon which trade must rest; remove them, and its destruction is inevitable. The maxim, that private vices are public benefits, has sunk into contempt, with the deist* who endeavoured to establish it.

All civilized states have agreed in cherishing those privileged orders whose rank or wealth made them the proper patrons of learning and the fine arts, and the encouragers of all the happy efforts of mechanical industry. From persons thus circumstanced, society demands munificence, splen-

* Mandeville.

dour, and hospitality. Liberality, elegance, and refinement, are the required characteristics of their immediate inferiors. The third degree should be contented to be distinguished by benevolence, œconomy, and propriety. Humanity, diligence, and frugality, become indispensable duties to the fourth class. Industry, humility, and general good-will, are so suited to the lowest state of life, that when the poor part with these virtues, they deprive themselves of their best consolation and richest possessions.

Let us look back on the times that are just past, and estimate the present by them. Soame Jenyns's popular description of the embarrassment of a country knight's family at an unexpected visit, would not now suit the domestic situation of a creditable farmer. Several steps in society have therefore,

therefore, been passed in the progress of refinement since the publication of Dodsley's Miscellanies. I have heard a well-attested tradition of a country lady who was the heiress of large possessions, and, what was then called, genteelly educated. It was determined by the females of the family met in council upon the occasion, that she should appear in the great hall clear-starching lawn ruffles, when she received the first visit of a favoured admirer. It is impossible to calculate how many degrees of manners are here passed, since the few who still continue to be notable blush to be thought so: yet this event happened about the beginning of the last century. I need not multiply anecdotes of this kind; the archives of every family can supply numerous attestations in point.

In low life, the gradation used to be from rags and dirt to tidiness; from thence to comfort; from comfort, improvement proceeded to superfluity. But even the pauper, if she move at all, now strides from filth to finery. May not the discontent and depravity of the lower orders be attributed to this circumstance? and that such discontent and depravity do exist, those who have the opportunity of close observation cannot doubt, though it has not yet assumed sufficient ripeness to attract legislative attention *. When pining want beheld its neighbour rising to decent comfort by unremitting industry and frugality, the possibility of obtaining equal advantages stimulated him to equal exertions. But the enormous wages

* In Letter XIVth. this subject is resumed.

which

which artisans now receive in many trades * support a style of living, to which the most rigorous toil of the day-labourer, the worsted weaver, or many other less profitable occupations, would be totally inadequate. If the males in the artisan's family are sober and industrious, their earnings are sufficient for the maintenance of the whole household: the wife, no longer feeling the daily necessity of adding to the common stock by the notability of herself and her daughters, is often induced, not only to *remit vigilance*, but to *allow of waste*. A style of appearance is assumed, the expense of which leaves them totally unprovided in an hour of sickness and misfortune;

* In several branches of the woollen trade, common hands may earn two guineas a week; yet even a short illness reduces them to extreme distress.

and also, by its absurdity and impropriety, deprives them of the good opinion of their superiors, who certainly would have been inclined to have extended their kind aid to alleviate that distress, against which prudence had in vain endeavoured to provide an adequate defence. What sort of servants, or poor men's wives, young women bred in idleness, and dressed in taste, are likely to make, is not *now* my inquiry: I speak of the effects of this unsuitable, and indeed useless abundance, upon the mind of the really indigent man; and surely it must render his tattered garb still more comfortless, and his brown crust more unsavoury and degrading. He could have passed by the magnificent mansion of the gentleman, the elegant residence of the rector, or the comfortable dwelling of the farmer, without heaving a sigh

or

or uttering one complaint at his hard lot; but the luxuries and indolence of those whose birth and education are the same as his own, wring his soul with anguish; and he supposes himself injuriously treated, since all ranks may be idle and extravagant except his own. Perhaps if we were so situated, we might be equally faulty. The contented cottager, quiet, sober, laborious, and cheerful, is fast disappearing from our rustic haunts; wretchedness, with all its attendant train of vices, or thoughtless, and I may add insolent extravagance, the result of great gains and little foresight, supply his place.

And is the nation really benefited by this change of manners? The loom may have more employment; the straw-manufacturer may have a greater demand; indeed, trade of every kind may receive a momentary impetus; but morals, which are the vital part of society, are attacked by a mortal disease. The middle ranks no longer feel ashamed of being in debt; the lower do not blush at receiving (I should rather say demanding) parochial relief, though œconomy might have preserved to them the blessing of independence. In vain does the mistress advise her servants to save the gains of prosperity; she is answered, that what they earn is their own; this is a land of liberty, and they have no notion of screening their parishes. To assume a more dictatorial tone, even to paupers, is impossible; they would tell you, that God made all men equal, and question your title to that preeminence which permits you to reprove them.

These are the effects of flourishing

trade and prosperous manufacture: are they symptoms of national prosperity, or internal decay? Allow me to quote the words of an eloquent writer*; who, having observed that this country was flourishing in all the arts of civil life, remarks, that "per-
"haps it is running the same course
"which Rome had done before; from
"virtuous industry to wealth; from
"wealth to luxury; from luxury to
"impatience of discipline, and cor-
"ruption of morals; till by a total
"degeneracy, and loss of virtue, being
"grown ripe for destruction, it falls
"a prey to some hardy oppressor;
"and, with loss of liberty losing every
"thing that is valuable, sinks gra-
"dually again into its original barba-
"rism." Such an oppressor, my dear

---

* See Dr. Middleton's Life of Cicero.

Miss M——, seems near at hand. He wants neither ambition, hatred, boldness, nor inclination to destroy us; but let us hope that there still remains enough of true religion among us, to obtain a *respite* from that merciful God who promised to spare offending Sodom, if ten righteous, or rather religious people, could therein be found. And may we so profit by our present chastisements, as to see the necessity of checking that career of degeneracy which proved destructive to every nation that has preceded us in empire, wealth, and renown!

My conviction that luxury, and affected refinement, have already passed those bounds which defend private happiness and public security, would induce me to confine our correspondence entirely to those orders whose conduct is most important to society, and

and among whom the insinuating arts of dissipation have lately gained a most alarming preponderance; but a regard for my literary reputation, together with the zeal natural to all reformers, prompt me to endeavour to obtain a fair hearing for my remonstrances, which I am convinced my present labours never would receive, if I did not occasionally introduce my readers to *very good company.* The fascinating names of the Marquis, and Lady Elizabetha, have caused many a village nymph to toil through six long volumes of intricate adventure, of which they never would have perused six pages, had the same story been told of plain John and Betty. It is with some reluctance that I quit a field of observation in which I have few competitors, to pursue a *beaten* track, wherein I am also preceded by personal

sonal experience and superior ability. Remarks on the manners of the great world cannot come with a good grace from one who has seldom emerged from the bosom of retirement (I could almost say, of domestic seclusion), and who consequently must feel a doubt whether the pictures from which she copies really were correctly sketched. Yet since I have promised to make some observations on prevailing opinions, I must not omit those leading characters whose conspicuous situation draws the attention of the world, and who give law to numerous aukward copyists. Considered in this point of view, the manners and morals of the great assume an influential consequence that is highly important to society; though, if confined to themselves, their depravity is less intimately connected with national ruin,

than

than a dereliction of principle in the great mass of the people would be; and especially among those who, by being placed in the medium between riches and poverty, should present a barrier to the vices and temptations of either extreme, and at the same time offer an asylum to every thing which is intrinsically estimable in both. The political importance which this rank possesses in England; the general information, sound sense, and unsophisticated manners that were their marked characteristics; the blameless occupations, domestic tenderness, modesty, simplicity, and unaffected gentleness, that distinguished their wedded partners, all heighten my regret that these solid excellences should be bartered for German principles, illustrated by French practice. It is not that I believe the middle classes

classes to be the most corrupted; it is because that corruption, if it fix here, destroys the vital principle, that I address the females of this most enviable, this most respectable order, with energetic intreaties to check their vain pursuit of false fame and absurd importance, and to resume the genuine graces of their natural character; beseeching them to remember that none can become contemptible or ridiculous, unless they desert the post at which the God of Nature has commanded them to stand. But I must now forsake my compeers, to address a more elevated station; conscious of being in many respects unequal to the task of public censor, and presuming only to gather a few scattered observations that have been over-looked by my predecessors, or to discover some noxious weeds which have

have recently shot forth. A new subject seems a hint for me to conclude my present epistle, and gives me an opportunity to assure you how fervently I am, &c.

LETTER

LETTER IV.

Absurdities and Licentiousness among Women of Fashion.

MY DEAR MISS M——,

I RESUME our correspondence; happy in the assurance that you are interested in the subjects I have hitherto discussed; and presuming not only on the partial affection that you have long shown me, but also on your natural candour, which I know induces you to pardon inadvertencies wherein the head only is concerned, provided the heart be free from those bad intentions which transform imperfections into crimes. We will enter upon the topic proposed in the conclusion of my last letter, without the formality of a tedious prologue.

There

There are numerous and popular writers, who have employed themselves in traducing the order that we are about to scrutinize; describing it as an excrescence springing out of the body politic, and draining every useful member of its vital juices, in order to swell its own putrid mass into a most hideous and most dangerous deformity. I will tell you a few of the abusive terms bestowed on these " earth-treading stars," by an author who was at least free from the feminine fault of mincing her language, and spoke out without the least ambiguity. She considered "monarchy " and hereditary rank to be such evils, " as balanced all the advantages which " Europe derived from civilization; " and so unnatural, that, in order to " account for their introduction, men " *blasphemously* supposed the human " race

" race had burst from its orbit, like a
" lawless planet, in order to steal the
" celestial fire of reason; while the
" vengeance of heaven, lurking in
" the subtle flame like Pandora's box,
" afflicted the earth with these retri-
" butive curses to which all our mi-
" sery and error are owing." In fine,
she thought " that it was the pesti-
" ferous purple, and the honours that
" flow from it," which had reduced us
poor women to the state of woeful degradation in which her writings found
us, namely, without political rights,
without masculine strength, compelled
to be obedient to our husbands, and
inclined to expect filial obedience
from our children; accustomed also
to consider modesty and gentleness
as constituent parts of our own character; disposed to attend to religious
duties, and to look forward to another
world,

world, not as the place where our
" indefeasible perfectibility is to ex-
" pand," but as the region where the
promises of salvation shall be fulfilled.
If the inversion of the present orders
in society will also produce this change
in the relative situation of our sex,
how ought we to *cling* to the present
state of affairs, and *supplicate* its continuance!

I have quoted from a book * which,
by supereminent absurdity and audacity, exposed the principles that it
meant to support to profound contempt. It, indeed, amazed and confounded for a day; and it received all
the assistance which an elaborate
analysis could bestow, to elevate it
into lasting celebrity. It was soon
found, however, that the times were

* The Rights of Women.

not

not sufficiently illuminated to bear such strong doctrine; and the disciples of the school of equality have since found it more convenient to gloss and soften, than misrepresent. The same democratic principles, however, pervade many popular works, especially dramatic performances, to which the *privileged* orders (as the nobility and gentry are cabalistically called) have most unwisely lent their patronage; and that not merely by countenancing the author, or applauding the scenic representations that are deeply tainted with the leaven of democracy. Party rage may now boast the same sacrifices as public virtue formerly enjoined; and though we have not our Curtii or our Decii, who *immolate* themselves to save their country, we have many men of birth and rank who seem inclined to pile their

their possessions and honours on the very brink of a precipice, to exalt the minion of the faction which they espouse. The first people in the kingdom have not scrupled to support, not merely the *equality*, but the *supremacy* of the mob, during the frenzy of a democratical contention for parliamentary honours; and thus they virtually signed the testimonial of their having long usurped unjustifiable ascendancy, and the certificate of their deserved degradation; little thinking that the sentiments and principles which they instilled into their clamorous adherents, would abide with them, and produce serious effects, when the temporary purpose for which they were promulgated was forgotten How far ambitious motives may justify gentlemen in thus endeavouring to *assassinate* their own importance, is not the present question. Modern patriotism may determine, that it is noble to reverse the part of Sampson when he was prisoner among the Philistines, and to pull down the pillars of your own state, when you find that you cannot climb into its upper story. But since our sex are happily *prevented* from engaging in these turbulent scenes, by native delicacy, by regard to their general reputation, and even by their fears, I do not feel myself called upon to vindicate them from the charge of being accessary to that general contempt for their superiors, which is so marked a feature among the populace. Imbibing the spirit of Mrs. Candour, in that masterly (though in some respects dangerous) play, "The School for Scan-"dal," I am resolved, "let the news-"papers say what they please of canvassing

" vassing beauties, haranguing toasts,
" and mobbing demireps," not to believe one syllable; and if " I repeat
" such anecdotes," it is only to usher in my observation that the world is grown so censorious, it even credits *impossibilities.* I wish I could acquit the illustrious culprits of every other proof of their being concerned in a conspiracy against their own order and consequence, with as much expectation of being *credited,* at least by my *country* readers.

But though I profess myself a steady advocate for that gradation of wealth and rank, which, if not positively appointed by God in scripture, is there shown to have been nearly coeval with the world that we inhabit; and which is not only the natural consequence of the moral government of the Almighty, but also the medium through which

which he thinks fit to convey a greater portion of happiness to the human race than it could otherwise enjoy; I am not so infatuated, as to maintain that the blessings of education, wealth, rank, leisure, authority, and reputation, are granted to a few with uncontrollable occupation; but rather that their possessors should employ them to the benefit of the whole community; that such as labour may not have cause to reproach those who rest for being drones in the state. The God and Judge of the whole earth does not bestow his spiritual or temporal blessings by any arbitrary rules of unconditional preference. When a talent is given to any one, an account is opened with the giver of it, who appoints a day in which he will arrive and " re-demand his own with usury." Nor are these children of prosperity

in

in reality so much better situated than their lowly fellow-creatures, as the jaundiced eye of envy is apt to believe: at least, ignorant envy is sure to fix upon a wrong person, and to select, as the object whose affluence causes her pining discontent, some besotted sensualist, who, forgetting his stewardship, presumes to turn the estate of which he is guardian entirely to his own account, and not only to " eat " and drink till he is drunken," but also to neglect, and even misuse, his fellow-servants. Independent of that fearful sentence which hangs over him, suspended by the gossamer thread of this frail existence; namely, " the Lord when he cometh shall ap- " point him a portion with unbelievers, " where shall be weeping and gnash- " ing of teeth," the present situation of this self-devoted Dives is most miserable.

which he thinks fit to convey a greater portion of happiness to the human race than it could otherwise enjoy; I am not so infatuated, as to maintain that the blessings of education, wealth, rank, leisure, authority, and reputation, are granted to a few with uncontrollable occupation; but rather that their possessors should employ them to the benefit of the whole community; that such as labour may not have cause to reproach those who rest for being drones in the state. The God and Judge of the whole earth does not bestow his spiritual or temporal blessings by any arbitrary rules of unconditional preference. When a talent is given to any one, an account is opened with the giver of it, who appoints a day in which he will arrive and "re-demand his own with usury." Nor are these children of prosperity in reality so much better situated than their lowly fellow-creatures, as the jaundiced eye of envy is apt to believe: at least, ignorant envy is sure to fix upon a wrong person, and to select, as the object whose affluence causes her pining discontent, some besotted sensualist, who, forgetting his stewardship, presumes to turn the estate of which he is guardian entirely to his own account, and not only to " eat " and drink till he is drunken," but also to neglect, and even misuse, his fellow-servants. Independent of that fearful sentence which hangs over him, suspended by the gossamer thread of this frail existence; namely, " the Lord when he cometh shall ap- " point him a portion with unbelievers, " where shall be weeping and gnash- " ing of teeth," the present situation of this self-devoted Dives is most mi-

L 2 serable.

serable. Excessive indulgence breeds a thousand bodily pains and mental infirmities; even supposing that it does not proceed to what are called criminal gratifications, capricious humours and unseasonable wishes haunt that breast whose desires centre in self-enjoyment. The expectation that we may be for ever lulled on the bosom of delight, is thwarted by the constitution of the world, and even by our own physical qualities. Pain is necessary, or we should never truly value pleasure. Rest must be bought by exertion, or it begets *ennui*. We cannot taste the full blessing of success, if we have never known disappointment or anxiety. The animal gratifications of our nature must be preceded by privations, or our appetites will not be satisfied, but palled. When penury has toiled hard for a

scanty

scanty meal and a slight covering, it weakly supposes that rest, repletion, and sumptuous attire, must be felicity; the indolent victim of spleen, the surfeited voluptuary, and the capricious votary of vanity, whose tortured imaginations are ever pursuing something new and strange, could, if pride permitted them to make a frank disclosure, present a very different picture of enjoyment; and, in spite of its restrictions, the tortures of a diseased body, and the miseries of an afflicted spirit, often wring from them the agonizing regrets that they cannot change situations with the poor labourer who walks whistling by their window, returning cheerful from his daily task. Amid the numerous complaints with which discontent ungratefully assails Divine Providence, the most frequent arise from those who have squandered its bounty in such pursuits as are incapable of satisfying a rational being; or who have supposed that the cup of blessing could not be enjoyed, but by quaffing such immoderate draughts as produce intoxication.

Where a woman who is born to the possession of rank and affluence properly appreciates those blessings, and, instead of circumscribing them within the narrow sphere of self-enjoyment, endeavours to diffuse improvement and comfort wherever her influence extends; if, through the conviction of being merely an agent, she lift her eyes to him who intrusted her with ample powers, she feels in the consciousness of well doing, and in the serene delight of reflected bliss, the purest earthly gratification. Her heart frequently speaks to her in the inspired language of the royal Psalmist,
"The

" The lot is fallen unto me in a fair ground, yea I have a goodly heritage." On the other hand, if she suppose herself to be some " mighty leviathan," sent into the ocean of existence "to take her pastime therein," the chain which held her to society is broken, or at least held together only by the fragile tie of interested dependence. She did not participate in the griefs of others, her own sorrows therefore shall be *all* her own; she sought not to make her fellow-creatures happy, they will not therefore rejoice in her prosperity. Now sorrow is a lonely sensation, and may be endured with heart-breaking poignancy without any partaker, or even witness; nay, it is ever most intolerable and overwhelming, when unrelieved by sympathy, and unsoftened by pity; but happiness, at least that species of it which selfish characters pursue, is a superadded quality, and subsists by the agency, or at least upon the opinion, of the multitude. The proudest beauty, when shining in the full glare of magnificence, is more dependent than any of the wondering spectators, past whom she glides with affected disdain; for, in reality, it is a persuasion that they admire her, which swells her vain heart with imaginary consequence. Does the mercenary bride, who sacrifices every prospect of domestic happiness to a stately equipage, a magnificent mansion, and a numerous retinue, really find her enjoyments increased in the hours of solitude by knowing that she possesses these baubles? No; it is while she shows her diamonds to a rival, or an enemy, that her vitiated taste appreciates their value; not by the

the pleasure they bestow, but by the pain they excite. For be it be remembered, that though the benevolent passions possess the sanative quality of healing their own wounds; or, to speak without a figure, though even disappointed goodness administers satisfaction to the soul; the selfish appetites and malignant propensities have but one miserable chance of affording a transient enjoyment; as soon as the animal exhilaration subsides, or the demoniacal conviction of having tormented another, has taken place, depression of spirits, and the stifled, yet powerful reproaches of the heart, convince the unhappy being who endures them, that she has mistaken her road to the bower of bliss.

Though the desire of living solely for themselves has been the characteristic of misused power and affluence, ever since the days of Solomon, yet since commercial acquisitions, and mechanical inventions, have increased the number of luxurious enjoyments, and also the rage of competition, the temptations which beset the great and wealthy are in these days exceedingly multiplied; and whoever among them shall take that mistaken road to happiness which we have just described, will feel continually stimulated to deviate further from the right path, by that rash pursuit of their inferiors which was the subject of my last letter. Vanity ever labours to disprove the wise king's apothegm, "that "there is nothing new under the sun." She rejects the petition of every votary who cannot support his claim to eclat by the testimonial of novelty. What was esteemed great and elegant for a nobleman fifty years ago, would now be be vulgar and mean for a successful mechanic. Nay, the extravagancies of the last winter must be outdone by the present, on peril of your becoming *nobody*; a term of reproach, which, though not formidable in its sound to those who have not been initiated in the mysteries of fashion, is known by adepts to contain the very quintessence of abuse, and to be much more derogatory to the unhappy being to whom it is applied, than all the epithets that Billingsgate or the Rue de St. Honore could invent.

Novelty must, therefore, be obtained; but how can it be acquired? Though loosely arrayed, like the fair queen of Ogygia *, you sit and sing by your fires of cedar, in an apartment decorated by the purest rules of Attic

---

* Calypso.—See Telemachus, Book I.

simplicity; though you convert yourself into a beauteous Fatima, and recline on an embroidered carpet in your magnificent alhambra, where a thousand lamps reflect the blazing diamonds which clasp your robe; though the eastern and western Indies lavish their treasures on your board, where the fruits of the tropic blaze beneath the ice of the pole, the wife of some rich cit, whom you despise, will have a costume more truly Greek or Arabesque; she will sport finer diamonds, have richer flavoured wines, or produce her hot-house delicacies a fortnight before you. Did you ever resolve to effect by absurdity what you cannot do by taste, and to fetch your models from countries ignorant of just proportion and correct design, mandarines, dragons, and pagodas, may be purchased; pyramids and sphinxes can

can be procured; a sign-post painter can devise scrawls which ninety-nine out of a hundred will suppose are an hieroglyphic; and the rival lady and her villa will become completely Egyptienne, or la Chinoise, at the next gala. I scarcely think that the most glaring indelicacy, or the grossest vulgarity, would rescue you from the hazard of having that palm of celebrity which novelty bestows wrested from your grasp by fresh discoveries; for the fascination of a great name, and the magic charm of being *outré*, would soon so transmute our old ideas on those subjects, that we should think it was only owing to prejudice that we did not before discover the refinement of immodesty, and the delicacy of obscenity. The partial exposure of the person, or the limited rejection of those restraints, which formerly secured

cured good manners and good morals, have been found of no avail. Your insatiable pursuers have followed you with remorseless activity; they have discarded more drapery, and dashed with less squeamishness. I almost doubt whether it would be possible for you to set them at fault by sheltering in the bath of Diana, or even in a kraal of Hottentots. What then must become of you? If you stand still, you will not only be overtaken, but preceded; and, melancholy to add, if you once give up this struggle of competition, your former triumphs are of no avail. It will be useless to say, "I *was* in fashion in the year four;" fashion admits no tense but the present. If fifty ladies fainted at one of your routs *then*, the fifteen who died away *last* night, at Lady Jostle's furnishes conversation for the town

this

this morning. Though your supper-rooms resembled a grove of cherries last May, cherries at a guinea a pound this April overwhelms the remembrance. You have entered into the service of a severe task-master, who, though you are crippled and exhausted by your former efforts, will still demand the wonted tale of bricks with rigorous exactness.

What is then to be done? Renounce all allegiance to these arbitrary mandates. Recollect that, though in proportion to the abundance of your fortune, or the vincibleness of your family entails, you may be the first fashionist for one, two, or three seasons (none but Midas can hope to hold out longer), fresh competitors are every year starting; and, as the philosopher's stone is still undiscovered, you must at last be dethroned. Soften the

the pain of your certain humiliation, therefore, by a timely and graceful retreat. Resign the sceptre, even in the career of your glory, which you know you cannot long retain; and moderate the triumph of your successor, by appearing accessory to her exaltation. These, I grant, are the counsels of worldly prudence; but I am addressing those whom I suppose to be incapable of nobler motives.

Aware of the evanescent nature of that celebrity which is only founded on expensive inventions, some ladies of high ton have cherished the Satanical ambition of becoming pre-eminent in vice. Adopting the horrid sentiments ascribed to the prince of darkness, they declare by their actions, that "to reign is worth ambition, though in Hell." They have, therefore, torn off those coy disguises in in which sinners of past times enveloped their enormities, and with unblushing fronts have proclaimed to the questioning world, that they " dare " do every thing, because they dare." Their contempt of reputation, and bold defiance of mankind, were soon discovered by a species of writers that are fellow-labourers with those whom I mentioned in the beginning of this letter; these wishing to reduce the world to an equality in infamy, as the former do to introduce equality of misery. Aware that this marked effrontery of character shocked the feelings of all beholders too much to gain converts, they invented a set of phrases which softened its atrocity, and at the same time preserved its publicity. I know not where this new mode of language originated; but as it consists in nothing but the *inversion*

and

and *perversion* of terms, it cannot be considered as any great proof of genius. It has been as eminently successful in the diplomatic papers, and other state fabrications of our Gallic neighbours, as the wand of mercury in Dryden's Amphytrion; and has actually either charmed the world to sleep, or taught them that " black is " not black, nor white so *very* white;" so that, though a sound more threatening than the Indian war-whoop bellowed in their ears, they persisted in calling it the peaceful lullaby of their innocent rocker. John Bull's natural aversion to *Mounseer's* cradle has hitherto prevented him from being completely swaddled; but his disposition to believe that people are what they call themselves, makes him run some danger of being duped by a misconception of the words patriot, honour,

honour, and independence. The principles of John's wife have been attacked in a stronger manner by those liberal apologists for vice and folly, who, setting out perhaps with a misapplication of a scripture text in praise of mercy, or enjoining charity to repentant sinners, soon proceeded to infuse into the unwary mind a *charity that is not scriptural,* by apologizing for sinners *who do not repent*, nay, who glory in their crimes. Hence the unreflecting, but well-meaning reader, who possesses much candour and little information, is led to believe that the perjured adultress, from whom she shrunk with abhorrence, may be a most *amiable, elegant, interesting* creature, with only *one* failing, a too susceptible heart; but then that heart was so benevolent, so condescending to the wishes of others, or perhaps so sincere, so incapable of disguising its own emotions, that it could not sacrifice what it felt to be its *invincible* propensities to the opinions of the world; which, after all (for nothing is certain), are perhaps only founded on the dictates of prejudice. Here the guileless readers, whom I have supposed attending to this new ethical lecture, will perhaps start; but they are then gently reminded, that freedom of thought is the indisputable privilege of the inhabitants of this country; that many learned men (and here a long list of well-sounding names will be introduced, blending the obscure with the celebrated, to swell the pomp of evidence, and misquoting without fear of detection), men most *exact* in moral conduct, and most celebrated for social virtues, have *doubted* whether, all things considered, the present

present aspect of the world might not be considerably improved, by a departure from those very *rigid* rules which were built on a too literal interpretation of the Jewish classics and early Christian writers*. A few shining examples, such as Aspasia, Sappho, and Ninon de l'Enclos, will then be brought forward, to prove that women may be very eminent for taste and science, and continue to be much respected, who have not strictly adhered to the decorums prescribed to the sex. It will then be allowed, that these severe tenets have expedience to recommend them, and therefore they are highly necessary for the great body of the people, who, if the cords of discipline were relaxed, might run into

* These denominations have been most irreverently applied to that book which is dictated by the Spirit of God,

gross depravity; from which the refinement natural to cultivated minds, and polished manners, will inevitably preserve that part of our species which might properly claim to be exempted from law, as being capable of giving law to themselves. These well-bred authors will then proceed to call your attention to the improvements which philosophy has introduced into arts and sciences of late years, preparatory to the bold assertion that morals are a science, and as much capable of improvements and discoveries as mechanics, chymistry, or astronomy. They will then enter that metaphysical maze in which plain sense is sure to be bewildered, and talk to you concerning the origin of moral obligation; but whether you are taught that it is self-love which vibrates from the centre to the extremity of social being,

or

or whether you are assured that ethics originated from man's preposterously surrendering his natural rights in order to procure the doubtful blessing of society; in either case the freedom of man as an agent is preserved, and his right to do wrong, if he judges that wrong to be expedient to his well-doing, is implied. Some few, indeed, of these apostles of falshood have re-adorned the old necessitarian system, and, by making the human race the passive machines of over-ruling fate, have contrived to transfer our crimes either to our nature, or to the stars; but this scheme wants the gloss of novelty.

The principles thus laid down, the application follows. What would be highly criminal in the footman, and the chamber-maid, becomes a pardonable *levity*, when referred to the actions
of

of those whose rank in life secures the world from the political consequences of their indiscretions. The opprobrious terms of preciseness, uncharitableness, narrowness of sentiment, and littleness of soul, will be employed to deter you from thinking unfavourably of those *soft* indiscretions, which, though they may be somewhat wrong, hurt nobody else, and are accompanied by all the amiable virtues, and all the alluring graces. Perhaps, indeed, these apologists of licentiousness may proceed so far as to affirm, that it is not vice, but virtue, to obey the dictates of nature, and that the conscious mind is its own awful world. This, with an observation that no characters are faultless, that we must take people as we find them, that many mean very well who act a little indiscreetly, and that chastity is apt to
be

be scandalous and religion morose, includes, I think, most of the arguments which these seductive advocates of candour employ, to mislead innocence and excuse guilt.

The ramifications of this pseudo-liberality extend very far. They branch from that pernicious system of infidelity which has done such mischief in the world; and, though compelled to disguise its nefarious designs in England, still labours with unwearied but cautious diligence to sap the fair foundation of our national fame. It is supposed, that there are but few *tainted* characters in England, who are not willing to allow the political expediency of religious institutions. They, however, mostly engraft somewhat of papistical principles on deistical practices, and seek to commute with the laws of their country,

try, by an occasional observance of one of its injunctions; I mean attendance on public worship. I know not whether this solemn mockery of the Deity be not more prejudicial to religion and morals than if they "stood "forth all infidel confest," and verbally denied the authority which their actions disclaim. Certainly, the national church is exposed to much undeserved odium on account of the scandalous lives of these political conformists, who cannot be justly ranked among her members. I have often heard it remarked, that the eyes of the congregation are naturally directed, during the reading of the commandments, to the conspicuous gallery in which some high-born violater of these positive precepts lolls with graceful negligence, hears the divine vengeance plainly pointed at his

his offence, and perhaps articulately joins in the petition to be preserved from the cherished sin that he is determined to hug in his bosom. The effect of such mockery upon the minds of a large assembly, inferior in station and education, probably also in ability, must infinitely overbalance all the good which could be derived from the most impressive discourse that Christian zeal and Christian knowledge ever delivered from a pulpit. Nothing, indeed, but that supernatural grace which the Almighty has promised to those who ask it of him, can protect *all* who witness such hypocritical effrontery from feeling their faith and hope affected by its contaminating influence.

It is, indeed, much to be wished, that the church of England would again exert its *inert,* but not *rescinded* authority, and banish notorious profligates from the house of God, while they continue to glory in their shame. It would be well too (I mean prudentially well) if these bold defiers of public opinion would recollect, that the populace, whose suffrages they court on other occasions, cannot be so very despicable, as to be unworthy of being even treated with the decencies of outward observance. It would be fruitless to tell the arrogant infidel, or lofty debauchee, that the souls of those whom he puts in jeopardy by thus triumphantly displaying his impenetrable vices, will rise with him at the last day, equal in rank, equal in duration of existence, and will accuse him at the judgment-seat of an impartial God, for having acted the part of the arch-apostate, by betraying those who rashly confided in his superior intel-

intelligence and more enlarged information. To those who are armed with that shield of licentious derision which is only vulnerable in the days of sickness or calamity, I must only address temporal dissuasives. I must shew them that it is indiscreet, and madly adventurous, to thrust their crimes upon the observation of those who, however ignorant or misjudging, perfectly understand the equalizing nature of ignominy. The grosser vices receive no exaltation from being clad in ermine; their nature is so very brutal, that their combination with education, rank, splendour, and affluence, cannot diminish their hideous aspect, or lessen the contempt of those who know that it would be very easy to rise to such "a bad emi-"nence." The dutchess who has violated her marriage oath, who is discarded

carded by her husband, and married to her gallant, is but the same degraded creature as the porter's wife who is transferred at Smithfield to a new purchaser. The reproachful epithets that we bestow upon the vulgar sinner, are by her scornfully rebanded to her dignified copartner in guilt; and let not the offender, who has only birth and wealth to boast, flatter herself that the world in general thinks those distinctions sacred. Public opinion is not yet so illuminized as the ear-tickling flatterers of greatness represent; and if they value their possessions more than they do their vices, they must rejoice that "many thou-" "sand knees in 'Britain' have never "yet bowed to the false gods" of sophisticated morality. The virtues of probity and chastity are closely allied; and prescription will be found to

be

be but a feeble support, where the solid pillars of affection and respect are undermined. But to return from, I hope, an improbable contingency, to what really happens: though the opprobrious epithets which the adulteress merits may not reach her own ears, they echo through a space proportioned to the circle which she was originally intended to enlighten and inform. She is there estimated, not by those arbitrary rules which her own depraved associates decree shall supersede common sense and moral obligation, but by the principles which, when she lies upon her death-bed, she will own are the unswerving dictates of rectitude and truth. At the bar of public opinion, the titled courtezan receives little mercy. Every plea which might be urged in favour of the poor night-wanderer, who of-fends for bread, turns into an aggravation of the guilt of her who *courted* temptation. The friendless outcast, whom no one acknowledges, sins, deeply sins against her own soul; but she who was hedged in from ruin by fortune, fame, and family, involves a host of distinguished connexions in her disgrace, and stamps a stigma of opprobrium on every part of her (perhaps till then unsullied) lineage. The pennyless prostitute is precluded from repentance; for will any one afford her an asylum, to try if that repentance be sincere? The prostitute of high life has only to stop in her shameless course, and to retreat to that retirement which is ever ready to shelter her disgrace and confirm her contrition. The former was most likely the child of ignorance, who knew little of good or evil till experience

ence taught her a severe lesson, by which she became wise too late. Her passions were probably unrestrained by discipline or precept, and some seducer spread a snare for her personal chastity, before reflection and observation taught her its value. I fear I shall say too much, if I suppose that the noble wanton has been early trained in the principles of truth and holiness; but we must allow that she has been taught the necessity of restraining her passions, accustomed to respect the opinion of the world, and to regard those decorums in her *outward manners* which awe the licentious. If she were a wife (and I grieve to say that in high life the major part of lost characters belong to the matronly order,) the libertine was deterred from " assaying by his devilish art to reach "the organs of her fancy," by the apprehension of those large fines by which the law has lately attempted to deter adulterers, holding out the certain prospect of long imprisonment, or banishment from their native country, to that tribe of led captains, and " second brothers to men of quality," who are most apt to arrange themselves in the ranks of cecisbeos and gallants. But whether the lady be wife or spinster, she was equally defended by those laws of honour which compel the fashionable rake to be an expert swordsman before he aspires to be a seducer; and few of our gay Lotharios would choose to run the gauntlet with husbands, fathers, and brothers, unless pre-assured that the guardians of their Calista's honour, "fierceness and pride

"would

"would soon be charmed to rest," and the yielding fair be content to give up all for them.

Such are the inferences which common sense always draws from a story of criminal intrigue; and however the eloquence of the bar may seek to divert indignation, and ingeniously palliate the frail fair one's guilt, by representing her as the victim of her gallant's unremitting assiduity, or as being so supereminently endowed with taste, eloquence, and beauty, that all who beheld her must love; this rigid censor, inflexible as a British judge on the bench of justice, adheres to the honest bluntness of her original conclusion: taste, eloquence, and beauty, are too common adjuncts of polished society to disarm her severity; and she determines that there must be a great degree of criminal levity in the conduct of a woman of rank and fortune, before any man, especially a mere opera lounger, or genteel dependant on the family, could dare to assail her with a criminal proposition. Here, therefore, the term seduction must be misapplied, except when the criminality, or studied negligence of the husband, has made him the active agent of his own disgrace. In this case, common sense may feel inclined to extenuate the lady's offences; but it will only be by lamenting that the manners of the age have an alarming tendency to promote conjugal infidelity, by sanctioning conjugal indifference; but she will still insist, that though a libertine, or contemptuous husband, must make his wife miserable, it is her own indiscretion that makes her criminal. An agreeable insinuating young man * is too dange-

---

* See Letter XII.

rous a companion for a resentful offended woman, to be admitted to confidence and intimacy. If her sorrows are too poignant to be confined to her own bosom, let her find a *female* friend with whom she may more safely repose them. If the solitude of home be insupportable, connexions may be formed, and amusements sought, which cannot endanger her fame, her virtue, or her peace. It is the madness of despair to rush into the arms of ruin, because she has drawn a blank in the lottery of connubial happiness. Let a lady shew, by her conduct, that though her wedded protector deserts his charge, she still respects herself; and she will excite those sentiments of esteem, and chastised admiration, which suit the hallowed and indelible character that she has assumed; nor will she be often called upon to repress

the

the insulting attentions of **presumptuous audacity.**

But, beside these prudential restraints, which the free censures of a really enlightened age should impose on that elevated station whose actions are most conspicuous, the democratical turn which public opinion has lately taken, offers still more *imperiously* momentous considerations to check the rash career of *open* profligacy. The melancholy fall of birth and grandeur in a neighbouring kingdom, may convince those who possess such distinctions in our own, that neither law, justice, nor power, can preserve their present superiority, if the voice of popular frenzy decree their overthrow. With whatever severity we may justly reprobate the mischievous doctrines which impose on the **commonalty,** and persuade them **to** imagine

imagine that the suppression of rank and opulence would contribute to their own exaltation, or even advantage, I must execrate the unblushing vices of those conspicuous sinners, who court publicity, and defy reproach; for they are a still surer engine of destruction to overwhelm our well-poised state. If our nobility and gentry are swept away from remembrance, their ruin must be accelerated by an act of self-murder; I should rather say, by fratricide. In proof of what I have alleged, that the lower orders perfectly understand that vice puts all upon a level, I appeal to the tumultuary applause which has crowned that scene in the play of John Bull, where the brazier seizes the chair lately occupied by the justice, on the latter refusing to receive the frail daughter of the mechanic with open arms into his

his family, as a suitable wife for his libertine heir. Have not the boxes learned, during the almost innumerable representations of this popular piece, that when they echo the laugh of the galleries, they virtually degrade their own order?

This, though a striking, is only one instance of the reigning humour of the times. To represent the higher ranks as mean, absurd, vicious, mercenary, or tyrannical, seems a sure road to reputation among our dramatists; and the higher they have coloured the caricature, the more ample has been their success. Perhaps the passion for German imitation, which lately gave law to our stage, may have hurried our play-wrights into the adoption of a defamatory libel on greatness, without fully discerning its mischievous tendency. It is certain, that when

when they describe poverty as the native soil of exalted sentiment and disinterested virtue, they neither derive their inspiration from nature, nor the muse. But as this absurd passion for bombast fustian, trivial events, extravagant sentiment, outrageous liberality, and perverted morality, seems declining (thanks to the spirited satire with which it has been attacked), let us hope that dramas of really English growth will be clear from this foreign excrescence. Let our own admirable Shakspeare serve here, as in other instances, for the model. He drew the great as they really are, disgraced by crimes, or glorious for virtues, struggling with the temptations incident to their stations or their nature, but not necessarily degraded by moving in that sphere of life to which Providence limits their trials and their duties.

duties. He depicted the unlettered vulgar too in their genuine colour, and with " a master's hand and prophet's " fire." Two hundred years have not effaced the resemblance, notwithstanding the change of manners and opinions which luxury and opulence have introduced. Many a valiant Talbot and open-hearted Hotspur still support the honour of their country in the tented field; and the latter seems indeed again " the glass wherein our " noble youth do dress themselves." Many a pious Cordelia still ministers, in privacy, to the sorrows of a petulant unhappy father; and many a faithful Imogen pursues the steps of her truant lord, anxious to recover his affections, even at the expense of life and fortune. Be it remembered too, that many a ferocious Cade, and wrong-headed Bevis, panting for change,

change, yet ignorant of what change must produce, are watching and magnifying the crimes of a faithless Margaret, and intriguing Eleanor*. But to return.

Next to that base abdication of her own importance, which the abandoned woman of rank tacitly ratifies whenever she permits the world to bruit her shame, the increasing facility with which ladies of lost character are re-admitted to the once select and decorous circle of refined society, becomes a subject of alarm to considerate minds, intent on the preservation of every barrier to female inno-

---

* See Henry VI, part 2. The characters of these princesses are here spoken of in their poetical dress, not as they are preserved in the unprejudiced page of history, which does justice to the heroical constancy and conjugal affection of the magnanimous consort of " Holy Henry."

cence,

cence. The maxims which induced our ancestors to determine, that even if we "deplored our loss with tears, "one false step for ever damned the "fame" of women, though apparently severe, were in reality merciful. This degradation might, indeed, harden a few reprobates in vice, who would otherwise have been hypocrites; but it sent many a real penitent to that retirement which true repentance loves, and it preserved thousands of thoughtless impassioned victims from the allurements of guilty pleasure, by the consciousness that they could not endure a life of reproach. Whatever encouragement mercy and charity may hold out to a backsliding sister determined to renounce the evil of her ways, let not her who hesitates be excited to offend, by stripping vice either of its punishments or its horrors.

Let

Let the young and unexperienced ever think, that if they pass the bourne of chastity, society will disclaim them, and to return to it will be *impracticable*. If they venture on the guilty deed with the forethought encouragement, that they shall soon emerge from their night of shame, their sin is dreadfully aggravated. Our best divines maintain, that whatever hope the heavenly promise of forgiveness affords to true contrition, it is most desperate wickedness to transgress " that grace may abound." If, in that storm of passions which attends a strong temptation, reason can be heard to plead that it will be but a temporary disgrace, she has leisure to assert her natural superiority, and by betraying her trust, becomes the ally, instead of the curb, of incontinence.

We will suppose (which I fear is far from

from being the case) that the principles of matronly ladies are so fixed, that they run no danger of contamination by frequently hearing the soft glosses which conscious offenders must cast over the crimes of which they have been publicly *convicted*; yet let us compassionate the tender bloom of virgin innocence, and save the youthful part of our sex from the pestilential blast of infectious sophistry. We will suppose that a young lady has been not only innocently, but wisely educated; taught to esteem virtue, and to shrink with abhorrence from audacious vice; accustomed only to contemplate respectable characters, and full of those ideas of worth and honour which are generally associated in an ingenuous inexperienced mind. She steps from the school-room to the crowded rout, and beholds a lady splendid

splendid in her appearance, most fascinating in her manner, to whom every one pays obsequious court; the beaux crowd around her to catch her smiles and hear her whispers, and the belles shew their admiration by wearing her uniform. The unsuspecting tyro in the subtle game of life steps forward to inquire the name of this supposed paragon of the day, this Arria, this Cornelia, in whose hallowed form she fancies the domestic virtues are worshipped; and she hears with horror and astonishment that it is one who has been branded in the public prints, degraded by the clear evidence of impartial justice, exposed by obscene caricatures, and ridiculed by the lowest witticisms; in fine, that she is a creature whom no one can *defame*, and whom any one may *abuse* with impunity. She turns away shudder-

shuddering with disgust, and perhaps listens to the bon-mots of a faded courtezan, whose early days passed in the low haunts of vulgar licentiousness, but who, in the wane of life, has persuaded her uxorious keeper to give her the name of his wife; not that she may repent of her former errors, nor yet to secure her such a competence that "lack of means enforce her not "to evil;" but for the avowed purpose of introducing her into company high at least in rank, though low in ideas of decorum; and who must prepare themselves for her reception either by copious draughts of Lethe, or strong doses of candid sentiment. As I may suppose my fair novice possesses too much good sense to call such time-serving adulation compassion, or such egregious folly generous love, what must be her opinion of the women

men who thus boldly take the lead where they should not so much as wish to appear, and of the society who *suffer*, nay *court* the intrusion? Will she not, on comparing the world of manners and the world of books, exclaim, like the Roman patriot, "O "virtue! have I worshipped thee as "a substantial good, and art thou but "an empty name!"

It is pleaded, that society owes so many pleasures to agreeable talents and polished manners, that those who possess these passports should be allowed to go every where without being subjected to a rigorous examination. This is to weaken the basis of social intercourse, and to overload the superstructure; to endanger all the sacred "charities of father, "son, and brother," that we may return from the fatiguing crowd of routs and assemblies, amused by a few sprightly sayings, or soothed by the smoothness of polite attentions. Is not this folly similar to that of swallowing poison, because it has been dissolved in a well-flavoured menstruum? But, after all, are we certain that we make this dreadful sacrifice to real wit and true elegance; or has fashion played the cheat here, as she has done in various instances, and dressed up a false Florimel of her own creation to impose upon her short-sighted votaries? I know too little of the walks in which these phenomena move to determine this important inquiry. I can only speak by hear-say evidence, and must confess that, had I not been assured to the contrary, I should have referred what has been repeated to me as the pure Attic wit of these English Ninons, to the inspiration of streams less

less simple than the Pierian; while the manners and attitudes which the enraptured describer spoke of as copied from the graces, seemed to me the sign-post daub of effrontery, or the hasty sketch of capricious affectation. If we take our ideas of wit from Cowley's admirable definition, it seems impossible that any trace of it should remain in the mind of a woman who has so long renounced the distinguishing characteristic of her sex, that she can scarcely know how to ape its language, or to *guess* what were its pure ideas. And if we suppose Milton correct in his notions of elegance, what resemblance can the impenitent wanton bear to his picture of our general mother in her state of innocence?

" Grace was in all her steps, heaven in her eye,
" In every gesture dignity and love."

My limited knowledge of high life makes me suspect, that the blind infatuation of the worshipper often ascribes such piquancy to the manners and expressions of the idol, as could not possibly be tolerated in a well-bred circle; and therefore that these *veneered* ladies are not quite so impudent and overwhelming as they are described to be; yet I must insist, that when the mind is deeply contaminated it will speak through its bodily organs, in spite of the most guarded caution. The eye will converse in a language unknown to the timid glances of modesty; the turns of the countenance will betray secrets to which delicacy is a stranger; and decorum will be violated by a thousand minutiæ to which even the practised actress has wanted skill to attend. But the danger does not rest here: simplicity may unwarily

unwarily adopt what seems to procure celebrity; and, though it solely aim at being fashionable, may transform its exterior into a likeness that it would abhor. Thus, while debauchees and deists rejoice in the increasing freedom of what may still be called virtuous society, our manners are in the most imminent danger of losing the proud distinctions of delicacy and purity; compared with which, wit and elegance, even when genuine, are but what the setting is to the diamond.

But it may be asked, will not penitence revoke the severe interdict which bars the doors of society against female frailty? Most unquestionably, so far as friendship or kindred are concerned. A very able instructress[*]

[*] See Mrs. More's Essays, and Strictures on Education.

of our sex has determined, that true penitence will not wish to exceed those bounds, or to mix in the crowded haunts of public life. Nor let a decision be censured for severity, which is really the dictate of mercy, sanctioned by a thorough knowledge of the human heart, and proceeding from lively sympathy for those who, though no longer *offending*, continue to be *unfortunate*. When the soul is really awakened by the sense of its own backslidings, when it feels the reproofs of conscience and the shame of contrition, it will naturally shrink from returning to those scenes which it knows are dangerous to reputation and peace. Convinced of her own weakness, afraid to trust her scarcely confirmed resolutions, and concluding by the publicity of her story, that all who see her will look

look upon her either with contempt, reproach, or pity, the true Magdalen wishes alike to avoid the hazard of falling into new transgressions, and the contumely attending the past. She is deafer than the adder to the syren strains of adulation; she knows too well the "ills that spring from "beauty;" splendour has lost its attractions; she cannot derive amusement from crowds, because she can no longer mingle in them without feeling a sense of degradation. She considers too, that if she should again aspire to fashionable celebrity, her's would be an uphill painful task; every eye would be fixed upon her conduct; every tongue inclined to question the sincerity of her professions; what would be thought mere vivacity in unsuspected innocence, would in her be levity; and marked reserve would be construed into a prudish vizard thrown over the worst designs. Her whispers would be supposed to convey assignations, her reproofs would be called the splenetic dictates of jealousy. Besides, can she that has so weighty a task to perform afford to trifle away the important hours? Turn thee, backsliding daughter, turn to the cool sequestered vale of life, and thy troubled day may yet have a peaceful close. Rational amusement, renovated esteem, friendship, contentment, tranquillity, and religious hope, may still be all thine own.

It is not, therefore, the harsh decree of *outrageous* virtue, but the mild counsels of kindness and sympathy, that determine the preservation of those distinctions which custom has long preserved between unsuspected and forfeited characters. And if those, in in whose favour these barriers might be broken down with safety, are too well convinced of their expedience to require their abolition, let us determine to defend the privileges of innocence from the pertinacious attacks of impudence and hardened depravity. The increasing facility of intercourse between the most profligate and the most irreproachable women, which is a marked and peculiar feature of these times, threatens more than our manners. The transition is very easy, and generally very rapid, from unrestrained freedom of behaviour, to unrestrained freedom of conduct; and especially when the mind has not been deeply tinctured with religious truths, in which case the opinion of the world forms one of the strongest bulwarks of virtue. Banishment from parties of high ton, and estrangement from the amusements which every one talks of, have often intimidated the wavering fair one, and imposed a guarded decorum of manner on the determined wanton. Let us not then, when the cardinal virtue of our sex is assailed by unusual perils, resign one of its most material outworks: we have an encouraging example set before us, which it behoves us to copy. There is a circle, and that the highest, where the *convicted* adultress dares not show her audacious front. May this prohibition be coeval with the duration of our monarchy; and may the eyes of a British queen never be offended by the presence of such as glory in violating those laws of which her ivory sceptre constitutes her the guardian.

The next circumstance which has an unfavourable and alarming effect on female virtue is, that unremitting pursuit

pursuit of amusement so universal in the great world. "Commune with thy "own heart in thy chamber and be "still," is the precept of the royal penitent, who knew too well what watchful attention the human heart requires in order to subdue its propensity to evil. Shall I injure the fair fashionist, if I suggest that her bosom inmate demands as frequent examination, and as constant controul, as that of the highly endowed, though greatly offending David? Little did he think, when he twice spared the life of his inexorable enemy Saul, who denied him a shelter even among the rocks and wilds of his native land, that the time would come, when, securely sitting on the throne of Israel, he should meanly project the murder of the faithful veteran who bravely refused repose while the enemies of his king remained unsubdued. Can we trace any similitude between the self-commanding hero, who, like our own Sidney, on the fatal plains of Zutphen, refused to taste the eagerly desired waters of the well of Bethlehem; because it had been purchased by the jeopardy of the lives of three of his valiant captains, and the lustful tyrant whose insatiable appetites violated the honour of defenceless beauty? Yet it was the same man who acted in these different characters; it was he who was alternately, as supported or deserted by the Almighty, the shepherd conqueror of Goliath, whom the virgins of Israel extolled in their songs, and the aged forlorn fugitive who fled from his rebellious offspring. Modern times are not destitute of examples to prove, that honour and prosperity are alike unstable; nor can we preserve either

either our spiritual or temporal affairs from disorder, but by continued vigilance. We are now considering the former; and let me remind all who shall honour these reflections with a perusal, that the road from the heights of virtue to the depths of vice does not lead you down a *steep* precipice, but a *gradual* slope. A slight indiscretion, which scarcely alarms the most scrupulous conscience, if suffered to pass without observation, prepares the mind for a serious error; error delivers it over to crime; and crime, when often repeated, petrifies the moral feelings into insensible depravity. The sensibilities of virtue should be cherished with as much care as the sensibilities of temper should be modified; and unless we allow the soul time to whisper to us in retirement, we can never catch

catch its still soft voice amid the busy turmoil of dissipation.

Were the Christian duty of self-examination rigorously performed, I am persuaded the world would exhibit a very different appearance, both with respect to sin, and to its constant associate, sorrow. Enfeebled virtue would recover its stability; nay, the seducer himself would pause in his guilty career, and perceive "consideration come like an angel to whip the offending Adam out of him," and to show him the little value of what he seeks to purchase at the risk of eternal perdition. Nor are the uses of reflection and meditation confined to our moral conduct, though their exercise is here most important. It is by these means that the difficulties of science are conquered, and the refinements of

taste

taste acquired. The skilful artist is formed by this self-communion; and the plans of the statesman and the warrior are thus ripened into perfection. Even that which is known by the name of pleasure is more truly enjoyed by retrospection in the silence of your own apartment, than when the gaudy scene actually passed your staring eyes, and the confused buz of sound agitated your ears. Such an act of the memory may be compared to the animal faculty of rumination; we at first swallow pleasure in the gross, and are too anxious to devour much, to discover of what it is composed; but when re-masticated, we discern its peculiar pungency. A load of undigested pleasure (suffer me to continue the allusion) palls the satiated appetite; a small quantity, taken after proper intervals, exhilarates the spirits,

rits, and infuses alacrity into every part. This is especially true of the pleasures which arise from conversation. Refined wit and brilliant sense communicate an inward degree of satisfaction every time we recall them to our remembrance. Genius, whether we seek her in the walks of the imitative arts, or in the " nobler growth of " thought," does not immediately pour her full radiance on our eyes; we must study her splendour before we can ascertain its degree of brightness. Even elegance and beauty, when they belong to the higher degrees of excellence, solicit *minute* attention, and refuse to unveil their coy graces to the careless gaze of the hurried beholder.

Are those then, may we not ask, true voluptuaries, who fly from pleasure to pleasure, eager to grasp all, and

and yet securing none? No, my dear young friend, they are only another order of those *drudging* slaves of *vanity*, who would impose themselves upon us rustics as free and happy beings; or, to speak in fashionable *slang*, as people of very high ton. "Some "demon whispered to them, have a "taste;" but as nature had withholden from them that property, they determined to affect one. Without any real gusto to determine their choice, and perplexed by the decrees of fashion, as arbitrary as those of the Medes and Persians, but more variable than the shape of the clouds in a squally day, these unhappy people, without a relish for any thing, are forced to see all that is to be seen, and to go every where, lest they should omit the one amusement on which their eclat depends. You, who are

accus-

accustomed to spend a happy evening in the enjoyment of domestic tranquillity, would laugh to observe the multitudes which the world of fashion pours forth as soon as the world of business has retired to repose. Did you see that incessant routine of carriages which nightly pour through the streets and squares at the westend of the town, you would at least conclude that rest and domestic comfort were sacrificed to some exquisite enjoyment; and that no one would reverse the order of nature without having some equivalent to balance the privations they must endure. Satisfied that the owners are going to be very happy, I suspect that your humane disposition will lead you to pity the servants, and even the horses, who must be exposed for many hours to the inclemency of the weather; but could

could you look within these splendid vehicles, you would confess that the real objects of pity were there. Languid and spiritless, the fine lady sets out upon her nightly round, more reluctant than the watchman does on his monotonous task. She must step in at all the places that are marked in her visiting list; but as time presses, and dispatch is necessary, she can only just look in and see who is there before she flies to another quarter. She must go to such a public amusement, because it is the first night of an exhibition which every body talks of; she can, however, do no more than make her entry and exit, for her time is minuted, and a vast deal of generalship depends upon the expedition of her coachman. Ask this votary of fashion, whether she liked her preceding evening, and her account will

will only add to Solomon's mournful catalogue of deceitful vanities. She cannot tell you what was said or what was done; it is almost impossible for her to recollect whom she saw. There was the usual set at one place, and a very vulgar-looking party at another. At a third house, she heard some detestable music; and every body seemed sleepy and stupid at a fourth. She made an attempt to look in at the dear duchess's; but the crowd was so immense, that she could proceed no farther than the anti-room; in returning, she heard the most violent screaming, and her own carriage was broke to pieces. On the whole, she never was so alarmed nor so weary in her life; and this morning she is annoyed by an insufferable headache, which makes her miserable. Still, however, she has not a moment to spare; a party waits for

for her àt Madame Lanchester's; from thence she must go to the Exhibition, where she can only run round the rooms, as she has six calls to make in her way to the Park; from whence she must return in time to dress for a dining party; then to the Opera; and after that she meets a few private friends at a *petite souper*. Observe, *inclination* and *pleasure* are never assigned as the motives for these Herculean labours; *compulsion* and *necessity* oblige these violent efforts? She dislikes all that she sees, the fatigue is insupportable, she knows it will kill her; but rigid duty proscribes reflection and repose. To whom, you will ask, does she owe this duty; to her God, her King, or her family? No, she owes it to *vanity*, who calls this a life of pleasure. The toiling millhorse is not a greater slave, nor are his

his motions circumscribed by more arbitrary injunctions. For do not suppose that a certificate of your having driven about town all night is sufficient to acquit you of being a humdrum; you must prove that you have been at the very high parties, and exactly at the genteel hour. You may naturally admire the graces of the tragic and comic muses; but let not the names of Siddons and Jordan tempt you to enter a side-box till near the end of the third act; and be sure never to look at the stage till the former stabs herself, or the latter blindfolds Jack Bannister. In short, be content to see what fashion requires, and do not venture even *incog.* to what was only a last year's amusement. Learned pigs, invisible girls, and phantasmagorias, *have been*, I dare not venture to pronounce what are; for only a Sybil's
prescience

prescience could enable a countrywoman to name "the Cynthia of the 'minute."

The same rule must regulate your *friendships*: I believe this term is still preserved in the vocabulary of polite life, though, as it only means herding together, it ought to be changed to gregarious assemblages. Be sure to go always late enough to cut Mrs. Plainly's early party, and just in time to take up Lady Bab Frightful as she returns from the Countess of Hurricane's; though you may think the Plainlys very pleasant people, and Lady Bab and the Countess detestable; but then the two latter are *ton*, and the former knows nobody. You may visit the Squanders, though they had an execution in the house last week, because Lady Modely has decided that they ought to be countenanced;

tenanced; but never think of calling on the Overdo family, for they went quite out the moment it was *known* that they had spent their fortune. Be equally exact in your eating, and imprint upon your mind, that as fashion and nature are antipodes in climate, it is right to devour voraciously in April, what you faint at the sight of in August. This is called eating well, and really is a most complex science, involving so many concurrent circumstances, that a fine lady must devote much of her time and thoughts to this study before she can hope to see her dinners announced in the Morning Post, or have the honour of employing the toothpicks of the most sapient epicures of the season; whose landaulet's at your door as surely attest your cook's abilities, as a flight of vultures do the triumphs of a general.

I should

I should be a most merciless tyrant, if I supposed it possible for a lady who lives in this continued bustle " to ex-" amine her ways," or to " commune " with her own heart." Once, indeed, the sabbatical rest would have allowed her a few composed moments, which she might have allotted to useful reflection; but now, " Sunday shines " no day of rest " for the daughters of dissipation. Some time ago this interregnum of amusement was appropriated to sleep or indisposition; but fashion is now unwilling to suspend her law of perpetual motion even for one day, and boldly disputes the palm with exhausted nature. Her votaries must continue upon the whirl; and as ladies can do nothing else during the early hours of Sunday morning, they put on the mantle of devotion, and drive to some chapel that is blessed with a *fashionable* auditory and an *elegant* preacher. But for fear the liturgical offices of our church should make a disagreeable impression, they must hurry from thence to Kensington gardens, to sport their promenade dresses, and observe who and who are together. During the sitting of parliament, this is the day for dining parties; which, with a concert in the evening, keeps them employed all day long, and renders them as happily forgetful of the services with which it commenced, as if they had devoted their morning to the worship of Morpheus.

It frequently happens, that these scenes of continual hurry and confusion so exhaust the frame, and dissipate the spirits, that the heart loses both its inclinations and its sympathies; and the fine lady becomes a
mere

mere self-moved automaton, incapable of either tenderness, resentment, or compassion. To a being that can neither be *roused* to virtue nor *seduced* to vice, cautions are unnecessary; but many a heart escapes the frigid cold of this arctic circle, and repines with secret sorrow, or frets with fruitless wishes, while the vacant eye seems only to ponder the fantastic scene of which it is an unconscious witness. To a person thus situated, consideration becomes of most momentous importance; for the wish should be analyzed, and the sorrow traced to its source. It ought to be known, whether her bosom anguish originates in her own faults, or belongs to that species to which she can only oppose the defence of patience and resignation. Her desires too should be so scrutinized, as to discover whether they

they are of that innocent kind which she may pray God to prosper; or whether she should not cast them from her heart, as she would the deadly worm of Nile. We shall not *materially* slander the circles of dissipation, if we embody this *grief* in the shape of a negligent or faithless husband; and connect those *wishes* with the person of an agreeable cecisbeo, whose attentions are the only pleasant interruption of the tediousness of high life. It would prove me to be a mere Goth, if I supposed that a man and his wife could *designedly* appear in the same party; but I presume it may by chance happen, that my lord's chair may arrive before my lady's chariot is ordered up; and that she may be under the necessity of seeing that his early appearance is really in consequence of an assignation with the person she has

long

long suspected to be his *chere amie*. Can any situation more peculiarly require the exercise of consideration, even if a fashionable Bronzely were not whispering agreeable nothings in her ear at that very moment, and forming, by his observance, a marked contrast to the *nonchalance*, or perhaps *hauteur*, of her husband? Yet she must hurry to some other scene, as joyless and as dangerous as what she now witnesses; and consideration is deferred to those agonizing hours, when her mind, torn with jealousy and vain regret, denies repose to her wearied body, by conjuring up the phantoms of stern ingratitude and respectful assiduity.

Surely, my dear young friend, fashion never passed any decree so injurious to the interests of conjugal fidelity, as when it ordained that the husband

"Though well I knew that dreadful post of honour
"I gave thee to maintain. Ah! who could bear
"Those eyes unhurt?"   THE REVENGE.

You, my dear Miss M——, will readily conceive that I am not pleading for the treacherous friend or the recreant wife; I believe that genuine virtue, when strengthened by Christian principle, and supported by divine grace, can vanquish every temptation; but I know that divine grace is only given to those who ask it; and, I fear, Christian principles are not the predominant rules of conduct among the gay and giddy votaries of pleasure. Chastity, even when supported by such invulnerable guardians, should not be wantonly exposed to severe trials; and surely, when she cannot boast such protectors, the fragility of all human aids is too indisputable, to render it safe to put her upon such hard probation.

probation. Prudence may be pacified by precaution, pride can be soothed by flattery, reserve is often conquered by obsequiousness. When, instead of founding female honour on the immutable decrees of an omnipotent God, we build it upon the opinion of the world, we have only to be assured that no eye seeth, and virtue and vice lose their identity. Affection for our wedded partners will not be an equivalent barrier; for affection is but a vagrant property, that may be subdued by ill-treatment, destroyed by contempt, restored by generosity and tenderness, or even created by assiduity and solicitation. We may appeal to those melancholy records of depravity which the archives of our civil courts will transmit to posterity, in proof of the transient nature of that preference which occasions what are commonly called

called love, matches. The start of passion, which leads a lady to Scotland to become a wife, too often proceeds from some romantic expectations of eternal affection and consummate excellence, which is not, and indeed cannot be, realized; and if she never experiences more than casual neglect or common infirmities, she will have more reason to bless her good fortune, than her precipitation in choosing deserved. But if, instead of "the faultless monster whom the "world ne'er saw," a being much beneath the general run of humanity starts up, in the form of a stern tyrant, or negligent coxcomb, and still deems himself entitled to the continuance of that warm affection which she once professed, merely because "she had eyes and chose him;" I fear, affection would here be found a very brittle

brittle chain. If a husband, thus circumstanced, should think himself justified in pursuing pleasure through every haunt in which he supposes he may meet it, and conceives his own humour entitled to full license, provided his lady has a beau to attend her if she likes to go out; let not such a man complain of being *injured*, either in friendship or in love, though his wife drink deep of the cup of infamy.

But it is my own sex that I chiefly hope to benefit by my admonitions; and here let me earnestly entreat those ladies whose will gives law to the world of fashion, to endeavour to rescue matronly manners from that extreme affectation of levity, which is now become so general, that it is considered to be the associate of perfect innocency of intention. The shrine of virgin beauty is now deserted by its most desirable worshippers, who hover round the chair where loveliness, already "link'd and wedlock bound," dispenses her *unmeaning* or *criminal* smiles. The married dame trips through the light maze of the dance, and shows her gay youthful partner to the provoked spinster, who is obliged to some antiquated *caro sposo* for not suffering her to sit shivering on the ottoman all the evening. A married lady may go any where, mix in all companies, dress in any style, say any thing, and do every thing not absolutely scandalous, without impeachment of her fair fame. If any allowance ought to be made for levity, should it not be granted to youthful inexperience, to indiscreet simplicity, and to the too frank disclosure of that wish to win hearts which is very natural to the early part of our lives?

Why

Why should a woman who has pledged her vows at the altar, and is thereby appropriated to one man by the laws of God and her country, try to gain admiration, which, if acquired, can only become a snare to her virtue or her peace? Her choice is made; it will therefore be in vain for her to try to captivate hearts which she must immediately restore. Will it add to her felicity, to discover that a gentleman superior to her husband in merit, fortune, or rank, considers her as the most charming of her sex? will it not rather lead to most dangerous comparisons, to regrets fatal to every hope of happiness, or even content? But let the infatuated woman, who gratifies her vanity at the hazard of her peace and reputation, know, that perhaps her conquest is not so very certain as she supposes. Her victim may have very different

different ends in view from that of swelling her triumphs. His own gross passions may fix him in her train, not to be trampled upon by her tyranny, but to be *her* conqueror. Whatever she may suppose, or he profess, she never would have been "his happiest "choice," even had he seen her before she was assigned to another. He has too much aversion to the marriage yoke, for her charms to vanquish his prejudices; and her principal attraction, in his eye, is the conviction that he may flirt with her without an officious friend's requesting to know whether he has any serious intentions. This character is well described in the lively farce of the "Wedding Day;" the regret of Lady Contest at not having seen the engaging lord before she had tied herself to old Sir Adam, and her surprise at his declining the honour

honour of her hand when she was unexpectedly released from her former bonds, affords a valuable lesson to married coquettes.

Before I dismiss the subject of *matronly flirting*, allow me to answer one objection. Though particular attentions to one gentleman are confessed to be both suspicious and dangerous, general ease and freedom are defended, on the ground of improving the pleasure and vivacity of society. I am so great a lover of cheerfulness, that I am willing to admit every species of sprightliness into the manner of married ladies, that can be fairly affirmed to be destitute of either design or immodesty. I acknowledge, that they may with propriety take a greater share of conversation, and indulge in a more latitude of remark, than their *juniors*. You will perceive by that limitation,

mitation, that I consider these more as the privileges of age, than as part of the hymeneal dowry. Let a married lady endeavour to promote the social enjoyments of the circle in which she moves. Let her consult her glass, and allow me to add her purse also, in the choice of appropriate and becoming ornaments. I permit her to aspire to the character of a very agreeable woman; but let not that distinction be laid by on ordinary occasions, and only produced to male witnesses. If the best *bon-mots* are reserved for the beaux, if the favourite head-dress is only worn when Lord Gaylove is expected; if her *ennui* and head-ache are apt to be cured by a *tête-à-tête* with a man of fashion, if she finds female parties dull, and female conversation insipid; I must entreat the advocates for the ease and freedom of of married ladies to remember, that cheerfulness is of no sex, and is as likely to visit a party of old women with her agreeable sallies, as a circle of box-lobby loungers. Nay, it is more likely; for in the first instance it will be stimulated by the humane desire of amusing lassitude, while in the latter it will be checked by a modest apprehension of misconstruction. I should have premised, that these said old women should not be *splenetic;* for I do confess, ill-nature gives the *coup de grace* to vivacity.

We have dwelt so minutely on some of the increasing improprieties of fashionable manners, that we must pass others with less observation. A rage for education is one of the marked features of the great world; and it has been much increased by the labour of writers who belong to the

the new school of morals. The hope of forming something superior to the present race of mortals, by merely human means, is one of the wildest theories that ever entered the brain of a visionary reformer; yet it is seriously acted upon by many indefatigable mothers, who weary the patience and injure the constitution of their children by the most unremitting attention to a multiplicity of pursuits; in the hope of being able to exhibit in their own families this mechanical compound of ethical and scientifical perfection; which is to prove, that divine wisdom is not necessary either for informing our ignorance, or restraining our propensities to evil. All parents do not, indeed, aspire to this high standard of philosophical erudition and impeccability; but even that routine of masters
who

who are necessary to form a young lady into the accomplished amateur, which is now deemed an essential part of the character of every woman of fashion, subjects a young lady to more privations, as much bodily fatigue, and a far greater exercise of patience and attention, than yonder little spinner encounters, who by her industry procures her own subsistence. We must, however, allow due praise to this severe discipline, on the same ground as we commend the rigid injunctions of Lycurgus: no laws but his could have formed the stern, indefatigable, impenetrable Spartan; nor could a less inexorable course of self-denial and activity convert the artless happy girl into that extraordinary being, a woman of ton. Beside being compelled to pass through those extremes of climate, without discovering any sense

of

of bodily inconvenience, as Milton, by a bold flight of well-governed fancy, supposed to be part of the punishment of the fallen angels, the candidates for this fading glory are trained from their cradles to such habits of observance, patience, and control, in order to attract the attention of their fellow-creatures, as, if they were influenced by better motives, would secure them the approbation of beings of a higher order. What a pity, that so much pains should be exerted for such a subordinate purpose; and in which, since all those whom you seek to amaze are your competitors, your chance of success is so very limited! For if your daughter, after fourteen thousand hours* spent in the acquisition

---

* Mrs. More communicates this anecdote. The author cannot refer to the page, not being in possession

tion of music, prove at last but a second-rate performer; if, after all that the dancing-master has done in screwing her shoulders and modelling her steps, her person be inelegant and her motions ungraceful; if no expense nor waste of time can prevent her drawings from being daubs, or bagatelles, for what have the hours of early life been sacrificed? Taste and ton have no *degrees* of 'glory' to allot to their worshippers; nor can ardent devotion, here, claim that reward for its sincerity, to which it is not entitled by talent. All that can be done for the unsuccessful candidate for fashionable

---

session of that Lady's Strictures on Education, which she read at their first appearance, and took from them a few extracts; to which, while writing these Letters, she has occasionally referred She will feel much flattered, if the reader should also trace an incidental and undesigned resemblance, arising from similarity of opinion on various points.

eclat

eclat is, to remove her to some narrower sphere. A second-rate party, or a summer bathing-place, is the only meridian which she can hope to illumine; while all who witnessed her former pretensions are tempted to exclaim, " Ill-weav'd ambition, how " much art thou shrunk!" Might not prudence here suggest the expediency of applying to another master, who acts upon very different principles from the cruel despot Vanity, by giving a certain retribution to the *motives*, not the *success* of our actions?

" No cold neglect the faithful heart repays,
 ". Whose steadfast aim solicits His regard;
" Each wish for merit, each attempt to please,
 " He views, and His benignant smiles reward."
                                    CARTER's POEMS.

It must, however, be acknowledged, that the favour of this wise and holy Being cannot be acquired by such an
exercise

exercise of our faculties, or determination of our views; for he does not enjoin us to *excel* our fellow-creatures, but to *conquer* ourselves; nor will the splendour of the crown of immortality be decreased, because it blazes upon the brows of myriads of happy beings. Envy of successful competition, and jealousy of pre-eminent abilities, will never torment the bosom of the young Christian, who, engrossed by the necessity of looking at her own ways, ceases to be a fretful observer of the progress of others; being assured, that at the day of judgment she cannot be *overlooked* amid an infinite host of happy spirits who claim the kingdom of their Father, nor *concealed* by a multitude of sinners who call in vain on the rocks and mountains to hide them from an omniscient eye.

In judging of the folly of those who seek

seek to form their children upon the model which vanity presents, we must add, to the great hazard of success, the brevity of the acquisition. As the career of a fine lady is ever in danger of being arrested by rivals in expense and taste, so rivals in accomplishments are coming forward to dispute her pretensions to superiority. Nor is this all: every year brings in a new fashion, even in these particulars, and the business of education is never finished. If you choose to dance, paint, sing, and play, till you reach your climacteric, you must still have masters to teach you the *last* improvement, or you will be laid aside as old lumber. Our mothers, who danced all their lives to the tune of Lady Coventry's minuet, will scarcely conceive how ephemeral are the triumphs of the successors of that paragon, who had

the

the good fortune to flourish at a period when the empire of beauty and taste dreaded no other enemies than the small-pox and old age. The *minuet de la cour* and the *cotillon* were afterwards thought better calculated to display the female figure to advantage, and these lasted in fashion long enough for one generation of dancers; but reels, strathspeys, and waltzes now succeed each other with such rapidity, that only the most flexile form and fixed attention can rise to the praise of having learned the figure, before they must assume different contortions, and wind into another meander. The like observation extends to all other accomplishments: there is even a fashion in language; the accent must retreat, or advance, according as ton, not syntax, has ordained; and the word of the year must hold a prominent place in our conversation. Our passions and sensations must be subject to like control; we must either be immoderately happy, monstrously delighted, intensely charmed, or amazingly interested. But as expressions of extreme suffering are best adapted to the joyless career of a fine lady, we must allow that her task of learning will be chiefly bounded by the compound epithets of immensely dull, horribly fatiguing, and insufferably vapid. A few mornings' observation will show her what *misfortune* is most in vogue, and give the proper tinge to her *dolours* for the ensuing winter.

If the quackery of education only extended to the formation of vain and frivolous beings, we should have far less reason to complain of its prevalence. Many strong minds would resist these shackles, and disappointment

ment would divert ill-directed understandings to some nobler pursuit. But, as we have before observed, a system of morals is formed still more dangerous than this system of manners. The popularity of either mode of education seems to depend more on the situation than on the intellects of their respective partisans; yet it appears as if the frivolous system was most in repute among second-rate gentility; while the bold theory of human perfectibility seeks its converts among those who, feeling themselves to be above the immediate influence of the temporal considerations which restrain their fellow-creatures, would fain get released from the eternal consequences of indulging their guilty passions. A morality, therefore, which rejects the basis of religion, is admirably suited to people who, while they seem to

make

barriers sufficiently strong to prevent our frail natures from deviating into bye paths of error, unless she renounce the guidance of her own pale fires, and submit to be led by the clear radiance of the gospel*.

The deficiency of this new system of self-dependent virtue, is not more apparent in the weakness of its restraints, and the feebleness of its motives, than in the very limited circle to which it even *pretends* to direct its improvements. Many Christian graces are excluded from its good deeds; and the cardinal virtue of our ancestors, the very bond of social intercourse, is now little inculcated in education, or enforced by fashionable practice; I speak of moral honesty, and the simple but energetic principle of paying every

* The subject of education is resumed in Letters Vth and XIIIth.

one his just debts. The difficulty which I find in treating this point in such à manner as to render it palatable to polite readers, is a sufficient proof that the duty is *quite gone out.* Yet honour and honesty were once thought to have a reciprocal relation; and the alliance was so congenial, that I think the former quality has appeared to be in a hectic state ever since it has been separated from its co-relative. A person of strict honour and independent principles, in debt to every tradesman he deals with, and actually living, if not by shuffling and evasion, at least by the forbearance of people whom he despises, seems a contradiction in nature; for generosity, pride, and dignity of sentiment, are supposed to be blended with meanness, servility, and cruelty of conduct. To live, to breathe at the mercy of another, nay to feel that you are really injuring those on whose forbearance you depend, and introducing anxiety and distress into a rank of life of which you were born the guardians: how does this accord with the magnificent nobleman, or high-spirited commoner, who know themselves to be parts of the legislature of their country? Yet even in those important branches of the state, the art not only of ruining themselves, but of living after they are ruined, is practised by many adepts in (must I say) the mystery of swindling. Living within the bounds of your income is so far from being considered as the test of a gentleman, that in the world of high fashion it conveys the oblique insinuation, that you are a narrow soul, destitute of taste, or at best merely a good sort of *spiritless* creature.

ture. This propensity to squander the bounty of Providence with careless profusion, has unhappily descended from the high to the lowly scenes of life. Its effects upon the middle and inferior orders have been already considered; in the higher it may be lamented, not only on account of the individual distress that it occasions, but as tending to make the humble classes think still more meanly of their superiors. I have ever been of opinion that the influence of birth and rank was more beneficial to the community at large, than that of wealth, and that the faults of the former were less prejudicial. To instance in pride; which, when it proceeds from hereditary superiority, is generally polished by education, and softened by habitual restraint; whereas the pride of mere wealth mostly seizes an unimproved mind,

mind, at a period of life in which habits have been formed on vulgar models, and of course it must become more odious to those whom it affects. Whether it is ingrafted on native servility or rudeness, or on the lately-acquired consequence arising from the possession of money, ostentation and self-indulgence will be the result, unless checked by extraordinary goodness of disposition. The man of rank, on the other hand, knows his own title to the respect of his neighbourhood to be indefeasible, nor does he feel the necessity of continually defending the dignity which was handed down to him by his ancestors. He has been accustomed to the luxuries of life from his infancy, and his relish for them is too much palled by long indulgence to allow him to attach importance to such distinctions. This

appears

appears to be the natural bias of these two characters, unless they are diverted out of their course by any accidental impulse. Let it be remembered too, that attachment to hereditary patrons, and respect for the old manor house, (the antient possessors of which are deposited in the family vault under the parish church), are feelings congenial to the minds of the common people, and such as our constitution wisely cherishes. The influence which an ancient and respectable family possessed over its tenantry and neighbourhood, cannot be soon acquired by the nabob, or manufacturer, who purchases the estate, however estimable his character, or conciliatory his conduct. A series of years must elapse before they can form any tie but what interest creates; and till the generation which served the old family has passed away, the new will be considered as interlopers, who have risen on the ruins of a race that was far more deserving. I must observe, that in these times every thing which tends to weaken the tie that connects the poorest man in the kingdom with the highest, is to be deprecated; and I regret the degradation which rank and station suffer in the eyes of the community, not only by the contagious influence of unbounded expense, but by transferring its power to other hands, which, even if as well-disposed, will be less able to exert it beneficially.

Shall we not then, my dear Miss M——, reprobate that false candour, which induces us to give soft names to such a vice as extravagance? Heaven forbid that we should here withhold that pity from *undeserved* distress to which

which it is ever entitled! I am not speaking of those who, by unforeseen unavoidable misfortunes, by the pressure of domestic calamity, by the treachery of enemies, the uproar of the elements, or even by misplaced confidence, are involved in pecuniary difficulties. The sorrows of such are sacred; let the world compassionate, and, if it can, assuage them. I confine my censures to those who voluntarily offer their fair possessions, their extensive influence, and every other blessing of which God has made them the guardian, at the shrine of vanity. These I charge with contributing to the ruin of their country, as well as of themselves. I accuse them of perverting their highly responsible station to the corrupting of national habits, and to the subverting of the interests of the order to which they belong. These

offences

offences must not pass off with the slight censure, that they were very generous people, and no one's enemies but their own; and every eulogy on their taste, spirit, and hospitality, is a severe charge against them, for not bounding these propensities by their lawful ability of indulging them.

It is indeed allowed, that people eminently gifted with genius are apt to fall into these pecuniary embarrassments; and perhaps it is just, that a more lenient censure should attach to errors which seem rather to proceed from the limited faculties of our nature, than from intentional injustice to others, or overweening attachment to ourselves. The intenseness of thought which accompanies any extraordinary effort of intellect, whether it be engaged in " bodying forth the forms of things unseen," in developing

ing the abstruse mazes of science, or in conducting the intricate and cumbersome machine of public business, necessarily withdraws the attention from what seem comparatively petty considerations; and the harassed mind, fatigued by the painful stretch of its faculties, finds the hours of relaxation insufficient to recruit its exhausted powers. When such an excuse can be fairly urged for embarrassments, let us abstain from reproach; sufficient to such a culprit, is the punishment which the consequences of indiscretion must inflict; especially as people of this stamp are generally rather dupes than knaves, and suffer more from misplaced confidence, and the extravagance of their connexions, than from the ungoverned importunity of their own desires.

Few, however, are lighted to ruin

incumbrance, and acting as a faithful steward and intelligent agent in every affair which can be submitted to her management. Punctuality and regularity in money transactions are still acknowledged to be counting-house requisites. May they long continue to distinguish and give respectability to the commercial world! but why should they be discarded from being supporters to the shield of ancestry and the coronet of nobility. I have heard it remarked (and the observation was judicious), that arithmetic has been of more real service to the world, than all other remains of classical learning or science; and in what respect does considerate expenditure (we are now addressing a class to which the term frugality may seem unappropriate) imply the absence of any noble quality? Can generosity,

can

can benevolence subsist upon funds which are not your own? When you bestowed what belonged to your children or your creditor, you did not *give*, but *surreptitiously apply the possessions of another*. The character of Charles Surface, in that very superior comedy "The School for Scandal," if not the hasty sketch of inconsiderate genius unconscious of its dangerous tendency, must be deemed a marked attack on the probity which is our national distinction. In either point of view, his celebrated animadversions on the old proverb, "Be just "before you are generous," ought to be received with groans and hisses, not thunders of applause*. They are, indeed, characteristic of a dishonest spendthrift; but they bear no mark of

* See the scene between Charles and Rowley, in the fourth Act of the School for Scandal.

integ-

integrity hurried away by the violence of ill-regulated passions; for they do not result from the strong impression made by a recent tale of distress, but from a mind *resolved* to be unjust, and enamoured of its own baseness. The sentiment which restrains him from selling the picture of his friend and benefactor, ought to have taught him that the necessities of Old Stanley might be supplied, by discharging his four valets with their bags and bouquets; from whose attendance only a consummate coxcomb could derive satisfaction, and not from a misappropriation of what he owns belonged to his tailor and hosier. How can the audience in the last scene acquiesce in Maria's destiny? Charles indeed tells us, that he never more *can* err, because he shall now have a monitor and guide; but has he not already told us, that

that he does an imprudent action precipitately, lest he should be checked by the *monitor* within him? To such a character the sober paces of justice will ever appear "lame and hobbling;" but the misfortune is, it is not "Generosity," but dishonesty, which outstrips her. The insolvent must relinquish the sublime pleasure of relieving indigence, from an absolute *impossibility* of enjoying it. He may be *base*, he cannot be *benevolent* in any thing but desire. If he truly valued the ability of giving, he should have reserved some little remnant of his possessions from the gulph of dissipation, and saved his tender heart from the exquisite anguish of finding himself incapable of relieving misery.

Compassion is one of those inherent qualities of the female mind, which seem to defy the influence of situation. Even

is granted; but it is equally certain, that the human mind is armed with power sufficient to resist the attack of pain; because the same person who often sinks into the extremes of nervous depression, at other times may be produced as an instance of fortitude, by enduring extreme agony with cheerfulness. It is thus in the common affairs of life, we frequently see that mind irritated by " trifles light as air," which has sustained real affliction with unyielding heroism. The state of the case seems to be, that when by bad habits and excessive dissipation, or through long confinement, over-watchfulness, great anxiety, or severe misfortune, the spirits become broken and the body debilitated, every little addition of pain or inconvenience alarms us; self predominates in all our thoughts; we no longer

longer compare ourselves with others, and judge from a fair-drawn parallel; but we accumulate upon our own heads every calamity and every disease, hereditary or contagious, which we can carry to our own mountain of misery, by any extravagant stretch of fancy. The natural consequence is, that we sink under its pressure. I have bestowed the more time on this subject, from a conviction that this malady often assaults most amiable women, who would shrink from themselves with horror, could they foresee the uneasiness that they cause, or the lamentable *transformation* which they suffer, while they are under the influence of this "foul fiend;" whom, though it is almost impossible to *vanquish*, it is easy to *avoid*. As the champion of my sex, I here enter my protest against the forced construction, that I suppose hypochondria to be merely a feminine infirmity. As it either originates in, or is aggravated by the patients permitting the imagination to revolve on the narrow pivot of self, the lords of the creation are indebted to their more athletic frames and active occupations, if (which is certainly questionable) they are more exempt than we from the assaults of nervous irritability..

Susceptibility, proceeding from weakness of judgment, and badness of temper, takes a variety of forms. Sometimes it teases ourselves and our connexions in the shape of bodily complaint; but it often assumes the colour of an injured character, suffering from an ungrateful, perfidious, undiscerning world. It sharpens supposed neglects, creates imaginary afflictions, and delivers us over a prey
to

to fastidiousness, resentment, and spleen; or perhaps it assumes the aspect of excessive tenderness and tremulous philanthropy. In this disguise, it is so admirably delineated, by the pencil of an *unknown* master in the school of poetry, that I must recal these well-known lines to your recollection:

"Taught by nice scale to mete her feelings strong,
"False by degrees and exquisitely wrong,
"For the crush'd beetle first, the widow'd dove,
"And all the warbled sorrows of the grove,
"Next for poor suffering guilt, and last of all
"For parents, friends, a king's and country's fall.
"Mark her fair votaries, prodigal of grief,
"With cureless pangs, and woes that mock relief,
"Droop in soft sorrow o'er a faded flower,
"O'er a dead jackass pour the pearly shower *."

It is most true, my dear Miss M——, that this pseudo humanity always seats herself upon an inverted pyramid,

* New Morality, in the Poetry of the Anti-Jacobin.

which totters under her. The poor fly that is eaten by the spider, and the dear dog that *would* die of old age, form the basis of an ample superstructure; and her pity always increases in violence with her consciousness of its being utterly unavailing. She is most admirably described in a deservedly popular allegory*, as gazing through a telescope in search of distant distress, and overthrowing the petitioner who was at her elbow soliciting her hospitality.

The trials which arise from real sensibility governed by good sense, are of that improving kind which immediately proceed from the will of Divine providence, and bring with them present complacency and future reward. Some severe sects of Christians seem desirous, by their too rigid interpreta-

* Progress of the Pilgrim Good Intent.

tion

tion of particular texts of scripture, to deprive us of all the consolation arising from conscious well doing. It is true, if we compare our finite virtues with the purity and goodness of our Creator, the largest accumulation of mortal excellence must become as dust upon the balance. It is also acknowledged, that when our whole lives are referred to the test of his holy laws, they must fall so infinitely below the prescribed standard, as to compel us to trust for mercy on a surer foundation than our own righteousness. We grant that in many things we offend, and that our best deeds are tainted by infirmity. Yet virtue, circumscribed, imperfect, backsliding yet sincere virtue, still exists in the human heart. Her identity is acknowledged by every precept which requires her exertion; nay, she is even authorized to expect

and

and to claim a *reward* * from that God by whom she is exercised and sanctified.

Amid those qualities which will entitle their blessed possessors to shine like stars in the kingdom of their heavenly Father, genuine benevolence claims pre-eminence. Let us not, then, consider the tenderness of heart which leads our sex to exert this glorious quality, as one of our trials, but as our noblest distinction; a distinction which the concurrent voice of travellers determines to be limited to no climate, enfeebled by no external circumstances, but as active amid the privations and ignorance of savage life, as in the refinement and opulence of civilized society. In every age and nation, women are alike distinguished by their promptitude to assist the miserable, and to sympathise with the unfortu-

* Matt. xxv. 21 and 23.

nate,

nate, even at the expense of their own enjoyments.

But this world presents a mixed scene, in which artifice and fraud are constantly endeavouring to ensnare unsuspicious generosity; and hence arises the duty of placing our hearts under the guidance of our understanding, and of enlightening our judgments by the united radiance of knowledge and experience. The unavoidable trials of real sensibility chiefly arise from the difficulty of striking a due balance between the promptitude of a generous temper, and the caution of an intelligent mind. Only general rules can be prescribed for our direction in this instance; and as it is much easier to lay them down, than to apply them to individual cases, we must act for ourselves after all, and can seldom aspire to higher praise than purity of intention.

I forbear to mention the trials that proceed from change of fortune, from false friends, artful enemies, and opposite interests; from disappointed ambition and defeated enterprize; from accidental adventures, mysterious intrigue, and intricate business. To these troubles we are less exposed than men; and, speaking collectively, we only feel them in their rebound. Providence has withdrawn us from the turmoil of worldly contention; and it is only some peculiar circumstances, or the improper encouragement of a busy disposition, which removes us from our proper sphere, domestic retirement.

Instead of presuming, with culpable hardihood, to question the wisdom or the justice of that dispensation which has determined our lot in life, let us direct our attention, from what we might have been, to what we are; and if we find, by the general constitution of our bodies, and the frame of our minds, that we are rightly placed; if we discover, too, that our relative situation in society has many real advantages, let dissatisfaction and disobedience yield to acquiescence and gratitude.

Our weaker strength and more delicately organized frame evidently point out our unfitness for those laborious and dangerous exertions, which the common wants of civilized life demand from man. The necessity for our being thus exempted is further apparent, because the future generation would immaturely perish, or languish in the miseries incident to neglected infancy, if at one period we were exposed to severe fatigue and alarming perils, and at another were compelled by extreme toil to desert our feeble offspring, who, unlike the brute creation, plead b their helplessness for indulgence to their mothers. The laborious and hazardous undertakings to which women are compelled to submit in savage countries, are considered as the preventive of such an increase of inhabitants as would prove too redundant for their scanty supply of provisions. And if these physical causes present insurmountable obstacles to our engaging in athletic or dangerous employments, there seems to be no less substantial moral reasons for our withdrawing from that species of public business in which the labours of the head are principally required. An eccentric writer, who thought audacity a proof of genius, and mistook insubordination for independence and greatness of soul, seemed to suppose that the professions of a lawyer, a physician, and a merchant, were no ways incompatible with women. Little ingenuity is necessary to

disprove a theory which puzzled for an hour, and then sunk into oblivion, overwhelmed by the weight of its own absurdity, till it was fished up again by some second-hand dealers in paradox and innovation. That we can neither gain happiness nor advantage, from renouncing the habits which nature communicated and custom has ratified, is evident, by considering the qualities for which we have been most valued, and how far they would accord with an alteration in our relative situation. Could modesty endure the stare of public attention; could meekness preserve her olive wand unbroken amid the noisy contention of the bar; could delicacy escape uninjured through the initiatory studies of medicine; could cautious discretion venture upon those hazardous experiments which private as well as public utility often require;
could

could melting compassion be the proper agent of impartial justice; or, would gentleness dictate those severe but wholesome restraints, which often preserve a nation from ruin? Though I am inclined to think highly of my own sex (so highly, that I fear all my claims in their behalf will not be readily allowed), I confess that I can see nothing in the Utopian scheme of an Amazonian republic, which is not in the highest degree absurd and laughable. My conviction that we should make wretched generals, patriots, politicians, legislators, and advocates, proceeds from my never having yet seen a private family well conducted, that has been subjected to female usurpation. Notwithstanding any degree of science or talent which may have illuminated the fair vicegerent, the awkward situation of the *good man* in the *corner* has always excited

excited risibility, and awakened such prying scrutiny into interior arrangements, as has never failed to discover "something rotten in the state of Den- "mark." For, alas! my dear Miss M——, it is not only the temperament of our virtues which indicates the necessity of our being shielded from the broad glare of observation; there is, generally speaking, (and, you know, Providence acts by general rules both in the natural and moral world) too much impetuosity of feeling, quickness of determination, and locality of observation, in women, to enable us to discharge public trusts or extensive duties with propriety. The warmth of our hearts overpowers the ductility of our judgments; and in our extreme desire to act *very* right, we want forbearance and accommodation, which makes our best designs often terminate

exactly

exactly opposite to what we proposed. The qualities that we possess are admirably fitted to enable us to perform a second part in life's concert; but when we attempt to lead the band, our soft notes become scrannel and discordant by being strained beyond their pitch; and our tremulous melodies cause a disgusting dissonance, if they attempt to overpower the bold full tones of manly harmony, instead of agreeably filling up its pauses.

Experience, which enables men to penetrate into the designs of others, and to develope specious characters, is the result of such intimate knowledge of the world as must by us be very dearly bought. Fertility of resource and boldness of invention, which in the comprehensive mind of man become the parents of stupendous efforts, when modified by female passions, are

apt

apt to degenerate into petty craft. More energetic and sanguine, but less endowed with courage and perseverance, we should, I doubt not, make well-intentioned and active, but rash and hasty reformers. Soon roused and soon intimidated; eager to adopt or to reject; unwilling to doubt, to temporize, or to examine; distracted by a multiplicity of cares, yet engrossed by one, how could we successfully manage the jarring interests and contending passions of the instruments that we should find it necessary to employ? Those nice susceptibilities of character, and that acuteness of moral feeling, which induce us to attend even to "the grace, the manner, and the decorum" of virtue, would never permit us to connive at a smaller evil in order to escape a greater; nor could we, consistently with our ingenuousness,

nuousness, act upon the politic principle of "divide and conquer." Our compassion and tenderness would never authorize us to exert that necessary severity, which is often obliged to devote a part to save the whole; yet both public and private affairs must often be conducted upon these principles. Our impatience of calumny would, on the one hand, urge us to that hasty vindication of our motives and actions, which would cause a premature disclosure of our designs; while, on the other, our strong perception of impropriety, and horror of reproach, would restrain us from adopting such measures as did not carry on their face their own justification. In fine we have too little of the "serpent's worldly wisdom" to indemnify us for bringing the "harmless dove" from its rural nest. Our adminis-

administration, whether of public or private affairs, would want the great desiderata of vigour, consistency, and extension; and we should ourselves be mere visionary perfectionists, the dupes of the specious, and the prey of the ambitious. Would this change in our destination promote general happiness? Should we ourselves have cause to rejoice in it?

It is possible, I allow, to produce many illustrious examples of female heroism and capacity; but *singular* occurrences do not overthrow the general conclusions of experience. The reigns of some of our British Queens may be fairly urged in proof of women being capable of discharging the most arduous and complicated duties of government with ability and perseverance. My observations are not designed to recommend the expediency

diency of a Salique law of exclusion from *hereditary* rank; but to strengthen the principles which consolidate *domestic* harmony. Besides, the sceptre's being ostensibly grasped by a female hand does not reverse the general order of government. The representative of authority is then indeed changed in gender; but power is lodged in the same sex which was wont to exercise it; men still execute the measures which men advise; and the sovereign is but an heiress, whose conduct is restricted and influenced by those laws which are virtually her guardians. But, to relieve the tedium of a discussion which I fear you will think dry and unnecessary, suppose we indulge in a slight historical digression. Will you deem me very hardy, if I attempt to strengthen my argument by

by some observations on the instances which our own island has afforded us of female supremacy? I will not derive them from the *supposed* influence of royal consorts or mistresses, but from the reigns of our actual queens.

The history of the first Mary is directly in point. She was, indeed, destitute of those amiable qualities of mercy and gentleness, which are considered as our best and most natural endowments; but in lieu of these, she was possessed of tremendous perseverance and sanguinary consistency. Good intentions, or at least sincerity of purpose, was never denied her; she aimed at what she thought reformation; she unquestionably wished her people to become " wise unto sal- " vation " in her own way; and her narrow mind presented no better expedients to make them so, than the faggot and the block. In her eagerness to obtain the desired end, she overlooked impossibilities: hence her marriage, in the decline of life, with a young foreign prince; hence her mal-administration of the domestic concerns of the state, and of its continental alliances. Her reign is a melancholy expansion of the passions of a weak woman, driven to cruelty and self-disgust by the opposition of her subjects, the bigotry of her advisers, and her own ignorance, rashness, and obstinacy.

I shall not be driven from the tenets that I have defended by the bright splendour of the Elizabethian æra; for no writers, except the parasites of her own court, ever ascribed *feminine* virtues to that *renowned* princess. Her education, conformably to the general taste of that age, was
learned

learned and comprehensive; and her understanding possessed the rare advantage of being alike solid and penetrating. The difficulties of her early life taught her discretion, and may I not also add dissimulation? while her long prospect of the throne which she was one day to ascend, induced her to study the science of government before she was called to wield the sceptre. In all but vanity, her mind was masculine. This vice certainly led her into a perfidious, though perhaps political sacrifice of a lovely competitor; and induced her, when past her grand climacteric, to court the praise of beauty, which even in youth she never possessed; and, unmindful of the deathless laurels which crowned her vigorous and successful administration, to decorate her withered brows with the myrtle of affected gallantry.

gallantry. If we compare her latter years with those of our first Edward, whom in her public actions she much resembled, our sex must feel humbled at the parallel.

The miseries of the unhappy Queen of Scotland, so evidently ascribable to the graces, the virtues, and the failings of her sex, must, while they still draw the tear of pity for her fate, excite our lively sympathy for every woman who is called to the dangerous estate of sovereign power; especially in a realm where the fundamental rights of the constitution and the bounds of prerogative are not *decidedly* settled. How beautiful was the picture which she exhibited in early life of conjugal virtue and domestic felicity! how must we regret the death of Francis, which banished her from " Fair France," and sent her to a kingdom barren of social
delights,

delights, the haunt of ambition, and the den of morose fanaticism! How do we participate in her reluctance to relinquish the charms of elegance and refinement; in her endeavours to soften the harsh character of her subjects, and to conciliate the alarmed suspicion of Elizabeth, to whose superior and more wisely cultivated understanding, she could only oppose graces and accomplishments, which were to her not only useless, but actually hastened her fall! We see the weak precipitation of her sex in her rash assumption of her rival's title, and her hasty marriage with Darnley; and we discover the unrestrained feelings of wounded sensibility, in her avowed contempt of him after her discovery of his ingratitude and meanness. The events immediately following are so perplexed by contradictory statements, that though general opinion now seems inclined to consider her conduct rather as imprudent than wicked, I will pass them, and hasten to the last scenes of her life; when, sinking with fatigue, destitute of friends, abandoned, helpless, and forlorn, the lovely fugitive threw herself upon the mercy of a sister queen; and, through eighteen years of tedious confinement, saw the sun only rise

"To mark how fierce her angry guardians frown'd,
To mark how fast her waning beauty flew."

To the last period of her mournful days, she felt no other effect of her royal birth, than from its elevating her to be the alternate mark of jealousy and ambition. The symmetry of her person, the susceptibility of her temper, the graces of her manner, the elegance of her accomplishments, the warmth of her attachments, all that
made

made the woman amiable, destroyed the queen.

Our second Mary only occasionally held a delegated sceptre; and as her tuneful panegyrist * justly observes, was " instructed to command," by obeying the hero William. Her regencies may be produced as the brightest example of female administration, combining all those qualities of firmness, promptitude, vigour, prudence, and clemency, which constitute the definition of a well-ordered state. Yet this wise and amiable Princess certainly knew that the passive virtues were best suited to her sex. " Never," says a cotemporary author, "were the reins of government " more reluctantly assumed, more " wisely managed, nor more willingly " resigned." Her conjugal deportment

* Prior.

to a husband whom she eclipsed in amiable qualities, is a shining example of discreet acquiescence in general laws. Her positive refusal to accept a *solitary* sceptre, was not affectation, but wisdom. Her political interference was always marked by beneficial effects, because it was never unnecessarily obtrusive. The revered character of this exemplary lady, the sacred theme of Prior's chaster muse, adorned by every public and every private excellence, still call the muses to weep over her early tomb. Should her imperial robes be destined to array another English queen, may they, like the mantle of Elijah, convey a portion of her hallowed spirit; and may the inheretrix of her regalia resemble the blessed spouse of William, in all but her premature exchange of an earthly for a heavenly diadem!

The

The royal sister of this illustrious princess ascended the throne with equally good intentions, but with inferior abilities. The splendid successes that attended her public administration are confessedly attributable to the wisdom of her statesmen, and the heroism of her naval and military commanders. Her private infelicities, and the distractions of her latter years, are a proof of the unfitness of women to manage the intricate perplexities that arise from contending parties, or to struggle against those gentler sympathies of nature which in elevated situations must give place to the sterner virtues that extensive responsibility imposes. Her subservience to those violent tempers whom her station authorized her to overawe; her desire to accomplish ends which were utterly incompatible, and to reconcile characters essentially discordant;

discordant; her attachment to her exiled disinherited brother, and to many ungrateful favourites who had recommended themselves to her esteem by specious qualities, rendered her dignity a crown of thorns, which pressed hard on the aching brows of inbecile sickness. Yet, considered as a woman, what can we censure in Queen Anne? Pious and sincere as a Christian, anxious for peace, compassionate to the afflicted, affectionate to her kindred, an excellent wife, disposed to friendship, sincere, placable, and compliant.

I allow, that the reigns of many of our kings present as many, or I will say more enormous errors than the worst of those which I have specified; but let it be remembered, that their maladministration arose from what, it must be acknowledged, were their errors or their

their vices. In most cases, it was from the predominance of some amiable *female* quality, that our queens erred in their public duties. You well know, that it is not my aim to affirm our absolute unfitness to take the lead, whenever peculiar circumstances enforce the necessity of our so doing; for we may then, equally with the other sex, hope for that supply of preventing and restraining grace which will enable us to do our duty in the state of life to which we are *called*; and whenever the exaltation of a woman to a highly responsible situation can be foreseen, a particular regard to her education and early habits may enable her to blend the authoritative, magnanimous, and discriminating qualities that her station will require with the milder virtues of her sex. These assistances we cannot hope to possess, if we rush madly from our sphere, and resolve, uncalled, to venture on untried and forbidden paths. Cheerful acquiescence in the will of him who disposes of the lot, and steady application to the improvement of the talents with which we are intrusted, is our duty; we have already proved, that it is also our interest.

The propriety of our seclusion from public affairs is necessarily interwoven with domestic subjection. The humour of the present age leans so strongly to the aspiring qualities, independence and self-controul have such attraction in their magical sound, that I must prudently shelter my opposition to their delusive enchantment under the protection of mighty names, when I pronounce the dependant situation of our sex *advantageous*. "One very " common error," says Dr. Paley,
" misleads

" misleads the opinions of mankind on
" this head; viz. that, universally, au-
" thority is pleasant, and submission
" painful. In the general course of
" human affairs, the very reverse of
" this is nearer the truth : command
" is anxiety, obedience ease." While
applying this admirable observation to
ourselves, as dependant upon the wills
of our near connexions, I shall not
become the advocate of male tyranny.
Referring to the origin of authority
and submission, we may be assured,
that they were imposed for mutual
benefit. " Men do not," as another
great divine observes, "claim the su-
" premacy for any inherent superio-
" rity, nor for their own individual
" solace; but rather, that domestic
" peace may not be violated by per-
" petual competition. The right of
" command must be placed some-
" where,

" where, or how could the little re-
" public be regularly ordered; where
" then shall it be properly bestowed?
" Shall it be confided to strength and
" courage, enterprize and activity; or
" shall these qualities be made subser-
" vient to weakness, apprehension,
" gentleness, and a love of repose?
" Would not this be to constitute a
" state of perpetual warfare, as the
" qualities of the governor and go-
" verned would be diametrically op-
" posite to what their respective duties
" required?"

No portrait can be more truly amiable, than that of a well-disposed well-informed woman ordering her domestic affairs with propriety, and guided in the more important concerns of life by the judgment of a worthy intelligent husband; and if we meant also to draw a picture of human felicity, we
could.

could not do better than copy from the same original. A well-disposed mind, conscious of its own imperfections (and no mind which is well disposed can avoid feeling them), shrinks from the burden of unnecessary responsibility. It can make allowances for the errors and failings of others; it cannot so lightly pardon its own. By committing our affairs to the disposal of one in whom we can confide, we always propose to ourselves quiet and self-enjoyment; but in a voluntary choice every degree of mismanagement subjects us to the reproach of misplaced confidence; where the choice is made for us, acquiescence is at least entitled to the solace of conscious rectitude: the authority of the agent will not prevent the effects of his weakness or mismanagement, but our submission is then justifiable.

Domesti

Domestic retirement is not only the scene where the passive virtues display their heavenly energies; it is also their secure asylum. From how many temptations is our sex preserved, by being placed in this enviable shade! We are so hedged in, and separated from the contagion of many vices by general opinion, established customs, and even by the natural repugnance of our own minds, that we must use violence before we can burst through the sacred enclosure, and solicit, or rather seize, contamination. We will mention, as instances, intemperance, profaneness, treachery, and cruelty. Even in the eyes of debauchees, a female bonvivant is contemptible; and indecorum of expression startles the most profligate, when it proceeds from that sex, whose presence is acknowledged to be such a restraint upon the boldest.

blasphemer,

blasphemer, as only ignorance and ill manners can surmount. Well might the inspired writer observe, that "there "is no wickedness like the wicked- "ness of a woman;" for the effrontery which enables her to brave infamy, ascertains the annihilation of those lively sensibilities which might have led her back to commiseration and contrition. It is observed in the lower walks of vice, that when a woman is concerned in a robbery, murder generally follows; this is a probable consequence, for cowards are always cruel; and those small remains of generosity, which even a course of rapine cannot always eradicate, are foreign to a heart which has only conquered the restraints, but not the selfishness of fear. In men we have often seen ambition united with many excellent qualities; it has even been styled the error of great

great minds. Conscious of ability,
and insatiate of renown, conquerors
and statesmen have generally been
solicitous to do that "holily which they
" would do highly;" but when woman
has delivered herself up to unlawful
cravings, her lively passions, and her
eager desire to attain her purpose,
combating with the sense of her weakness, has generally driven her upon
the most detestable means of accomplishing a bad design. Macbeth, in
the very act of murder, retains somewhat of the " milk of human kindness ;" but " his fiend-like queen " has
no other thought than self-security.
Do not object that we contemplate
these historical characters through
the medium of fiction; their portraits
are delineated with the most perfect
resemblance to human nature. That
of Lady Macbeth presents what, I
believe,

believe, is rather rare in the annals of vice, a woman *genuinely* ambitious; for in our sex ambition is commonly a subaltern quality, stimulated by love, hatred, revenge, fear, or vanity. Like **Kenrida** in Shenstone's elegies, the aspiring female mostly anticipates. " How sweet are slumbers on a couch of state," or else wishes "To crown at " once the lover and the love." But the same baleful effects proceed from the mixed as from the primary passion; whenever an Athaliah covets undue pre-eminence, she arises with a determination "to cut off all the seed-royal." These observations, my dear Miss M——, are not wholly irrelative to the million. Ambition presents other temptations beside crowns, and has less bloody, though equally destructive consequences as those to which we have just alluded. I am

persuaded

persuaded that we must refer to this passion, when, under the guidance of vanity, many of those extravagancies which we shall be called upon to lament in the course of our correspondence, as ruinous to domestic peace, and derogatory to female character.

I do not think that women have less temptation to anger than men; because in the routine of family affairs they generally meet with perpetual, though trivial, trials of meekness; and we know, that the solid rock is more likely to be fretted by continual droppings, than broken by the rushing of a hasty cataract; but the present forms of society, and I grieve to add, its seemingly irresistible propensities, may make us enumerate as one of our advantages, that anger is not likely to involve *us* in very serious consequences. While the only sinful part of chivalry is preserved from that oblivion which has involved its high-souled chastity, integrity, and generosity, we must congratulate ourselves that we are not likely to be *called out* for an unguarded expression, perhaps uttered unconsciously in a moment of temporary delirium. You will smile at my enumerating this security amongst our advantages; but the bloody register of false honour is become so voluminous, that it really is a consolation to reflect, that the whizzing ball or gliding steel are not likely to be classed in the list of *our* mortal diseases.

The customs of society give us advantages not highly valuable of themselves, but capable of being converted to real benefit. The attentions that we receive as women may certainly be, as Mary Wolstonecraft terms them, " engines of refined voluptuousness," when they minister to our caprice, our vanity, and our frivolity; but they are capable of a higher direction, and may be so received, and so directed, as to reform the morals of those from whom we require them. Gallantry (I here use that term in its *inoffensive* signification) has been so modified and curtailed by prevailing manners, that it is to be hoped women will not join in a conspiracy to annihilate the small degree of knightly courtesy which yet exists, by themselves assuming the deportment of amazonian boldness, or affecting amazonian independence. By indelicacy of habit, by unblushing confidence in conversation, and by the discovery of a vindictive disposition, we forfeit the respect to which the passive virtues, our natural endowments, are entitled, and must receive from all but brutes or monsters.

The passive virtues, my dear young friend, are not mean, servile, or cowardly. Dr. Paley places them in such a point of view, as may excite the emulation of the most aspiring mind. His definition is, "passive virtues are "of all others the severest, the most "sublime, and perhaps the most ac- "ceptable to the Deity." The foundation on which they stand is fortitude, magnanimity, and disinterestedness; and their sure reward is self-possession, and that peace of God which passeth understanding. The overstrained softness of affected refinement is as inimical to these heavenly qualities, as the fury of a virago; a life of uselessness and indulgence can never be a life of happiness. Whoever erects herself into the golden idol of self-importance will be perpetually harassed, by seeing inflexible integrity refuse to fall prostrate before her. Whatever painted gauds may pass upon the world as the trappings of happiness, it can only reside in the bosoms of those who are exercised in good works. The offices which are daily required of women, enable us to lay claim to this enviable distinction. Our relative situation in life preserves us from many temptations; we are more guarded by our natural propensities from some vices; and from others, we are more secured by habit and general opinion. We are in less danger of having our integrity censured by the allurements of fraud, ambition, or contending interests; but these are not our best advantages: our most glorious distinction is, that we are better fitted for receiving the tenets and obeying the precepts of that faith which will make us wise unto salvation; for, however infidels may misrepresent and cavil at lowliness and singleness of heart, these are the dispositions which fit us for the reception of the stupendous plan of redemption, and

and prepare us for evangelical holiness. Credulity and terror may make us superstitious, and obstinacy and ignorance may beget bigotry; but bigotry and superstition are mere opprobrious appellations when applied to true religion, and only reflect odium on the bestower. Here, then, our peculiar qualities give us advantages, which strength, courage, and wisdom, when unsanctioned by piety, cannot impart. A consciousness of infirmity is the admonition of nature, bidding us look up to "the rock from whence "we were hewn," and depend upon the power that has promised "to save "all who trust in him." Our general habits of submission and constraint tend to subdue our stormy passions, and to eradicate our corrupt desires; the humble offices of life in which most of us are engaged, make us acquainted

quainted with the wants of our fellow-creatures, and also dispose us to relieve the sorrows in which we have such full participation; while all the emotions of hope, fear, joy, grief, affection, and gratitude, to which our susceptible hearts are so peculiarly alive, form the very basis for a pure but animated devotion. Surely, then, my dear Miss M——, contemplating these inestimable privileges, these securities from vice, these incentives to virtue, these helps of grace and hopes of glory, we may adopt the language of a nervous, though now neglected instructor * of our sex, and "thank God that we were born women." Leaving you to improve these reflections as your piety will best suggest, I remain, &c.

* The Author of the Ladies' Calling.

LETTER

LETTER III.

Change of Manners in the Middle Classes.

MY DEAR MISS M——,

From the consideration of what we are designed to be by Providence, the proposed series of our correspondence leads us to inquire, what we become when we renounce the obligation of duty, and submit to be new-modelled by caprice or affectation. Though the woman of fashion boasts of having emancipated herself from those restraints which fetter the inclination of the woman of propriety, we shall discover that she really is in a state of bondage, and has voluntarily submitted to injunctions no less numerous, and far more servile, than those which she has rejected. She has her trials too; for the wisdom of Divine Providence never suffers any glaring violation of its laws to brave its authority, without being reproved, or at least feeling the internal consequences of its pertinacity. We need not extend our researches to the comforts and advantages of a life of voluptuous dissipation, or indolent self-indulgence; they possess none. The punishments of the wicked do not, like the corrections of the faithful, heal the heart they are intended to probe.

Moralists are always censured for giving an exaggerated caricature of their own times. I am ready to admit, that in some respects we have improved upon our ancestors; that vice ceases to be gross, and manners are no longer stiff or pedantic; that society is governed by more agreeable and
convenient

convenient laws, and that dress, when it does not outrage modesty, is regulated by a purer taste, than that which ordained long waists, long ruffles, high pokes, and farthingales. It is also acknowledged, that our comforts are materially increased by mechanical and mathematical discoveries, and that knowledge is more generally diffused. I believe the learned are agreed, that in profound studies, which do not depend upon experimental philosophy, mechanical contrivance, or natural history, this age cannot sustain a comparison with those which laid the foundation of our church, and perfected our civil constitution. If the most proper study of mankind is man, our ancestors had the advantage of us in knowledge. Nor can we claim uncontested pre-eminence in charity; because donations from those ample stores which internal peace and commerce have diffused over this nation, must not be rated in arithmetical proportion with the *pittance* that could be spared from the urgent necessities of individuals, at a period when agriculture was ill understood, and often interrupted by civil wars, and when arts and manufactures were unknown. The benevolence, public spirit, and magnificent liberality of those perilous and needy times, are proved by the irrefragable testimony of many religious and charitable foundations, by stately edifices devoted to the advancement of learning, by splendid asylums for infancy and sickness, and by comfortable habitations for age and penury.

Charity is therefore only, what it ever has been, a striking feature in our national character. It is, indeed, so predominant a distinction, that even
selfish-

selfishness, languishing in the dissipation and luxury of what is called high life, cannot avoid imparting some of its superflux to the poor and needy. Justice should be always done even to the least deserving; and it is to be lamented, that the author of a very spirited and well-principled satire*, while describing the "barren and dreary de-" sert of the fashionable world," has neglected to mark out the green Oasis † of charity. Perhaps it would have been false candour to have applied the name of this sublime Christian grace to the liberality of philanthropy; however, as even that indicates some remnant of moral feeling, some interrup-

---

* The Fashionable World Displayed.

† This term is used by modern travellers in North Africa, to signify those spots of cultivation which occasionally diversify the immense deserts that lie between Barbary and Negro-land.

tion of the frigid cold of a life of pleasure, it should not be passed over without commendation, though its motives do not entitle it to the praise of religious obedience.

It is no new observation, that the extremes of society are unfavourable to virtue. Wise Agur formed a wish upon this head three thousand years ago *, which for piety and prudence is alike entitled to everlasting remembrance. The levity and dissipation of the middle ranks are the singular and alarming characteristics of the present times. A dissolute sensual nobility is no novelty. It is also upon record, that the lower orders in these kingdoms have been dissatisfied, clamorous, negligent of their proper duties, and inclined to assume political

* Prov. xxx. 8.

supremacy. But the middle classes, where temperance, diligence, and propriety used to reside, the favourite abode of rectitude, good sense, and sound piety, have undergone a change within the last fifty years which must startle every considerate mind; so far as it relates to women, either as to the cause or the cure, it presents a topic demanding our close attention.

Though the effects of commercial prosperity are in some degree generally diffused over the nation, it has principally affected the intermediate orders. Successful adventure, professional skill, patient diligence, or laborious industry, often bring a rapid increase of wealth to families that have not, either by habit or education, been taught the proper use of it. The first blessing which fortune seems to offer to an ill-regulated or ill-informed mind is self-enjoyment, the second is distinction; hence arise luxurious modes of living, and absurd exhibitions of grandeur. It would be well, if the consequences of these errors were limited to what inevitably follows extreme indulgence, I mean disease and contempt; but the effects are rarely confined to the faulty individual. The gains of successful adventure are soon lost by a reverse of fortune; the savings of diligence and industry cannot supply the waste of carelessness and indolence; the profits of the professional man die with him, and nothing remains to his family but the hoard which frugality reserved in the hour of prosperity. Yet if people so circumstanced will vie in expense with hereditary wealth, what must be the consequence? what indeed, but that which we hourly see, in bankruptcies, suicides, helpless widows and destitute orphans, in every species of nefarious fraud, extortion, and swindling imposition; we must also add, that the ruin caused by this rage for luxury and show is visible in the madness of gaming-houses, and in the licentious haunts of prostitution.

Would to heaven our sex could be vindicated from the heavy censure that must fall upon those who, to purchase the *eclat* of a few years, not the *happiness* of an hour, involve themselves and families in destruction! An impartial review of living manners compels me to confess, that we are in this point often more culpable than our weakly indulgent partners. It is Eve who again intreats Adam to eat the forbidden fruit: he takes it, and is undone. Men in this rank of life have generally less *taste* than women; they are amused by their business through the day, and at its weary close they would generally be contented with the relaxation which their own families afforded, if those families were social, domestic, cheerful, and desirous to promote their amusement. But since the potent decree of fashion determined it to be unfit for the wife of a man in reputable circumstances to employ herself in domestic arrangements, or useful needle-work, time has proved a severe burden to people who are destitute of inclination for literature. To relieve themselves from a load, the weight of which they are too proud to acknowledge, they have felt obliged to mingle with what is called the world. Did any of these adventurous dames consider the heavy services which this association requires, did they fairly rate the fatigue, the perplexity, the slavery of being *very genteel* upon a *limited* scale, they would think it better to prefer a plain system of social comfort, even at the expense of that ridicule

ridicule which, I lament to say, such a deviation from refinement would incur. Yet, when there is no housekeeper in the spice-room, nor butler at the sideboard, an elegant entertainment occasions more labour and perplexity to the mistress of the house, than she would undergo by a regular performance of services highly beneficial and praiseworthy. What anxiety is there that every part of the splendid repast should be properly selected, well dressed, and served in style! What care to keep the every-day garb of family economics out of sight, and to convince the guests that this is the usual style of living; though, if they credit the report, it must only confirm their suspicion that their hostess is actually insane. What blushing confusion do these *demi*-fashionists discover, if detected in any employment that seems to indicate a little re-maining regard for prudence and œconomy! What irregularity and inconvenience must the family experience during the days immediately preceding the gala! what irritation of temper, what neglect of children, what disregard of religious and social offices! And for what is all this sacrifice? to procure the honour of being talked of; for happiness, or even comfort, are rarely expected at such entertainments. Notwithstanding all due preparation, something goes wrong, either in the dinner or the company. The face of the inviter displays mortification, instead of exultation; and the invited disguise the sneer of ridicule under the fixed simper of affected politeness Nor let the giver of the feast complain of disappointment. She aimed not to please, but to dazzle; not to gratify her guests by the cheerful hilarity of her table, but to announce her

her own superiority in taste or in expense. When the hospitable hostess spreads her plain but plentiful board for friendship and kindred, for those whom she loves or respects, those whom she seeks to oblige, or those to whom she wishes to acknowledge obligation, where vanity and self are kept out of sight, and real generosity seeks no higher praise than that of giving a sufficient and comfortable repast with a pleasant welcome, a fastidious observance of any accidental mistake, or trivial error, might be justly called ill-nature and ingratitude; but when ostentation summons her myrmidons to behold the triumph, let ridicule join the party, and proclaim the defeat.

But this insatiable monster, a rage for distinction, is not content with spoiling the comforts of the cheerful regale; luxury has invented a prodigious number of accommodations in the department of moveables; and the mistress of a tiny villa at Hackney, or a still more tiny drawing-room in Crutched Friars, only waits to know if her Grace has placed them in her baronial residence, to pronounce that they are comforts without which no soul can exist. Hence it becomes an undertaking of no little skill, to conduct one's person through an apartment twelve feet square, furnished in *style* by a lady of *taste*, without any injury to ourselves, or to the fauteuils, candelabras, consoletables, jardiniers, chiffoniers, &c. Should we, at entering the apartment, escape the workboxes, foot-stools, and cushions for lapdogs, our debut may still be celebrated by the overthrow of half a dozen top-gallant screens, as many perfume jars, or even by the total demolition of a glass cabinet stuck full of stuffed monsters. By an inadvertent remove of our chair backwards, we may thrust it through the paper frame of the book-stand, or the pyramidal flower-basket; and our nearer approach to the fire is barricadoed by nodding mandarines and branching lustres. It is well, if the height of the apartment permits us to glide secure under the impending danger of crystal lamps, chandeliers, and gilt bird-cages inhabited by screaming canaries. An attempt to walk would be too presumptuous, amidst the opposition of a host of working-tables, sofas, rout chairs, and ottomans. To return from a visit of this description without having *committed* or *suffered* any depredation, is an event almost similar to the famous expedition of the Argonauts. The fair mistress, indeed, generally officiates as pilot; and by observing how she folds

or

tresses, and the studiously inconve
nient situation of her ornaments, proclaim an airy sylph, a Grecian nymph,
a "mincing mammet," or, to speak i
her own language, a very fine lady:
they cannot possibly denote the indus
trious housewife, or the help-mate o
man.

'The pursuits of this *lusus naturæ*,
this creature formed to feed on the
toils of industry, consist of laborious
idleness. As, after all her exertions,
her situation in life does not allow of
her being genteel in *every* thing, parsimonious œconomy and heedless expense take their turn. To be as smart,
not as her equals, but as her superiors,
it becomes necessary that she should
excel in contrivance; I do not mean
in that prudent forethought, which
enables a good wife to proportion the
family expenditure by the regular or-
    der

der of necessities, comforts, conveniences, and superfluities: this gradation must be reversed, and superfluities take the lead. French wines may be introduced on great occasions, by a daily retrenchment of small beer; and wax-lights may be had for routs, by limiting the number of kitchen candles. If her husband and children dine on hashed mutton, she can provide ices in the evening; and by leaving their bed-chambers comfortless and inconvenient, she can afford more drapery for the drawing-room. Even white morning dresses will not be so very expensive, provided you are expert in haggling with the washer-woman, and do not dislike being dirty when you are invisible; and if you know cheap shops, and the art of driving bargains, you may even save money by making *useless* purchases. New modelling

modelling your household and persona ornaments is, I grant, an indispensabl duty; for no one can appear thre times in the same gown, or have si parties without one additional vandyk or festoon to the window-curtains These employments will therefore oc cupy your mornings till the hour o visiting arrives; then you must take care to dismiss the bed-gown and work-bag, and, having crammed every thing ungenteel out of sight, assume the airs of that happy creature who has nothing in the world to do, and nothing to think of but killing time. Fashions are now to be discussed, public places criticised, shopping schemes adjusted, and evening parties fixed. After your morning ramble, you will just get time to treat your own family with a little of that spleen and chagrin which have been excited by your having seen an
acquaintance

acquaintance in her carriage while you were still compelled to be on foot, or by having met one better dressed than yourself, whose husband cannot *half* so well afford it. You must, in compliance with the pressure of time, hurry over the business of the toilette; and if during the remainder of the evening, you are not quite in so great a crowd as a duchess, you may at least console yourself with the consideration that you are as useless to your family.

My dear young friend will smile when I add, that our second-rate ladies plead that they undergo all this from motives of *conjugal duty* and *maternal affection*. It is necessary, they say to keep up connections; their husband's credit depends upon their appearance; nobody notices them if they do not live like other people; or

perhaps

perhaps the good man himself insists upon their being very smart and living in style. When this latter excuse happens to be the fact, we certainly must seem to sail with the stream; but the plans of expense which we dare not openly oppose, a regard to our children, and indeed self-love, should induce us to counteract gradually. Vanity is rarely a prevailing feature in a man's character; men sometimes, indeed, choose that their wives should be gaily adorned, and hurried through a round of amusements, because they are their property; but much oftener they do this out of gallantry, with a view to gratify them, and by way of showing them their attachment. In the latter case, it is very possible to decline, with affection and steadiness, every expensive attention which prudence disapproves; and in the former, this mania

mania of unconjugal *ostentation* may be checked, by appearing rather to *endure* than to *enjoy* the exhibition. Men are far more sensual than vain; they are less influenced by general opinion, and less affected by petty detraction. The passion of self-indulgence leads them into expensive habits. Disdaining the fictitious happiness which depends upon the breath of others, dissipated men pursue what they call *substantial* bliss. They know that the club will at least for an hour exclude sorrow and ensure gaiety. The circulating glass has with them the united properties of Lethe and Helicon. To a man of this cast, the society of his wife and children is vapid, or at least not sufficiently poignant to be long entertaining. If his tavern-engagements can be counteracted by a well-dressed dinner, and a few a few cheerful friends at home, a woman is justified in resorting to these measures, by way of weaning him from his more dangerous propensities; even though she should be obliged to sacrifice those pure domestic pleasures, which happy wedlock affords those people whose fortunes are equal to their wants;

> " An elegant sufficiency, content,
> " Retirement, rural quiet, friendship, books,
> " Ease and alternate labour, useful life,
> " Progressive virtue, and approving heaven."

I cannot admit the generally-received excuse, that convivial meetings and tavern associations are promoters of business; because I have known men transact a great deal, and even rise from low life to opulence, by means of an established character for probity, integrity, and sobriety. The general habits of the superior part of the mercantile

cantile world confirm my opinion. But, granting that the convenience of driving a bargain, or forcing trade, may withdraw the husband from the domestic circle, the dissipation of the wife is left without excuse. The craft of deceiving by false appearances is followed by too many, to be a profitable *speculation* any longer; and wealthy people, whom it is desirable to make dupes, are much sooner induced to trust a man by the appearance of order and œconomy in his family, than by hearing that it is the gayest in the street; which cautious traders often think is the surest omen of approaching bankruptcy. Nor is the wisdom of the mother more apparent than that of the wife, in thus cultivating taste at the expense of propriety, from a design of procuring respectable connexions for her daughter;

which intention is almost sure to be frustrated by one circumstance: every body is embarking in the same traffic; and the market is so full of well-dressed spinsters, who are adepts in the art of spending money, that if our laws permitted the same plurality of wives to men of fortune as the Koran sanctions, still many an elegant belle would be in want of a good *establishment*. The nymphs of modern times, who spend their days in music and dancing, differ much from the ancient heroines of pastoral and romance; for these latter, if they fed at all, subsisted upon the wild productions of groves and meads, quaffed the limpid stream, and reposed under umbrageous trees; so that they really were very *cheap* companions. But now, ornaments are no longer composed of natural flowers, unless, like Lady Teazle, the fair one

pur-

purchases roses at Christmas. Penelope (except we seek for her in the circle of royalty) cannot fabricate a vest for her son or sire; and even " white-handed Phyllis " disdains "to dress herbs and other country messes for Corydon and Thyrsis;" and indeed I much fear that those gentlemen would no longer find them " savoury." The rich gudgeon, for whom *portionless* elegance drops such numerous baits, often possesses that most ungallant acquirement, arithmetic; and, having discovered that a dowerless wife will have the same conjugal anxiety to support his pecuniary reputation, seems inclined to ally himself to a gold-fish. Compassionating the claims of those numerous young women, who found their expectation of being supported on their total inability of helping themselves, I would advise,

advise, by way of experiment, that some few mothers would show a wish of furnishing the next generation with *wives*, by cultivating those qualities in their daughters which will prevent them from being converted into *mistresses*. Diffidence, frugality, and industry, are indeed quite out; but, for that very reason they will certainly be stared at, and may give their possessor that notoriety, which those who only herd with a crowd never can obtain; and it is even possible that some whimsical humourist may take a fancy to such vulgarity, and, remembering his old grandmother's proverb, may overlook the want of fortune with a wife, when there appears to be something in her which promises to wear well. I grant that such a man must be a quiz; yet quizzes have made good husbands; at least, it is better to be
the

the wife of such a one, than to be eternally transforming an old tambour muslin into fresh nets to entangle a Titus or a Brutus, who, being himself upon his preferment, perfectly understands the mystery of *entrapment*.

I can no longer support a strain of irony. My soul is moved to the liveliest indignation, and keenest sorrow, at the wilful degradation of my sex. With what propriety do we complain of the state of dependence in which God and the laws of our country have placed us, when we render ourselves infinitely more helpless, more destitute (shall we not say more servile and despicable?) by deserting our proper sphere, by neglecting the useful duties that we might perform, by sacrificing the interest and the affections of our families, not to be even an object of admiration, distinguished for elegant

gant frivolity and expensive nothingness; but for the sake of starting in a crowd to run the race of folly, of echoing a forged tale of happiness and splendor, which has been too often told to be even specious? For let me once again repeat the often-urged fact, dissipation, finery, and extravagance, are *too frequent to attract attention.* Even if you strain the bursting nerves of credit, and not only squander every shilling of your children's property, but ruin every one whom you can ensnare, some rival, equally unprincipled, but better situated, will outshine you. Could these poor slaves of vanity, who judge by the supposed opinion of the world, hear the contemptuous sarcasms which this unsuitable parade and expense excite from those whom they attempt to propitiate, it is possible that the dread of ridicule might
prove

prove a more powerful restraint, than the reproachful tears of their ruined offspring, and the curses of their creditors. In the higher circles, a more costly dress than the occasion requires is considered as an indelible proof of vulgarity; the grandeur of the lady's paraphernalia is contrasted with the pettiness of her attendant lacquey, the shabbiness of her buggy, or the leanness of her laborious Rozinante; and the suitability of the *tout ensemble* must be arranged with no common skill, if it escapes the prying glance of piqued superiority. An uncommon assemblage of feathers, a treble accumulation of train, a double row of plaited Valenciennes, or a sleeve decorated till it reminds one of Petruchio's whimsical description*, as in-

---

* "What! up and down, carv'd like an apple-tart,
"With snip, and nip, and cut."
SHAKSPEARE.

disputably announce the entry of some would-be fine lady to a well-bred assembly, as a copper complexion does a native American to the Canadian settlers; and the company wait, with the *nonchalance* of good breeding, till some cockney misapplication of the W., or provincial inversion of the aspirate, determines the stranger's tribe and latitude. For let it not be supposed, that the propensity to appear what we are not is limited to crowded cities: few retirements are so sequestered, as to prevent their being explored by the visitations of this ostentatious passion for *saleable* refinement. The village madam hopes her showy array, and fastidious scrupulosity, will convince you that her husband cannot be a farmer; and, at the peril of a brisk retort, you must forbear to insinuate to the market-town *elegante*, that she may be wanted in the shop.

They

They suppose that it is very vulgar to be thought useful; and the acknowledgment of an honest avocation is to them a reproach. Yet, though wealth and commerce have rendered the *externals* of the gentlewoman so attainable, that she is no longer to be distinguished by her habit; it is left to more patient and less prosperous times to transcribe the complaisance, affability, condescending attention to the claims of others, love of propriety, and regard for decorum, which are the *essentials* of this desired distinction: the adoption of these latter qualities is too arduous an undertaking, and requires too many privations. Rudeness of habit is soon cast aside, rudeness of manner is more adhesive. The country lass doffs the former at the dress maker's, where she leaves her red cloak and her humility; but she is infinitely too much delighted with her transformation, to suppose respect to superiors, or civility to equals, can be necessary, now that the Miss Stitchwells have pronounced her *quite another thing*. Is there, my dear Miss M——, a more disgusting produce than insolence engrafted on awkwardness? or are any airs so ridiculous, as those which are assumed by purse-proud ignorance?

Your excellent mother filled a situation in life too decidedly respectable to derive any real elevation from attempting to outstep the modesty of nature. Her good sense taught her both to perceive and preserve its advantages. I enjoy a soothing gratification from reflecting, that as, by avoiding the extremes of parsimony and extravagance, she gave an example of prudence to people of her own rank;

rank; so the wisdom of the maxims by which she governed her conduct was *generally* useful. When the pressure of the times presented those claims to which country gentlemen are especially exposed, she did not plead public exigency as a reason for restraining private benevolence; nor did she make her domestics miserable by penurious restrictions. " The " world," she observed, " will always "allow you to spare from yourself. " If you never attempt to outshine " your neighbours, they will pardon " your old gown, and permit you to " stay at home unquestioned." By limiting our wardrobe, or giving up an excursion, it is possible to avoid the censure of being mean, and the pain of knowing that we embarrass our husband's affairs.

It is worth considering, at how much

much less expense of time, fortune, and comfort you may purchase the reputation of solid, than you can of brilliant qualities, provided you are contented with being a good *plain* character; for few are inclined to contest the right of a claimant to that distinction. I do not advise you to gain it by struggling against the torrent, but by getting out of its way, and suffering it to glide quietly by you. If the attention of your superiors be the object at which you aim, this is the surest way to obtain it; for, to return to the observations of my deceased monitor, "though every rank "in life has pressed into the station "immediately preceding, none seem "conscious of their own advancement, "while all are piqued at the exalta-"tion of their inferiors." The clergyman's daughters will express much indigna-

indignation that the Misses Flamborough have imitated their Sunday hat, at the very moment that they are fabricating a head-dress resembling what the baronet's lady wore at the last county assembly. It is in vain, therefore, to rush forward with precipitation; our superiors will only suffer us to overtake them for one moment; and then, with a smile of contempt, they will vault on a higher eminence, where you must try to perch beside them, or else be thrown down by the crowd of jostling inferiors, who are pressing hard upon you. To step aside is the only wise method; and, to be convinced of the absolute necessity for our so doing, let us for a moment turn our eyes on the lower orders of society. Our attention shall be first directed to that with which we are most connected, domestic servants.

vants. What is their appearance; what are their pursuits; what, generally speaking, is their moral character? The propensity to appear what they are not, has operated so strongly in this class, that few mistresses, however besotted themselves, can refrain from complaining of its ill effects; and it is impossible to go into a mixed company, without being assailed with narratives of the extravagance, ignorance, folly, and finery of maid-servants. Yet, to say that they only faithfully copy the examples which are set before them, would not (generally speaking) be too severe an answer. But this subject must be reserved for future discussion*.

We have seen, that no speculative advantages can accrue either to our husbands, or our daughters, by our

* See Letter XIVth.

extra-

extravagance. Suppose we now estimate the pleasure really enjoyed by a woman who devotes herself to expensive gratifications, who wears the most elegant dress, gives the most sumptuous entertainments, goes every where, and sees all that is to be seen. I allow that the being thus occupied must be too much devoted to self-enjoyment to feel anxious about her deserted family; to care whether her children are brutes, idiots, or cripples, further than as they affect herself; to be solicitous how her husband amuses himself in her absence; to shrink at the apprehension of the carelessness or the dishonesty of her servants; or to mind having her morning slumbers broken by a levee of clamorous duns. We may deny that she ever attains what she pursues, pleasure; and our proof of this assertion is derived from

the

the palling effect of satiety on tl
physical constitution of our bodie:
and from the certain fact, that ple
sure ever flies away the fastest wh(
it is most eagerly pursued. The r
tional dame, who spares one evenir
in the week from domestic occupation
will enjoy a lively party, a well-act(
play, a concert, or a ball. She w
feel the force of contrast; and ever
agreeable incident will be engrav(
on her memory, for the purpose
amusing the beloved group, who w:
crowd around her next morning,
inquire the history of the gay evenin;
She has a still greater chance of bein
gratified, as she will enter the fest
scene with spirits undepressed by th
load of bodily debility which sleeple
nights and listless days must occasio1
beside, amusement is not the busine
of her life; and if what she ente

in

into falls short of her expectation, it is but a petty disappointment, and she has other resources.

"The sleep of the labouring man " is sweet," says the inspired penman; and surely nothing is so delightful, as, after a day spent in the peaceful exercise of some honest calling, to sink upon our pillows, conscious of well-meant endeavours, and confiding in that God who has promised to accept them. Fatigue of this kind never injures the animal frame; it is repaired by rest and refreshment; and the morning, which renews the *demand* for exertion, revives the *power* of compliance. The fatigue which arises from excessive dissipation is of another description. The exhausted body has lost the ability of revivification; the clamour of music, the clashing of carriages, assail its feverish slumbers;
the

the mazes of the dance, and the glare of theatrical scenery, still flit before the frequently unclosed eyes; the passions are not yet calm in the throbbing bosom; envy enumerates the ornaments of a rival, and chagrin dwells upon the slight curtsey of an opulent acquaintance. The votary of pleasure rises unrefreshed, and a listless yawning morning is the penalty which she must pay to nature for having forced her beyond her ability. These are the moments that engender spleen; the dissatisfaction that she feels is averted from herself, on whom it ought to fall; but, as she really is unhappy, it must fix somewhere. Very probably, she will discover that her evening's chagrin was owing to her husband, who either *looked* as if he did not wish her to go out, or *prevented* her making a more pleasant party, or *restrained*

restrained her expenses, or *dropped* some harsh expression which broke her spirits, always meek and tenderly sensitive. Perhaps the children are troublesome, cross, humoursome, and want more attention than she has leisure to give them; or perhaps the French governess may be negligent, the abigail impertinent, or the cook tipsey. It is happy when the disease fixes in some remote part, and only prompts the sufferer to treat her family with a detail of the cruel usage that she has undergone; and a pathetic explanation of the extreme hardship, that she, who has such a relish for pleasure, should never be permitted to taste it. Mistaken creature! who told thee that this world was made for butterflies? Call me not too severe, nor suppose that I overcharge the portrait. I know the depravity

pravity of the human heart too well (shall I own too experimentally?) not to be convinced that they who have no time for self-consideration, and religious communing, may be esteemed fortunate if they do not fall into still grosser faults and misfortunes.

To descend a little from the line of society that we have been considering: I have often contemplated the good city pair, who set out for their box in the country on Saturday night, and return time enough to open shop on Monday morning. We rustics might suppose, that after the fatigue of six days they would look forward to the sabbatical rest with ecstacy; and that their purpose for going into the country was to enjoy the heavenly blessings of reflection and devotion in retirement. Quite the reverse; their intention is to have a party of friends. The
travelling

travelling vehicle is laden with provisions; and though the mistress of the "snug retreat" arrives at it late and weary, she must unpack her plate, dust her china, and arrange her dessert that evening. A little indulgence next morning would be excusable, provided the family were in readiness to perform the appropriate duties of the Sabbath; but, unhappily, there is a multiplicity of reasons to prevent this observance. The church is a long way off; it is cold and damp; the pew is in an obscure corner; the weather is suspicious, and a shower would destroy the patent net mantle; or perhaps (which is a still more insurmountable difficulty) the patent net mantle was left in London. The kitchen too now begins to give "dreadful note of preparation;" not from " armourers accomplishing the knights,"

knights," but from the shop-maid's chopping force-meat, the apprentice's cleaning knives, and the journeyman's receiving a *practical* lesson in the art of waiting at table. For, do not suppose that the entertainment is to be merely comfortable and social. No; it is to be a display, a set out, and as much intended to elevate and surprise as a Grosvenor-square gala. Certainly it is fortunate, that the legislature still prohibits opening shop of a Sunday; as but for this remission of worldly toil, many people would be obliged to leave the garden of taste quite uncultivated. The company at length arrive; they admire the furniture, praise the garden, and declare their intention of *coming very often;* for it is so delightful to be out of the smoke of London. Dinner is now served; and then "they eat, they drink," but probably

bably not "in communion sweet;" nor do they "quaff immortality and joy," because they neglect to visit the fount where those blessings are dispensed. Surely, if it were not for being a *little* in the fashion, a quiet domestic religious Sunday would be quite as comfortable. But I betray my ignorance in using this term: comfort is abjured by all who enlist in the ranks of vanity; and as, among the high ton, the eclat of the fête depends upon the violence of the squeeze; so, among second ton, the prodigiousness of the preceding fuss determines the pleasure that your visitors are to give you. One morning's trouble would be enough for a common-councilman's wife; but who would mind being perplexed in the extreme for a whole week, provided one could say that we gave

gave a dinner to *Alderman* Marrowfat, and *all* his family.

Permit me to attend to an apology which is often made for this style of gentility; I mean, that it is patriotic; though, in refuting this pretence, I may deviate a little from the prescribed bounds of female authorship. It is allowed, that fine ladies of all descriptions are *nuisances* in their own families; but then it is said they are *public* benefits; they force trade, promote the circulation of cash, and reward the ingenuity of manufacturers. To preserve the metaphor, whatever is forced must be proportionably delicate and hazardous. If luxury, by becoming universal, increases the wealth of the community, the artificial wants of each individual are also multiplied; and though the
merchant

merchant receives more for his commodities, the demands of his family, and the frequent insolvency of his connexions, leave him in a worse situation, than when frugality and moral honesty were more prevalent. Those, indeed, are the solid pillars upon which trade must rest; remove them, and its destruction is inevitable. The maxim, that private vices are public benefits, has sunk into contempt, with the deist* who endeavoured to establish it.

All civilized states have agreed in cherishing those privileged orders whose rank or wealth made them the proper patrons of learning and the fine arts, and the encouragers of all the happy efforts of mechanical industry. From persons thus circumstanced, society demands munificence, splen-

* Mandeville.

dour, and hospitality. Liberality, elegance, and refinement, are the required characteristics of their immediate inferiors. The third degree should be contented to be distinguished by benevolence, œconomy, and propriety. Humanity, diligence, and frugality, become indispensable duties to the fourth class. Industry, humility, and general good-will, are so suited to the lowest state of life, that when the poor part with these virtues, they deprive themselves of their best consolation and richest possessions.

Let us look back on the times that are just past, and estimate the present by them. Soame Jenyns's popular description of the embarrassment of a country knight's family at an unexpected visit, would not now suit the domestic situation of a creditable farmer. Several steps in society have therefore,

therefore, been passed in the progress of refinement since the publication of Dodsley's Miscellanies. I have heard a well-attested tradition of a country lady who was the heiress of large possessions, and, what was then called, genteelly educated. It was determined by the females of the family met in council upon the occasion, that she should appear in the great hall clear-starching lawn ruffles, when she received the first visit of a favoured admirer. It is impossible to calculate how many degrees of manners are here passed, since the few who still continue to be notable blush to be thought so: yet this event happened about the beginning of the last century. I need not multiply anecdotes of this kind; the archives of every family can supply numerous attestations in point.

In low life, the gradation used to be from rags and dirt to tidiness; from thence to comfort; from comfort, improvement proceeded to superfluity. But even the pauper, if she move at all, now strides from filth to finery. May not the discontent and depravity of the lower orders be attributed to this circumstance? and that such discontent and depravity do exist, those who have the opportunity of close observation cannot doubt, though it has not yet assumed sufficient ripeness to attract legislative attention *. When pining want beheld its neighbour rising to decent comfort by unremitting industry and frugality, the possibility of obtaining equal advantages stimulated him to equal exertions. But the enormous wages

---

* In Letter XIVth. this subject is resumed.

which

which artisans now receive in many trades * support a style of living, to which the most rigorous toil of the day-labourer, the worsted weaver, or many other less profitable occupations, would be totally inadequate. If the males in the artisan's family are sober and industrious, their earnings are sufficient for the maintenance of the whole household: the wife, no longer feeling the daily necessity of adding to the common stock by the notability of herself and her daughters, is often induced, not only to *remit vigilance*, but to *allow* of *waste*. A style of appearance is assumed, the expense of which leaves them totally unprovided in an hour of sickness and misfortune;

* In several branches of the woollen trade, common hands may earn two guineas a week; yet even a short illness reduces them to extreme distress.

and also, by its absurdity and impropriety, deprives them of the good opinion of their superiors, who certainly would have been inclined to have extended their kind aid to alleviate that distress, against which prudence had in vain endeavoured to provide an adequate defence. What sort of servants, or poor men's wives, young women bred in idleness, and dressed in taste, are likely to make, is not *now* my inquiry: I speak of the effects of this unsuitable, and indeed useless abundance, upon the mind of the really indigent man; and surely it must render his tattered garb still more comfortless, and his brown crust more unsavoury and degrading. He could have passed by the magnificent mansion of the gentleman, the elegant residence of the rector, or the comfortable dwelling of the farmer, without heaving a sigh

or

or uttering one complaint at his hard lot; but the luxuries and indolence of those whose birth and education are the same as his own, wring his soul with anguish; and he supposes himself injuriously treated, since all ranks may be idle and extravagant except his own. Perhaps if we were so situated, we might be equally faulty. The contented cottager, quiet, sober, laborious, and cheerful, is fast disappearing from our rustic haunts; wretchedness, with all its attendant train of vices, or thoughtless, and I may add insolent extravagance, the result of great gains and little foresight, supply his place.

And is the nation really benefited by this change of manners? The loom may have more employment; the straw-manufacturer may have a greater demand; indeed, trade of every kind

kind may receive a momentary impetus; but morals, which are the vital part of society, are attacked by a mortal disease. The middle ranks no longer feel ashamed of being in debt; the lower do not blush at receiving (I should rather say demanding) parochial relief, though œconomy might have preserved to them the blessing of independence. In vain does the mistress advise her servants to save the gains of prosperity; she is answered, that what they earn is their own; this is a land of liberty, and they have no notion of screening their parishes. To assume a more dictatorial tone, even to paupers, is impossible; they would tell you, that God made all men equal, and question your title to that preeminence which permits you to reprove them.

These are the effects of flourishing

trade and prosperous manufacture: are they symptoms of national prosperity, or internal decay? Allow me to quote the words of an eloquent writer*; who, having observed that this country was flourishing in all the arts of civil life, remarks, that "per-
"haps it is running the same course
"which Rome had done before; from
"virtuous industry to wealth; from
"wealth to luxury; from luxury to
"impatience of discipline, and cor-
"ruption of morals; till by a total
"degeneracy, and loss of virtue, being
"grown ripe for destruction, it falls
"a prey to some hardy oppressor;
"and, with loss of liberty losing every
"thing that is valuable, sinks gra-
"dually again into its original barba-
"rism." Such an oppressor, my dear

* See Dr. Middleton's Life of Cicero.

Miss M——, seems near at hand. He wants neither ambition, hatred, boldness, nor inclination to destroy us; but let us hope that there still remains enough of true religion among us, to obtain a *respite* from that merciful God who promised to spare offending Sodom, if ten righteous, or rather religious people, could therein be found. And may we so profit by our present chastisements, as to see the necessity of checking that career of degeneracy which proved destructive to every nation that has preceded us in empire, wealth, and renown!

My conviction that luxury, and affected refinement, have already passed those bounds which defend private happiness and public security, would induce me to confine our correspondence entirely to those orders whose conduct is most important to society, and

and among whom the insinuating arts of dissipation have lately gained a most alarming preponderance; but a regard for my literary reputation, together with the zeal natural to all reformers, prompt me to endeavour to obtain a fair hearing for my remonstrances, which I am convinced my present labours never would receive, if I did not occasionally introduce my readers to *very good company*. The fascinating names of the Marquis, and Lady Elizabetha, have caused many a village nymph to toil through six long volumes of intricate adventure, of which they never would have perused six pages, had the same story been told of plain John and Betty. It is with some reluctance that I quit a field of observation in which I have few competitors, to pursue a *beaten* track, wherein I am also preceded by personal

sonal experience and superior ability. Remarks on the manners of the great world cannot come with a good grace from one who has seldom emerged from the bosom of retirement (I could almost say, of domestic seclusion), and who consequently must feel a doubt whether the pictures from which she copies really were correctly sketched. Yet since I have promised to make some observations on prevailing opinions, I must not omit those leading characters whose conspicuous situation draws the attention of the world, and who give law to numerous aukward copyists. Considered in this point of view, the manners and morals of the great assume an influential consequence that is highly important to society; though, if confined to themselves, their depravity is less intimately connected with national ruin,

than

than a dereliction of principle in the great mass of the people would be; and especially among those who, by being placed in the medium between riches and poverty, should present a barrier to the vices and temptations of either extreme, and at the same time offer an asylum to every thing which is intrinsically estimable in both. The political importance which this rank possesses in England; the general information, sound sense, and unsophisticated manners that were their marked characteristics; the blameless occupations, domestic tenderness, modesty, simplicity, and unaffected gentleness, that distinguished their wedded partners, all heighten my regret that these solid excellences should be bartered for German principles, illustrated by French practice. It is not that I believe the middle classes

classes to be the most corrupted; it is because that corruption, if it fix here, destroys the vital principle, that I address the females of this most enviable, this most respectable order, with energetic intreaties to check their vain pursuit of false fame and absurd importance, and to resume the genuine graces of their natural character; beseeching them to remember that none can become contemptible or ridiculous, unless they desert the post at which the God of Nature has commanded them to stand. But I must now forsake my compeers, to address a more elevated station; conscious of being in many respects unequal to the task of public censor, and presuming only to gather a few scattered observations that have been over-looked by my predecessors, or to discover some noxious weeds which
have

have recently shot forth. A new subject seems a hint for me to conclude my present epistle, and gives me an opportunity to assure you how fervently I am, &c.

LETTER

LETTER IV.

Absurdities and Licentiousness among Women of Fashion.

MY DEAR MISS M——,

I RESUME our correspondence; happy in the assurance that you are interested in the subjects I have hitherto discussed; and presuming not only on the partial affection that you have long shown me, but also on your natural candour, which I know induces you to pardon inadvertencies wherein the head only is concerned, provided the heart be free from those bad intentions which transform imperfections into crimes. We will enter upon the topic proposed in the conclusion of my last letter, without the formality of a tedious prologue.

There

There are numerous and popular
writers, who have employed themselves
in traducing the order that we are
about to scrutinize; describing it as
an excrescence springing out of the
body politic, and draining every useful member of its vital juices, in order
to swell its own putrid mass into a
most hideous and most dangerous deformity. I will tell you a few of the
abusive terms bestowed on these
" earth-treading stars," by an author
who was at least free from the feminine fault of mincing her language,
and spoke out without the least ambiguity. She considered "monarchy
" and hereditary rank to be such evils,
" as balanced all the advantages which
" Europe derived from civilization;
" and so unnatural, that, in order to
" account for their introduction, men
" *blasphemously* supposed the human
" race

" race had burst from its orbit, like a
" lawless planet, in order to steal the
" celestial fire of reason; while the
" vengeance of heaven, lurking in
" the subtle flame like Pandora's box,
" afflicted the earth with these retri-
" butive curses to which all our mi-
" sery and error are owing." In fine,
she thought " that it was the pesti-
" ferous purple, and the honours that
" flow from it," which had reduced us
poor women to the state of woeful degradation in which her writings found
us, namely, without political rights,
without masculine strength, compelled
to be obedient to our husbands, and
inclined to expect filial obedience
from our children; accustomed also
to consider modesty and gentleness
as constituent parts of our own character; disposed to attend to religious
duties, and to look forward to another
world,

world, not as the place where our "indefeasible perfectibility is to expand," but as the region where the promises of salvation shall be fulfilled. If the inversion of the present orders in society will also produce this change in the relative situation of our sex, how ought we to *cling* to the present state of affairs, and *supplicate* its continuance!

I have quoted from a book * which, by supereminent absurdity and audacity, exposed the principles that it meant to support to profound contempt. It, indeed, amazed and confounded for a day; and it received all the assistance which an elaborate analysis could bestow, to elevate it into lasting celebrity. It was soon found, however, that the times were

* The Rights of Women.

not sufficiently illuminated to bear such strong doctrine; and the disciples of the school of equality have since found it more convenient to gloss and soften, and misrepresent. The same democ... principles, however, pervade many popular works,—especially dramatic performances, to which the *privileged* orders (as the nobility and gentry are cabalistically called) have most unwisely lent their patronage; and that not merely by countenancing the author, or applauding the scenic representations that are deeply tainted with the leaven of democracy. Party rage may now boast the same sacrifices as public virtue formerly enjoined; and though we have not our Curtii or our Decii, who *immolate* themselves to save their country, we have many men of birth and rank who seem inclined to pile their

215

their possessions and honours on the very brink of a precipice, to exalt he minion of the faction which they spouse. The first people in the kingom have not scrupled to support, ot merely the *equality*, but the *suremacy* of the mob, during the frenzy f a democratical contention for paramentary honours; and thus they irtually signed the testimonial of eir having long usurped unjustifiable scendancy, and the certificate of their eserved degradation; little thinking hat the sentiments and principles hich they instilled into their clamoous adherents, would abide with hem, and produce serious effects, when the temporary purpose for which hey were promulgated was forgotten How far ambitious motives may jusify gentlemen in thus endeavouring o *assassinate* their own importance,

is

is not the present question. Modern patriotism may determine, that it is noble to reverse the part of Sampson when he was prisoner among the Philistines, and to pull down the pillars of your own state, when you find that you cannot climb into its upper story. But since our sex are happily *prevented* from engaging in these turbulent scenes, by native delicacy, by regard to their general reputation, and even by their fears, I do not feel myself called upon to vindicate them from the charge of being accessary to that general contempt for their superiors, which is so marked a feature among the populace. Imbibing the spirit of Mrs. Candour, in that masterly (though in some respects dangerous) play, "The School for Scan-
" dal," I am resolved, " let the news-
" papers say what they please of canvassing

"vassing beauties, haranguing toasts, and mobbing demireps," not to believe one syllable; and if "I repeat such anecdotes," it is only to usher in my observation that the world is grown so censorious, it even credits *impossibilities*. I wish I could acquit the illustrious culprits of every other proof of their being concerned in a conspiracy against their own order and consequence, with as much expectation of being *credited*, at least by my *country* readers.

But though I profess myself a steady advocate for that gradation of wealth and rank, which, if not positively appointed by God in scripture, is there shown to have been nearly coeval with the world that we inhabit; and which is not only the natural consequence of the moral government of the Almighty, but also the medium through which

which he thinks fit to convey a greater portion of happiness to the human race than it could otherwise enjoy; I am not so infatuated, as to maintain that the blessings of education, wealth, rank, leisure, authority, and reputation, are granted to a few with uncontrollable occupation; but rather that their possessors should employ them to the benefit of the whole community; that such as labour may not have cause to reproach those who rest for being drones in the state. The God and Judge of the whole earth does not bestow his spiritual or temporal blessings by any arbitrary rules of unconditional preference. When a talent is given to any one, an account is opened with the giver of it, who appoints a day in which he will arriv[e] and "re-demand his own with usury[.]" Nor are these children of prosperi[ty]

in reality so much better situated than their lowly fellow-creatures, as the jaundiced eye of envy is apt to believe: at least, ignorant envy is sure to fix upon a wrong person, and to select, as the object whose affluence causes her pining discontent, some besotted sensualist, who, forgetting his stewardship, presumes to turn the estate of which he is guardian entirely to his own account, and not only to " eat " and drink till he is drunken," but also to neglect, and even misuse, his fellow-servants. Independent of that fearful sentence which hangs over him, suspended by the gossamer thread of this frail existence; namely, " the Lord when he cometh shall ap-
" point him a portion with unbelievers,
" where shall be weeping and gnash-
" ing of teeth," the present situation of this self-devoted Dives is most miserable.

serable. Excessive indulgence breeds a thousand bodily pains and mental infirmities; even supposing that it does not proceed to what are called criminal gratifications, capricious humours and unseasonable wishes haunt that breast whose desires centre in self-enjoyment. The expectation that we may be for ever lulled on the bosom of delight, is thwarted by the constitution of the world, and even by our own physical qualities. Pain is necessary, or we should never truly value pleasure. Rest must be bought by exertion, or it begets *ennui*. We cannot taste the full blessing of success, if we have never known disappointment or anxiety. The animal gratifications of our nature must be preceded by privations, or our appetites will not be satisfied, but palled. When penury has toiled hard for a

scanty

scanty meal and a slight covering, it
weakly supposes that rest, repletion,
and sumptuous attire, must be felicity;
the indolent victim of spleen, the surfeited voluptuary, and the capricious
votary of vanity, whose tortured imaginations are ever pursuing something
new and strange, could, if pride permitted them to make a frank disclosure, present a very different picture
of enjoyment; and, in spite of its restrictions, the tortures of a diseased
body, and the miseries of an afflicted
spirit, often wring from them the agonizing regrets that they cannot change
situations with the poor labourer who
walks whistling by their window, returning cheerful from his daily task.
Amid the numerous complaints with
which discontent ungratefully assails
Divine Providence, the most frequent
arise from those who have squandered

its

it's bounty in such pursuits as are incapable of satisfying a rational being; or who have supposed that the cup of blessing could not be enjoyed, but by quaffing such immoderate draughts as produce intoxication.

Where a woman who is born to the possession of rank and affluence properly appreciates those blessings, and, instead of circumscribing them within the narrow sphere of self-enjoyment, endeavours to diffuse improvement and comfort wherever her influence extends; if, through the conviction of being merely an agent, she lift her eyes to him who intrusted her with ample powers, she feels in the consciousness of well doing, and in the serene delight of reflected bliss, the purest earthly gratification. Her heart frequently speaks to her in the inspired language of the royal Psalmist,

"The

"The lot is fallen unto me in a fair ground, yea I have a goodly heritage." On the other hand, if she suppose herself to be some "mighty leviathan," sent into the ocean of existence "to take her pastime therein," the chain which held her to society is broken, or at least held together only by the fragile tie of interested dependence. She did not participate in the griefs of others, her own sorrows therefore shall be *all* her own; she sought not to make her fellow-creatures happy, they will not therefore rejoice in her prosperity. Now sorrow is a lonely sensation, and may be endured with heart-breaking poignancy without any partaker, or even witness; nay, it is ever most intolerable and overwhelming, when unrelieved by sympathy, and unsoftened by pity; but happiness, at least that species of it which selfish characters pursue, is a superadded quality, and subsists by the agency, or at least upon the opinion, of the multitude. The proudest beauty, when shining in the full glare of magnificence, is more dependent than any of the wondering spectators, past whom she glides with affected disdain; for, in reality, it is a persuasion that they admire her, which swells her vain heart with imaginary consequence. Does the mercenary bride, who sacrifices every prospect of domestic happiness to a stately equipage, a magnificent mansion, and a numerous retinue, really find her enjoyments increased in the hours of solitude by knowing that she possesses these baubles? No; it is while she shows her diamonds to a rival, or an enemy, that her vitiated taste appreciates their value; not by the

the pleasure they bestow, but by the pain they excite. For be it be remembered, that though the benevolent passions possess the sanative quality of healing their own wounds; or, to speak without a figure, though even disappointed goodness administers satisfaction to the soul; the selfish appetites and malignant propensities have but one miserable chance of affording a transient enjoyment; as soon as the animal exhilaration subsides, or the demoniacal conviction of having tormented another, has taken place, depression of spirits, and the stifled, yet powerful reproaches of the heart, convince the unhappy being who endures them, that she has mistaken her road to the bower of bliss.

Though the desire of living solely for themselves has been the characteristic of misused power and affluence, ever since the days of Solomon, yet since commercial acquisitions, and mechanical inventions, have increased the number of luxurious enjoyments, and also the rage of competition, the temptations which beset the great and wealthy are in these days exceedingly multiplied; and whoever among them shall take that mistaken road to happiness which we have just described, will feel continually stimulated to deviate further from the right path, by that rash pursuit of their inferiors which was the subject of my last letter. Vanity ever labours to disprove the wise king's apothegm, "that "there is nothing new under the sun." She rejects the petition of every votary who cannot support his claim to eclat by the testimonial of novelty. What was esteemed great and elegant for a nobleman fifty years ago, would now be be vulgar and mean for a successful mechanic. Nay, the extravagancies of the last winter must be outdone by the present, on peril of your becoming *nobody*; a term of reproach, which, though not formidable in its sound to those who have not been initiated in the mysteries of fashion, is known by adepts to contain the very quintessence of abuse, and to be much more derogatory to the unhappy being to whom it is applied, than all the epithets that Billingsgate or the Rue de St. Honore could invent.

"Novelty must, therefore, be obtained; but how can it be acquired? Though loosely arrayed, like the fair queen of Ogygia *, you sit and sing by your fires of cedar, in an apartment decorated by the purest rules of Attic

---

* Calypso.—See Telemachus, Book I.

simplicity; though you convert yourself into a beauteous Fatima, and recline on an embroidered carpet in your magnificent alhambra, where a thousand lamps reflect the blazing diamonds which clasp your robe; though the eastern and western Indies lavish their treasures on your board, where the fruits of the tropic blaze beneath the ice of the pole, the wife of some rich cit, whom you despise, will have a costume more truly Greek or Arabesque; she will sport finer diamonds, have richer flavoured wines, or produce her hot-house delicacies a fortnight before you. Did you ever resolve to effect by absurdity what you cannot do by taste, and to fetch your models from countries ignorant of just proportion and correct design, mandarines, dragons, and pagodas, may be purchased; pyramids and sphinxes can

can be procured; a sign-post painter can devise scrawls which ninety-nine out of a hundred will suppose are an hieroglyphic; and the rival lady and her villa will become completely Egyptienne, or la Chinoise, at the next gala. I scarcely think that the most glaring indelicacy, or the grossest vulgarity, would rescue you from the hazard of having that palm of celebrity which novelty bestows wrested from your grasp by fresh discoveries; for the fascination of a great name, and the magic charm of being *outré*, would soon so transmute our old ideas on those subjects, that we should think it was only owing to prejudice that we did not before discover the refinement of immodesty, and the delicacy of obscenity. The partial exposure of the person, or the limited rejection of those restraints, which formerly secured

cured good manners and good morals, have been found of no avail. Your insatiable pursuers have followed you with remorseless activity; they have discarded more drapery, and dashed with less squeamishness. I almost doubt whether it would be possible for you to set them at fault by sheltering in the bath of Diana, or even in a kraal of Hottentots. What then must become of you? If you stand still, you will not only be overtaken, but preceded; and, melancholy to add, if you once give up this struggle of competition, your former triumphs are of no avail. It will be useless to say, "I *was* in fashion in the year four;" fashion admits no tense but the present. If fifty ladies fainted at one of your routs *then*, the fifteen who died away *last* night, at Lady Jostle's furnishes conversation for the town

this

this morning. Though your supper-rooms resembled a grove of cherries last May, cherries at a guinea a pound this April overwhelms the remembrance. You have entered into the service of a severe task-master, who, though you are crippled and exhausted by your former efforts, will still demand the wonted tale of bricks with rigorous exactness.

What is then to be done? Renounce all allegiance to these arbitrary mandates. Recollect that, though in proportion to the abundance of your fortune, or the vincibleness of your family entails, you may be the first fashionist for one, two, or three seasons (none but Midas can hope to hold out longer), fresh competitors are every year starting; and, as the philosopher's stone is still undiscovered, you must at last be dethroned. Soften the

the pain of your certain humiliation, therefore, by a timely and graceful retreat. Resign the sceptre, even in the career of your glory, which you know you cannot long retain; and moderate the triumph of your successor, by appearing accessory to her exaltation. These, I grant, are the counsels of worldly prudence; but I am addressing those whom I suppose to be incapable of nobler motives.

Aware of the evanescent nature of that celebrity which is only founded on expensive inventions, some ladies of high ton have cherished the Satanical ambition of becoming pre-eminent in vice. Adopting the horrid sentiments ascribed to the prince of darkness, they declare by their actions, that "to reign is worth ambition, though in Hell." They have, therefore, torn off those coy disguises in in which sinners of past times enveloped their enormities, and with unblushing fronts have proclaimed to the questioning world, that they " dare " do every thing, because they dare." Their contempt of reputation, and bold defiance of mankind, were soon discovered by a species of writers that are fellow-labourers with those whom I mentioned in the beginning of this letter; these wishing to reduce the world to an equality in infamy, as the former do to introduce equality of misery. Aware that this marked effrontery of character shocked the feelings of all beholders too much to gain converts, they invented a set of phrases which softened its atrocity, and at the same time preserved its publicity. I know not where this new mode of language originated; but as it consists in nothing but the *inversion* and

and *perversion* of terms, it cannot be considered as any great proof of genius. It has been as eminently successful in the diplomatic papers, and other state fabrications of our Gallic neighbours, as the wand of mercury in Dryden's Amphytrion; and has actually either charmed the world to sleep, or taught them that " black is "not black, nor white so *very* white;" so that, though a sound more threatening than the Indian war-whoop bellowed in their ears, they persisted in calling it the peaceful lullaby of their innocent rocker. John Bull's natural aversion to *Mounseer's* cradle has hitherto prevented him from being completely swaddled; but his disposition to believe that people are what they call themselves, makes him run some danger of being duped by a misconception of the words patriot, honour,

honour, and independence. The principles of John's wife have been attacked in a stronger manner by those liberal apologists for vice and folly, who, setting out perhaps with a misapplication of a scripture text in praise of mercy, or enjoining charity to repentant sinners, soon proceeded to infuse into the unwary mind a *charity that is not scriptural,* by apologizing for sinners *who do not repent,* nay, who glory in their crimes. Hence the unreflecting, but well-meaning reader, who possesses much candour and little information, is led to believe that the perjured adultress, from whom she shrunk with abhorrence, may be a most *amiable, elegant, interesting* creature, with only *one* failing, a too susceptible heart; but then that heart was so benevolent, so condescending to the wishes of others, or perhaps so sincere,

so

so incapable of disguising its own emotions, that it could not sacrifice what it felt to be its *invincible* propensities to the opinions of the world; which, after all (for nothing is certain), are perhaps only founded on the dictates of prejudice. Here the guileless readers, whom I have supposed attending to this new ethical lecture, will perhaps start; but they are then gently reminded, that freedom of thought is the indisputable privilege of the inhabitants of this country; that many learned men (and here a long list of well-sounding names will be introduced, blending the obscure with the celebrated, to swell the pomp of evidence, and misquoting, without fear of detection), men most *exact* in moral conduct, and most celebrated for social virtues, have *doubted* whether, all things considered, the present

present aspect of the world might not be considerably improved, by a departure from those very *rigid* rules which were built on a too literal interpretation of the Jewish classics and early Christian writers*. A few shining examples, such as Aspasia, Sappho, and Ninon de l'Enclos, will then be brought forward, to prove that women may be very eminent for taste and science, and continue to be much respected, who have not strictly adhered to the decorums prescribed to the sex. It will then be allowed, that these severe tenets have expedience to recommend them, and therefore they are highly necessary for the great body of the people, who, if the cords of discipline were relaxed, might run into

* These denominations have been most irreverently applied to that book which is dictated by the Spirit of God,

gross

gross depravity; from which the refinement natural to cultivated minds, and polished manners, will inevitably preserve that part of our species which might properly claim to be exempted from law, as being capable of giving law to themselves. These well-bred authors will then proceed to call your attention to the improvements which philosophy has introduced into arts and sciences of late years, preparatory to the bold assertion that morals are a science, and as much capable of improvements and discoveries as mechanics, chymistry, or astronomy. They will then enter that metaphysical maze in which plain sense is sure to be bewildered, and talk to you concerning the origin of moral obligation; but whether you are taught that it is self-love which vibrates from the centre to the extremity of social being, or or whether you are assured that ethics originated from man's preposterously surrendering his natural rights in order to procure the doubtful blessing of society; in either case the freedom of man as an agent is preserved, and his right to do wrong, if he judges that wrong to be expedient to his well-doing, is implied. Some few, indeed, of these apostles of falshood have re-adorned the old necessitarian system, and, by making the human race the passive machines of over-ruling fate, have contrived to transfer our crimes either to our nature, or to the stars; but this scheme wants the gloss of novelty.

The principles thus laid down, the application follows. What would be highly criminal in the footman, and the chamber-maid, becomes a pardonable *levity*, when referred to the actions of of those whose rank in life secures the world from the political consequences of their indiscretions. The opprobrious terms of preciseness, uncharitableness, narrowness of sentiment, and littleness of soul, will be employed to deter you from thinking unfavourably of those *soft* indiscretions, which, though they may be somewhat wrong, hurt nobody else, and are accompanied by all the amiable virtues, and all the alluring graces. Perhaps, indeed, these apologists of licentiousness may proceed so far as to affirm, that it is not vice, but virtue, to obey the dictates of nature, and that the conscious mind is its own awful world. This, with an observation that no characters are faultless, that we must take people as we find them, that many mean very well who act a little indiscreetly, and that chastity is apt to

be

be scandalous and religion morose, includes, I think, most of the arguments which these seductive advocates of candour employ, to mislead innocence and excuse guilt.

The ramifications of this pseudo-liberality extend very far. They branch from that pernicious system of infidelity which has done such mischief in the world; and, though compelled to disguise its nefarious designs in England, still labours with unwearied but cautious diligence to sap the fair foundation of our national fame. It is supposed, that there are but few *tainted* characters in England, who are not willing to allow the political expediency of religious institutions. They, however, mostly engraft somewhat of papistical principles on deistical practices, and seek to commute with the laws of their country,

try, by an occasional observance of one of its injunctions; I mean attendance on public worship. I know not whether this solemn mockery of the Deity be not more prejudicial to religion and morals than if they "stood "forth all infidel confest," and verbally denied the authority which their actions disclaim. Certainly, the national church is exposed to much undeserved odium on account of the scandalous lives of these political conformists, who cannot be justly ranked among her members. I have often heard it remarked, that the eyes of the congregation are naturally directed, during the reading of the commandments, to the conspicuous gallery in which some high-born violater of these positive precepts lolls with graceful negligence, hears the divine vengeance plainly pointed at his

his offence, and perhaps articulately joins in the petition to be preserved from the cherished sin that he is determined to hug in his bosom. The effect of such mockery upon the minds of a large assembly, inferior in station and education, probably also in ability, must infinitely overbalance all the good which could be derived from the most impressive discourse that Christian zeal and Christian knowledge ever delivered from a pulpit. Nothing, indeed, but that supernatural grace which the Almighty has promised to those who ask it of him, can protect *all* who witness such hypocritical effrontery from feeling their faith and hope affected by its contaminating influence.

It is, indeed, much to be wished, that the church of England would again exert its *inert*, but not *rescinded* authority, and banish notorious profligates from the house of God, while they continue to glory in their shame. It would be well too (I mean prudentially well) if these bold defiers of public opinion would recollect, that the populace, whose suffrages they court on other occasions, cannot be so very despicable, as to be unworthy of being even treated with the decencies of outward observance. It would be fruitless to tell the arrogant infidel, or lofty debauchee, that the souls of those whom he puts in jeopardy by thus triumphantly displaying his impenetrable vices, will rise with him at the last day, equal in rank, equal in duration of existence, and will accuse him at the judgment-seat of an impartial God, for having acted the part of the arch-apostate, by betraying those who rashly confided in his superior intel-

intelligence and more enlarged information. To those who are armed with that shield of licentious derision which is only vulnerable in the days of sickness or calamity, I must only address temporal dissuasives. I must shew them that it is indiscreet, and madly adventurous, to thrust their crimes upon the observation of those who, however ignorant or misjudging, perfectly understand the equalizing nature of ignominy. The grosser vices receive no exaltation from being clad in ermine; their nature is so very brutal, that their combination with education, rank, splendour, and affluence, cannot diminish their hideous aspect, or lessen the contempt of those who know that it would be very easy to rise to such "a bad emi-" "nence." The dutchess who has violated her marriage oath, who is discarded

carded by her husband, and married to her gallant, is but the same degraded creature as the porter's wife who is transferred at Smithfield to a new purchaser. The reproachful epithets that we bestow upon the vulgar sinner, are by her scornfully rebanded to her dignified copartner in guilt; and let not the offender, who has only birth and wealth to boast, flatter herself that the world in general thinks those distinctions sacred. Public opinion is not yet so illuminized as the ear-tickling flatterers of greatness represent; and if they value their possessions more than they do their vices, they must rejoice that "many thou-
"sand knees in 'Britain' have never
"yet bowed to the false gods" of sophisticated morality. The virtues of probity and chastity are closely allied; and prescription will be found to

be

be but a feeble support, where the solid pillars of affection and respect are undermined. But to return from, I hope, an improbable contingency, to what really happens: though the opprobrious epithets which the adulteress merits may not reach her own ears, they echo through a space proportioned to the circle which she was originally intended to enlighten and inform. She is there estimated, not by those arbitrary rules which her own depraved associates decree shall supersede common sense and moral obligation, but by the principles which, when she lies upon her death-bed, she will own are the unswerving dictates of rectitude and truth. At the bar of public opinion, the titled courtezan receives little mercy. Every plea which might be urged in favour of the poor night-wanderer, who of-fends for bread, turns into an aggravation of the guilt of her who *courted* temptation. The friendless outcast, whom no one acknowledges, sins, deeply sins against her own soul; but she who was hedged in from ruin by fortune, fame, and family, involves a host of distinguished connexions in her disgrace, and stamps a stigma of opprobrium on every part of her (perhaps till then unsullied) lineage. The pennyless prostitute is precluded from repentance; for will any one afford her an asylum, to try if that repentance be sincere? The prostitute of high life has only to stop in her shameless course, and to retreat to that retirement which is ever ready to shelter her disgrace and confirm her contrition. The former was most likely the child of ignorance, who knew little of good or evil till experience

ence taught her a severe lesson, by which she became wise too late. Her passions were probably unrestrained by discipline or precept, and some seducer spread a snare for her personal chastity, before reflection and observation taught her its value. I fear I shall say too much, if I suppose that the noble wanton has been early trained in the principles of truth and holiness; but we must allow that she has been taught the necessity of restraining her passions, accustomed to respect the opinion of the world, and to regard those decorums in her *outward* manners which awe the licentious. If she were a wife (and I grieve to say that in high life the major part of lost characters belong to the matronly order,) the libertine was deterred from " assaying by his devilish art to reach

"the

"the organs of her fancy," by the apprehension of those large fines by which the law has lately attempted to deter adulterers, holding out the certain prospect of long imprisonment, or banishment from their native country, to that tribe of led captains, and "second brothers to men of quality," who are most apt to arrange themselves in the ranks of cecisbeos and gallants. But whether the lady be wife or spinster, she was equally defended by those laws of honour which compel the fashionable rake to be an expert swordsman before he aspires to be a seducer; and few of our gay Lotharios would choose to run the gauntlet with husbands, fathers, and brothers, unless pre-assured that the guardians of their Calista's honour, "fierceness and pride,
"would

"would soon be charmed to rest," and the yielding fair be content to give up all for them.

Such are the inferences which common sense always draws from a story of criminal intrigue; and however the eloquence of the bar may seek to divert indignation, and ingeniously palliate the frail fair one's guilt, by representing her as the victim of her gallant's unremitting assiduity, or as being so supereminently endowed with taste, eloquence, and beauty, that all who beheld her must love; this rigid censor, inflexible as a British judge on the bench of justice, adheres to the honest bluntness of her original conclusion: taste, eloquence, and beauty, are too common adjuncts of polished society to disarm her severity; and she determines that there must be a great degree of criminal levity in the conduct of a woman of rank and fortune,

tune, before any man, especially a mere opera lounger, or genteel dependant on the family, could dare to assail her with a criminal proposition. Here, therefore, the term seduction must be misapplied, except when the criminality, or studied negligence of the husband, has made him the active agent of his own disgrace. In this case, common sense may feel inclined to extenuate the lady's offences; but it will only be by lamenting that the manners of the age have an alarming tendency to promote conjugal infidelity, by sanctioning conjugal indifference; but she will' still insist, that though a libertine, or contemptuous husband, must make his wife miserable, it is her own indiscretion that makes her criminal. An agreeable insinuating young man * is too dange-

* See Letter XII.

rous a companion for a resentful offended woman, to be admitted to confidence and intimacy. If her sorrows are too poignant to be confined to her own bosom, let her find a *female* friend with whom she may more safely repose them. If the solitude of home be insupportable, connexions may be formed, and amusements sought, which cannot endanger her fame, her virtue, or her peace. It is the madness of despair to rush into the arms of ruin, because she has drawn a blank in the lottery of connubial happiness. Let a lady shew, by her conduct, that though her wedded protector deserts his charge, she still respects herself; and she will excite those sentiments of esteem, and chastised admiration, which suit the hallowed and indelible character that she has assumed; nor will she be often called upon to repress the

the insulting attentions of presumptuous audacity.

But, beside these prudential restraints, which the free censures of a really enlightened age should impose on that elevated station whose actions are most conspicuous, the democratical turn which public opinion has lately taken, offers still more *imperiously* momentous considerations to check the rash career of *open* profligacy. The melancholy fall of birth and grandeur in a neighbouring kingdom, may convince those who possess such distinctions in our own, that neither law, justice, nor power, can preserve their present superiority, if the voice of popular frenzy decree their overthrow. With whatever severity we may justly reprobate the mischievous doctrines which impose on the commonalty, and persuade them to imagine

imagine that the suppression of rank and opulence would contribute to their own exaltation, or even advantage, I must execrate the unblushing vices of those conspicuous sinners, who court publicity, and defy reproach; for they are a still surer engine of destruction to overwhelm our well-poised state. If our nobility and gentry are swept away from remembrance, their ruin must be accelerated by an act of self-murder; I should rather say, by fratricide. In proof of what I have alleged, that the lower orders perfectly understand that vice puts all upon a level, I appeal to the tumultuary applause which has crowned that scene in the play of John Bull, where the brazier seizes the chair lately occupied by the justice, on the latter refusing to receive the frail daughter of the mechanic with open arms into his

his family, as a suitable wife for his libertine heir. Have not the boxes learned, during the almost innumerable representations of this popular piece, that when they echo the laugh of the galleries, they virtually degrade their own order?

This, though a striking, is only one instance of the reigning humour of the times. To represent the higher ranks as mean, absurd, vicious, mercenary, or tyrannical, seems a sure road to reputation among our dramatists; and the higher they have coloured the caricature, the more ample has been their success. Perhaps the passion for German imitation, which lately gave law to our stage, may have hurried our play-wrights into the adoption of a defamatory libel on greatness, without fully discerning its mischievous tendency. It is certain, that when

sary appendages to the votaries of vanity, without whose assistance every attempt to propitiate the idol they adore, or to outshine a rival, would be impossible. The aspect of a decoration painter, when he sets out an apartment in a style of elegance, is so very engaging, that if the obligations which are due to him were but heightened by passing through the alembic of German sentiment, they might become native alcohol; and no longer loading the feeble shoulders of the old beldame *Justice,* they would even increase the speed of Charles Surface's admired equestrian nymph *Generosity.* By perusing the items which form the debts of a genteel bankrupt, we might discover what portion should be assigned to honour, and what to honesty. I hope no well-bred person will deny, that expensive furniture, elegant

duties. He depictured the unlettered vulgar too in their genuine colour, and with " a master's hand and prophet's " fire." Two hundred years have not effaced the resemblance, notwithstanding the change of manners and opinions which luxury and opulence have introduced. Many a valiant Talbot and open-hearted Hotspur still support the honour of their country in the tented field; and the latter seems indeed again " the glass wherein our " noble youth do dress themselves." Many a pious Cordelia still ministers, in privacy, to the sorrows of a petulant unhappy father; and many a faithful Imogen pursues the steps of her truant lord, anxious to recover his affections, even at the expense of life and fortune. Be it remembered too, that many a ferocious Cade, and wrong-headed Bevis, panting for change,

change, yet ignorant of what change must produce, are watching and magnifying the crimes of a faithless Margaret, and intriguing Eleanor*. But to return.

Next to that base abdication of her own importance, which the abandoned woman of rank tacitly ratifies whenever she permits the world to bruit her shame, the increasing facility with which ladies of lost character are re-admitted to the once select and decorous circle of refined society, becomes a subject of alarm to considerate minds, intent on the preservation of every barrier to female inno-

---

* See Henry VI, part 2. The characters of these princesses are here spoken of in their poetical dress, not as they are preserved in the unprejudiced page of history, which does justice to the heroical constancy and conjugal affection of the magnanimous consort of " Holy Henry."

cence,

cence. The maxims which induced our ancestors to determine, that even if we "deplored our loss with tears, "one false step for ever damned the "fame" of women, though apparently severe, were in reality merciful. This degradation might, indeed, harden a few reprobates in vice, who would otherwise have been hypocrites; but it sent many a real penitent to that retirement which true repentance loves, and it preserved thousands of thoughtless impassioned victims from the allurements of guilty pleasure, by the consciousness that they could not endure a life of reproach. Whatever encouragement mercy and charity may hold out to a backsliding sister determined to renounce the evil of her ways, let not her who hesitates be excited to offend, by stripping vice either of its punishments or its horrors.

Let

Let the young and unexperienced ever think, that if they pass the bourne of chastity, society will disclaim them, and to return to it will be *impracticable.* If they venture on the guilty deed with the forethought encouragement, that they shall soon emerge from their night of shame, their sin is dreadfully aggravated. Our best divines maintain, that whatever hope the heavenly promise of forgiveness affords to true contrition, it is most desperate wickedness to transgress " that grace may abound." If, in that storm of passions which attends a strong temptation, reason can be heard to plead that it will be but a temporary disgrace, she has leisure to assert her natural superiority, and by betraying her trust, becomes the ally, instead of the curb, of incontinence.

We will suppose (which I fear is far
from

from being the case) that the principles of matronly ladies are so fixed, that they run no danger of contamination by frequently hearing the soft glosses which conscious offenders must cast over the crimes of which they have been publicly *convicted*; yet let us compassionate the tender bloom of virgin innocence, and save the youthful part of our sex from the pestilential blast of infectious sophistry. We will suppose that a young lady has been not only innocently, but wisely educated; taught to esteem virtue, and to shrink with abhorrence from audacious vice; accustomed only to contemplate respectable characters, and full of those ideas of worth and honour which are generally associated in an ingenuous inexperienced mind. She steps from the school-room to the crowded rout, and beholds a lady
splendid

splendid in her appearance, most fascinating in her manner, to whom every one pays obsequious court; the beaux crowd around her to catch her smiles and hear her whispers, and the belles shew their admiration by wearing her uniform. The unsuspecting tyro in the subtle game of life steps forward to inquire the name of this supposed paragon of the day, this Arria, this Cornelia, in whose hallowed form she fancies the domestic virtues are worshipped; and she hears with horror and astonishment that it is one who has been branded in the public prints, degraded by the clear evidence of impartial justice, exposed by obscene caricatures, and ridiculed by the lowest witticisms; in fine, that she is a creature whom no one can *defame*, and whom any one may *abuse* with impunity. She turns away shudder-

shuddering with disgust, and perhaps listens to the bon-mots of a faded courtezan, whose early days passed in the low haunts of vulgar licentiousness, but who, in the wane of life, has persuaded her uxorious keeper to give her the name of his wife; not that she may repent of her former errors, nor yet to secure her such a competence that "lack of means enforce her not " to evil;" but for the avowed purpose of introducing her into company high at least in rank, though low in ideas of decorum; and who must prepare themselves for her reception either by copious draughts of Lethe, or strong doses of candid sentiment. As I may suppose my fair novice possesses too much good sense to call such time-serving adulation compassion, or such egregious folly generous love, what must be her opinion of the women

men who thus boldly take the lead where they should not so much as wish to appear, and of the society who *suffer*, nay *court* the intrusion? Will she not, on comparing the world of manners and the world of books, exclaim, like the Roman patriot, " O " virtue! have I worshipped thee as " a substantial good, and art thou but " an empty name!"

It is pleaded, that society owes so many pleasures to agreeable talents and polished manners, that those who possess these passports should be allowed to go every where without being subjected to a rigorous examination. This is to weaken the basis of social intercourse, and to overload the superstructure; to endanger all the sacred " charities of father, " son, and brother," that we may return from the fatiguing crowd of routs and assemblies, amused by a few sprightly sayings, or soothed by the smoothness of polite attentions. Is not this folly similar to that of swallowing poison, because it has been dissolved in a well-flavoured menstruum? But, after all, are we certain that we make this dreadful sacrifice to real wit and true elegance; or has fashion played the cheat here, as she has done in various instances, and dressed up a false Florimel of her own creation to impose upon her short-sighted votaries? I know too little of the walks in which these phenomena move to determine this important inquiry. I can only speak by hear-say evidence, and must confess that, had I not been assured to the contrary, I should have referred what has been repeated to me as the pure Attic wit of these English Ninons, to the inspiration of streams

less

less simple than the Pierian; while the manners and attitudes which the enraptured describer spoke of as copied from the graces, seemed to me the sign-post daub of effrontery, or the hasty sketch of capricious affectation. If we take our ideas of wit from Cowley's admirable definition, it seems impossible that any trace of it should remain in the mind of a woman who has so long renounced the distinguishing characteristic of her sex, that she can scarcely know how to ape its language, or to *guess* what were its pure ideas. And if we suppose Milton correct in his notions of elegance, what resemblance can the impenitent wanton bear to his picture of our general mother in her state of innocence?

" Grace was in all her steps, heaven in her eye,
" In every gesture dignity and love."

My limited knowledge of high life makes me suspect, that the blind infatuation of the worshipper often ascribes such piquancy to the manners and expressions of the idol, as could not possibly be tolerated in a well-bred circle; and therefore that these *veneered* ladies are not quite so impudent and overwhelming as they are described to be; yet I must insist, that when the mind is deeply contaminated it will speak through its bodily organs, in spite of the most guarded caution. The eye will converse in a language unknown to the timid glances of modesty; the turns of the countenance will betray secrets to which delicacy is a stranger; and decorum will be violated by a thousand minutiæ to which even the practised actress has wanted skill to attend. But the danger does not rest here: simplicity may
unwarily

and summer excursions, leaves no opening. By learning the pursuits, resources, and difficulties of classes not remotely separated from their own, they would imbibe a strong attachment to the obligations of justice, and would correct that criminal thoughtlessness which impedes the fulfilment of the divine precept, " Whatsoever " ye would that others should do to " you, do ye even so to them." They would see (and surely to see is to admire) that blunt intelligence which forms a predominant feature in the true Englishman. They would observe boldness of remark, originality of idea, and all those peculiar traits of character which courtly refinement melts into one mass. A morning spent in unmeaning shopping, would then afford less retrospective pleasure to indolent beauty; and the foreseen perplexities

of our sex has determined, that true penitence will not wish to exceed those bounds, or to mix in the crowded haunts of public life. Nor let a decision be censured for severity, which is really the dictate of mercy, sanctioned by a thorough knowledge of the human heart, and proceeding from lively sympathy for those who, though no longer *offending*, continue *to be unfortunate*. When the soul is really awakened by the sense of its own backslidings, when it feels the reproofs of conscience and the shame of contrition, it will naturally shrink from returning to those scenes which it knows are dangerous to reputation and peace. Convinced of her own weakness, afraid to trust her scarcely confirmed resolutions, and concluding by the publicity of her story, that all who see her will
look

look upon her either with contempt, reproach, or pity, the true Magdalen wishes alike to avoid the hazard of falling into new transgressions, and the contumely attending the past. She is deafer than the adder to the syren strains of adulation; she knows too well the "ills that spring from " beauty;" splendour has lost its attractions; she cannot derive amusement from crowds, because she can no longer mingle in them without feeling a sense of degradation. She considers too, that if she should again aspire to fashionable celebrity, her's would be an uphill painful task; every eye would be fixed upon her conduct; every tongue inclined to question the sincerity of her professions; what would be thought mere vivacity in unsuspected innocence, would in her be levity; and marked reserve would be construed into a prudish vizard thrown over the worst designs. Her whispers would be supposed to convey assignations, her reproofs would be called the splenetic dictates of jealousy. Besides, can she that has so weighty a task to perform afford to trifle away the important hours? Turn thee, backsliding daughter, turn to the cool sequestered vale of life, and thy troubled day may yet have a peaceful close. Rational amusement, renovated esteem, friendship, contentment, tranquillity, and religious hope, may still be all thine own.

It is not, therefore, the harsh decree of *outrageous* virtue, but the mild counsels of kindness and sympathy, that determine the preservation of those distinctions which custom has long preserved between unsuspected and forfeited characters. And if those, in whose favour these barriers might be broken down with safety, are too well convinced of their expedience to require their abolition, let us determine to defend the privileges of innocence from the pertinacious attacks of impudence and hardened depravity. The increasing facility of intercourse between the most profligate and the most irreproachable women, which is a marked and peculiar feature of these times, threatens more than our manners. The transition is very easy, and generally very rapid, from unrestrained freedom of behaviour, to unrestrained freedom of conduct; and especially when the mind has not been deeply tinctured with religious truths, in which case the opinion of the world forms one of the strongest bulwarks of virtue. Banishment from parties of high ton, and estrangement from the amusements which every one talks of, have often intimidated the wavering fair one, and imposed a guarded decorum of manner on the determined wanton. Let us not then, when the cardinal virtue of our sex is assailed by unusual perils, resign one of its most material outworks: we have an encouraging example set before us, which it behoves us to copy. There is a circle, and that the highest, where the *convicted* adultress dares not show her audacious front. May this prohibition be coeval with the duration of our monarchy; and may the eyes of a British queen never be offended by the presence of such as glory in violating those laws of which her ivory sceptre constitutes her the guardian.

The next circumstance which has an unfavourable and alarming effect on female virtue is, that unremitting pursuit

pursuit of amusement so universal in the great world. "Commune with thy "own heart in thy chamber and be "still," is the precept of the royal penitent, who knew too well what watchful attention the human heart requires in order to subdue its propensity to evil. Shall I injure the fair fashionist, if I suggest that her bosom inmate demands as frequent examination, and as constant controul, as that of the highly endowed, though greatly offending David? Little did he think, when he twice spared the life of his inexorable enemy Saul, who denied him a shelter even among the rocks and wilds of his native land, that the time would come, when, securely sitting on the throne of Israel, he should meanly project the murder of the faithful veteran who bravely refused repose while the enemies of his

king

king remained unsubdued. Can we trace any similitude between the self-commanding hero, who, like our own Sidney, on the fatal plains of Zutphen, refused to taste the eagerly desired waters of the well of Bethlehem; because it had been purchased by the jeopardy of the lives of three of his valiant captains, and the lustful tyrant whose insatiable appetites violated the honour of defenceless beauty? Yet it was the same man who acted in these different characters; it was he who was alternately, as supported or deserted by the Almighty, the shepherd conqueror of Goliath, whom the virgins of Israel extolled in their songs, and the aged forlorn fugitive who fled from his rebellious offspring. Modern times are not destitute of examples to prove, that honour and prosperity are alike unstable; nor can we preserve either

either our spiritual or temporal affairs from disorder, but by continued vigilance. We are now considering the former; and let me remind all who shall honour these reflections with a perusal, that the road from the heights of virtue to the depths of vice does not lead you down a *steep* precipice, but a *gradual* slope. A slight indiscretion, which scarcely alarms the most scrupulous conscience, if suffered to pass without observation, prepares the mind for a serious error; error delivers it over to crime; and crime, when often repeated, petrifies the moral feelings into insensible depravity. The sensibilities of virtue should be cherished with as much care as the sensibilities of temper should be modified; and unless we allow the soul time to whisper to us in retirement, we can never

catch

catch its still soft voice amid the busy turmoil of dissipation.

Were the Christian duty of self-examination rigorously performed, I am persuaded the world would exhibit a very different appearance, both with respect to sin, and to its constant associate, sorrow. Enfeebled virtue would recover its stability; nay, the seducer himself would pause in his guilty career, and perceive "consideration come like an angel to whip the offending Adam out of him," and to show him the little value of what he seeks to purchase at the risk of eternal perdition. Nor are the uses of reflection and meditation confined to our moral conduct, though their exercise is here most important. It is by these means that the difficulties of science are conquered, and the refinements of

taste

taste acquired. The skilful artist is formed by this self-communion; and the plans of the statesman and the warrior are thus ripened into perfection. Even that which is known by the name of pleasure is more truly enjoyed by retrospection in the silence of your own apartment, than when the gaudy scene actually passed your staring eyes, and the confused buz of sound agitated your ears. Such an act of the memory may be compared to the animal faculty of rumination; we at first swallow pleasure in the gross, and are too anxious to devour much, to discover of what it is composed; but when re-masticated, we discern its peculiar pungency. A load of undigested pleasure (suffer me to continue the allusion) palls the satiated appetite; a small quantity, taken after proper intervals, exhilarates the spirits,

rits, and infuses alacrity into every part. This is especially true of the pleasures which arise from conversation. Refined wit and brilliant sense communicate an inward degree of satisfaction every time we recall them to our remembrance. Genius, whether we seek her in the walks of the imitative arts, or in the " nobler growth of " thought," does not immediately pour her full radiance on our eyes; we must study her splendour before we can ascertain its degree of brightness. Even elegance and beauty, when they belong to the higher degrees of excellence, solicit *minute* attention, and refuse to unveil their coy graces to the careless gaze of the hurried beholder.

Are those then, may we not ask, true voluptuaries, who fly from pleasure to pleasure, eager to grasp all, and

tizens, yet never bowed down to its idols. It is my wish to prevent that which is in itself detestable, from being adopted as fashionable; being aware that the unguarded are often cheated out of those principles by the magic of a name, which they would not sacrifice to passion, or yield to criminal importunity.

Your lenient temper may probably think that I have treated the mere fine lady, the pretty butterfly of vanity, with too much severity; but if I could awaken these triflers from their dangerous torpor, surely severity would be mercy. They are probably responsible for many misemployed talents, at least they are sporting with that important trust, existence. While they falsely conceive themselves sent into the world to display their beauty, their accomplishments, and their taste, life glides

accustomed to spend a happy evening in the enjoyment of domestic tranquillity, would laugh to observe the multitudes which the world of fashion pours forth as soon as the world of business has retired to repose. Did you see that incessant routine of carriages which nightly pour through the streets and squares at the west-end of the town, you would at least conclude that rest and domestic comfort were sacrificed to some exquisite enjoyment; and that no one would reverse the order of nature without having some equivalent to balance the privations they must endure. Satisfied that the owners are going to be very happy, I suspect that your humane disposition will lead you to pity the servants, and even the horses, who must be exposed for many hours to the inclemency of the weather; but could

could you look within these splendid
vehicles, you would confess that the
real objects of pity were there. Languid and spiritless, the fine lady sets
out upon her nightly round, more reluctant than the watchman does on his
monotonous task. She must step in at
all the places that are marked in her
visiting list; but as time presses, and
dispatch is necessary, she can only
just look in and see who is there
before she flies to another quarter.
She must go to such a public amusement, because it is the first night of
an exhibition which every body talks
of; she can, however, do no more
than make her entry and exit, for her
time is minuted, and a vast deal of
generalship depends upon the expedition of her coachman. Ask this
votary of fashion, whether she liked
her preceding evening, and her account
will

will only add to Solomon's mournful catalogue of deceitful vanities. She cannot tell you what was said or what was done; it is almost impossible for her to recollect whom she saw. There was the usual set at one place, and a very vulgar-looking party at another. At a third house, she heard some detestable music; and every body seemed sleepy and stupid at a fourth. She made an attempt to look in at the dear duchess's; but the crowd was so immense, that she could proceed no farther than the anti-room; in returning, she heard the most violent screaming; and her own carriage was broke to pieces. On the whole, she never was so alarmed nor so weary in her life; and this morning she is annoyed by an insufferable headache, which makes her miserable. Still, however, she has not a moment to spare; a party waits for

for her at Madame Lanchester's; from thence she must go to the Exhibition, where she can only run round the rooms, as she has six calls to make in her way to the Park; from whence she must return in time to dress for a dining party; then to the Opera; and after that she meets a few private friends at a *petite souper*. Observe, *inclination* and *pleasure* are never assigned as the motives for these Herculean labours; *compulsion* and *necessity* oblige these violent efforts? She dislikes all that she sees, the fatigue is insupportable, she knows it will kill her; but rigid duty proscribes reflection and repose. To whom, you will ask, does she owe this duty; to her God, her King, or her family? No, she owes it to *vanity*, who calls this a life of pleasure. The toiling millhorse is not a greater slave, nor are his

his motions circumscribed by more arbitrary injunctions. For do not suppose that a certificate of your having driven about town all night is sufficient to acquit you of being a humdrum; you must prove that you have been at the very high parties, and exactly at the genteel hour. You may naturally admire the graces of the tragic and comic muses; but let not the names of Siddons and Jordan tempt you to enter a side-box till near the end of the third act; and be sure never to look at the stage till the former stabs herself, or the latter blindfolds Jack Bannister. In short, be content to see what fashion requires, and do not venture even *incog.* to what was only a last year's amusement. Learned pigs, invisible girls, and phantasmagorias, *have been*, I dare not venture to pronounce what are; for only a Sybil's
prescience

prescience could enable a countrywoman to name "the Cynthia of the "minute."

The same rule must regulate your *friendships:* I believe this term is still preserved in the vocabulary of polite life, though, as it only means herding together, it ought to be changed to gregarious assemblages. Be sure to be always late enough to cut Mrs. Plainly's early party, and just in time to take up Lady Bab Frightful as she returns from the Countess of Hurricane's; though you may think the Plainlys very pleasant people, and Lady Bab and the Countess detestable; but then the two latter are *ton,* and the former knows nobody. You may visit the Squanders, though they had an execution in the house last week, because Lady Modely has decided that they ought to be countenanced;

tenanced; but never think of calling on the Overdo family, for they went quite out the moment it was *known* that they had spent their fortune. Be equally exact in your eating, and imprint upon your mind, that as fashion and nature are antipodes in climate, it is right to devour voraciously in April, what you faint at the sight of in August. This is called eating well, and really is a most complex science, involving so many concurrent circumstances, that a fine lady must devote much of her time and thoughts to this study before she can hope to see her dinners announced in the Morning Post, or have the honour of employing the toothpicks of the most sapient epicures of the season; whose landaulet's at your door as surely attest your cook's abilities, as a flight of vultures do the triumphs of a general.

I should

which has been denied to genius enriched by learning, and enforced by those strong powers of argument which result from the united bounty of nature and education. A recollection of the candid treatment which I have formerly experienced from the public encourages me to hope that my motives for this undertaking will apologize for its deficiencies. Works on religion and morals, in this country, can rarely pretend to any novelty, beside the title and the arrangement; but the mere name of something new bestows a momentary celebrity on even *jejune* productions; while the sterling compositions which they modernize sleep in the library. But if, while employed in reading a recent appeal to their consciences, one profligate should be converted, one prejudiced mind illuminated, one wavering understanding

blessed with a *fashionable* auditory and an *elegant* preacher. But for fear the liturgical offices of our church should make a disagreeable impression, they must hurry from thence to Kensington gardens, to sport their promenade dresses, and observe who and who are together. During the sitting of parliament, this is the day for dining parties; which, with a concert in the evening, keeps them employed all day long, and renders them as happily forgetful of the services with which it commenced, as if they had devoted their morning to the worship of Morpheus.

It frequently happens, that these scenes of continual hurry and confusion so exhaust the frame, and dissipate the spirits, that the heart loses both its inclinations and its sympathies; and the fine lady becomes a
mere

mere self-moved automaton, incapable of either tenderness, resentment, or compassion. To a being that can neither be *roused* to virtue nor *seduced* to vice, cautions are unnecessary; but many a heart escapes the frigid cold of this arctic circle, and repines with secret sorrow, or frets with fruitless wishes, while the vacant eye seems only to ponder the fantastic scene of which it is an unconscious witness. To a person thus situated, consideration becomes of most momentous importance; for the wish should be analyzed, and the sorrow traced to its source. It ought to be known, whether her bosom anguish originates in her own faults, or belongs to that species to which she can only oppose the defence of patience and resignation. Her desires too should be so scrutinized, as to discover whether they are of that innocent kind which she may pray God to prosper; or whether she should not cast them from her heart, as she would the deadly worm of Nile. We shall not *materially* slander the circles of dissipation, if we embody this *grief* in the shape of a negligent or faithless husband; and connect those *wishes* with the person of an agreeable cecisbeo, whose attentions are the only pleasant interruption of the tediousness of high life. It would prove me to be a mere Goth, if I supposed that a man and his wife could *designedly* appear in the same party; but I presume it may by chance happen, that my lord's chair may arrive before my lady's chariot is ordered up; and that she may be under the necessity of seeing that his early appearance is really in consequence of an assignation with the person she has

long

long suspected to be his *chere amie.* Can any situation more peculiarly require the exercise of consideration, even if a fashionable Bronzely were not whispering agreeable nothings in her ear at that very moment, and forming, by his observance, a marked contrast to the *nonchalance*, or perhaps *hauteur*, of her husband? Yet she must hurry to some other scene, as joyless and as dangerous as what she now witnesses; and consideration is deferred to those agonizing hours, when her mind, torn with jealousy and vain regret, denies repose to her wearied body, by conjuring up the phantoms of stern ingratitude and respectful assiduity.

Surely, my dear young friend, fashion never passed any decree so injurious to the interests of conjugal fidelity, as when it ordained that the husband and the wife should *always* pursue different plans of pleasure. I do not wish the wedded pair to be inseparable; I know that occasional absence renders the dearest society more delightful; and that being engaged in different scenes gives spirit and variety to the conjugal *tête-à-tête.* But the duties of life impose a sufficient necessity for separation; and when the hours of amusement arrive, let the zest of pleasure be heightened by participation. General custom seems to imply that there is danger in public places; or why do ladies require protectors? and can a man of reflection expect to escape the reproach of wittol husband, who declines escorting *her* to those haunts of Comus, in whose preservation *he* is most interested? I am aware of the ridicule that a family party in a stage-box

must

must excite; but a gentleman in Westminster-hall often makes a more ridiculous, I might say detestable appearance. Much may be there said respecting the breach of a sacred trust; and many oratorical flourishes may be introduced about violating the laws of hospitality, and betraying the honour of confiding friendship; but unless the plaintiff can give better reasons for absenting himself from his wedded charge, than that he was in pursuit of some other amusement, reason and experience will condemn him for being guilty of culpable folly, in putting friendship to an unnecessary test. Were such husbands candid, they would exclaim, in the words of Carlos,

―――"The crime was mine,
"Who plac'd thee there, where only thou couldst
  "fail;
"Though

"Though well I knew that dreadful post of honour
"I gave thee to maintain. Ah! who could bear
"Those eyes unhurt?" THE REVENGE.

You, my dear Miss M———, will readily conceive that I am not pleading for the treacherous friend or the recreant wife; I believe that genuine virtue, when strengthened by Christian principle, and supported by divine grace, can vanquish every temptation; but I know that divine grace is only given to those who ask it; and, I fear, Christian principles are not the predominant rules of conduct among the gay and giddy votaries of pleasure. Chastity, even when supported by such invulnerable guardians, should not be wantonly exposed to severe trials; and surely, when she cannot boast such protectors, the fragility of all human aids is too indisputable, to render it safe to put her upon such hard probation.

Liberality looks as well as charity; conscious merit has a more imposing air than humility; a Sunday rout seems more pleasant than family devotion; and if faith and holiness are not necessary passports to a better state of existence, the woman of the world is for the most part a more desirable companion than the pious Christian. If the task of religious instruction be not begun while learning is a duty, I know not at what period of life the mind will feel its own deficiencies, and set about acquiring what it perceives that it can do very well without. The seeds of science are sown in childhood, and left to ripen with our years; and yet we do not hear of *prejudiced* geographers, astronomers, or mathematicians. As the understanding unfolds, clearer views are obtained; the rudiments by which we gained our
first

called love. matches. The start of passion, which leads a lady to Scotland to become a wife, too often proceeds from some romantic expectations of eternal affection and consummate excellence, which is not, and indeed cannot be, realized; and if she never experiences more than casual neglect or common infirmities, she will have more reason to bless her good fortune, than her precipitation in choosing deserved. But if, instead of "the faultless monster whom the "world ne'er saw," a being much beneath the general run of humanity starts up, in the form of a stern tyrant, or negligent coxcomb, and still deems himself entitled to the continuance of that warm affection which she once professed, merely because "she had eyes and chose him;" I fear, affection would here be found a very

brittle

brittle chain. If a husband, thus circumstanced, should think himself justified in pursuing pleasure through every haunt in which he supposes he may meet it, and conceives his own humour entitled to full license, provided his lady has a beau to attend her if she likes to go out; let not such a man complain of being *injured*, either in friendship or in love, though his wife drink deep of the cup of infamy.

But it is my own sex that I chiefly hope to benefit by my admonitions; and here let me earnestly entreat those ladies whose will gives law to the world of fashion, to endeavour to rescue matronly manners from that extreme affectation of levity, which is now become so general, that it is considered to be the associate of perfect innocency of intention. The shrine of virgin beauty is now deserted by its most desirable worshippers, who hover round the chair where loveliness, already "link'd and wedlock bound," dispenses her *unmeaning* or *criminal* smiles. The married dame trips through the light maze of the dance, and shows her gay youthful partner to the provoked spinster, who is obliged to some antiquated *caro sposo* for not suffering her to sit shivering on the ottoman all the evening. A married lady may go any where, mix in all companies, dress in any style, say any thing, and do every thing not absolutely scandalous, without impeachment of her fair fame. If any allowance ought to be made for levity, should it not be granted to youthful inexperience, to indiscreet simplicity, and to the too frank disclosure of that wish to win hearts which is very natural to the early part of our lives? Why

for they must improve their school-accomplishments, and make those ornaments in the morning which their evening engagements will call upon them to display. And yet, if they become Christians from conviction at this period of their lives, they must encounter the labours of a philosopher with the courage of a hero. They must be *argued* out of the deism in which they have been tutored, and *persuaded* to renounce the motives and habits which they have been taught to adopt. "It is one thing," says Dr. Waterland, " to understand the " doctrine, and quite another to be " master of the controversy." A girl with a common capacity, who has received an ordinary education on Christian principles, knows enough to entertain notions that are sufficiently clear to her own judgment, though she

different ends in view from that of swelling her triumphs. His own gross passions may fix him in her train, not to be trampled upon by her tyranny, but to be *her* conqueror. Whatever she may suppose, or he profess, she never would have been "his happiest "choice," even had he seen her before she was assigned to another. He has too much aversion to the marriage yoke, for her charms to vanquish his prejudices; and her principal attraction, in his eye, is the conviction that he may flirt with her without an officious friend's requesting to know whether he has any serious intentions. This character is well described in the lively farce of the " Wedding Day ;" the regret of Lady Contest at not having seen the engaging lord before she had tied herself to old Sir Adam, and her surprise at his declining the honour

honour of her hand when she was unexpectedly released from her former bonds, affords a valuable lesson to married coquettes.

Before I dismiss the subject of *matronly flirting*, allow me to answer one objection. Though particular attentions to one gentleman are confessed to be both suspicious and dangerous, general ease and freedom are defended, on the ground of improving the pleasure and vivacity of society. I am so great a lover of cheerfulness, that I am willing to admit every species of sprightliness into the manner of married ladies, that can be fairly affirmed to be destitute of either design or immodesty. I acknowledge, that they may with propriety take a greater share of conversation, and indulge in more latitude of remark, than their *juniors*. You will perceive by that limitation,

mitation, that I consider these more as the privileges of age, than as part of the hymeneal dowry. Let a married lady endeavour to promote the social enjoyments of the circle in which she moves. Let her consult her glass, and allow me to add her purse also, in the choice of appropriate and becoming ornaments. I permit her to aspire to the character of a very agreeable woman; but let not that distinction be laid by on ordinary occasions, and only produced to male witnesses. If the best *bon-mots* are reserved for the beaux, if the favourite head-dress is only worn when Lord Gaylove is expected; if her *ennui* and head-ache are apt to be cured by a *tête-à-tête* with a man of fashion, if she finds female parties dull, and female conversation insipid; I must entreat the advocates for the ease and freedom of of married ladies to remember, that cheerfulness is of no sex, and is as likely to visit a party of old women with her agreeable sallies, as a circle of box-lobby loungers. Nay, it is more likely; for in the first instance it will be stimulated by the humane desire of amusing lassitude, while in the latter it will be checked by a modest apprehension of misconstruction. I should have premised, that these said old women should not be *splenetic;* for I do confess, ill-nature gives the *coup de grace* to vivacity.

We have dwelt so minutely on some of the increasing improprieties of fashionable manners, that we must pass others with less observation. A rage for education is one of the marked features of the great world; and it has been much increased by the labour of writers who belong to the

the new school of morals. The hope of forming something superior to the present race of mortals, by merely human means, is one of the wildest theories that ever entered the brain of a visionary reformer; yet it is seriously acted upon by many indefatigable mothers, who weary the patience and injure the constitution of their children by the most unremitting attention to a multiplicity of pursuits; in the hope of being able to exhibit in their own families this mechanical compound of ethical and scientifical perfection; which is to prove, that divine wisdom is not necessary either for informing our ignorance, or restraining our propensities to evil. All parents do not, indeed, aspire to this high standard of philosophical erudition and impeccability; but even that routine of masters
who

who are necessary to form a young lady into the accomplished amateur, which is now deemed an essential part of the character of every woman of fashion, subjects a young lady to more privations, as much bodily fatigue, and a far greater exercise of patience and attention, than yonder little spinner encounters, who by her industry procures her own subsistence. We must, however, allow due praise to this severe discipline, on the same ground as we commend the rigid injunctions of Lycurgus: no laws but his could have formed the stern, indefatigable, impenetrable Spartan; nor could a less inexorable course of self-denial and activity convert the artless happy girl into that extraordinary being, a woman of ton. Beside being compelled to pass through those extremes of climate, without discovering any sense

of

of bodily inconvenience, as Milton, by a bold flight of well-governed fancy, supposed to be part of the punishment of the fallen angels, the candidates for this fading glory are trained from their cradles to such habits of observance, patience, and control, in order to attract the attention of their fellow-creatures, as, if they were influenced by better motives, would secure them the approbation of beings of a higher order. What a pity, that so much pains should be exerted for such a subordinate purpose; and in which, since all those whom you seek to amaze are your competitors, your chance of success is so very limited! For if your daughter, after fourteen thousand hours* spent in the acquisition

---

* Mrs. More communicates this anecdote. The author cannot refer to the page, not being in possession

tion of music, prove at last but a second-rate performer; if, after all that the dancing-master has done in screwing her shoulders and modelling her steps, her person be inelegant and her motions ungraceful; if no expense nor waste of time can prevent her drawings from being daubs, or bagatelles, for what have the hours of early life been sacrificed? Taste and ton have no *degrees* of glory to allot to their worshippers; nor can ardent devotion, here, claim that reward for its sincerity, to which it is not entitled by talent. All that can be done for the unsuccessful candidate for fashionable

---

session of that Lady's Strictures on Education, which she read at their first appearance, and took from them a few extracts; to which, while writing these Letters, she has occasionally referred She will feel much flattered, if the reader should also trace an incidental and undesigned resemblance, arising from similarity of opinion on various points.

eclat

eclat is, to remove her to some narrower sphere. A second-rate party, or a summer bathing-place, is the only meridian which she can hope to illumine; while all who witnessed her former pretensions are tempted to exclaim, " Ill-weav'd ambition, how " much art thou shrunk!" Might not prudence here suggest the expediency of applying to another master, who acts upon very different principles from the cruel despot Vanity, by giving a certain retribution to the *motives*, not the *success* of our actions?

" No cold neglect the faithful heart repays,
 ". Whose steadfast aim solicits His regard ;
" Each wish for merit, each attempt to please,
 " He views, and His benignant smiles reward."
                              CARTER's POEMS.

It must, however, be acknowledged, that the favour of this wise and holy Being cannot be acquired by such an exercise

exercise of our faculties, or determination of our views; for he does not enjoin us to *excel* our fellow-creatures, but to *conquer* ourselves; nor will the splendour of the crown of immortality be decreased, because it blazes upon the brows of myriads of happy beings. Envy of successful competition, and jealousy of pre-eminent abilities, will never torment the bosom of the young Christian, who, engrossed by the necessity of looking at her own ways, ceases to be a fretful observer of the progress of others; being assured, that at the day of judgment she cannot be *overlooked* amid an infinite host of happy spirits who claim the kingdom of their Father, nor *concealed* by a multitude of sinners who call in vain on the rocks and mountains to hide them from an omniscient eye.

In judging of the folly of those who seek

seek to form their children upon the model which vanity presents, we must add, to the great hazard of success, the brevity of the acquisition. As the career of a fine lady is ever in danger of being arrested by rivals in expense and taste, so rivals in accomplishments are coming forward to dispute her pretensions to superiority. Nor is this all: every year brings in a new fashion, even in these particulars, and the business of education is never finished. If you choose to dance, paint, sing, and play, till you reach your climacteric, you must still have masters to teach you the *last* improvement, or you will be laid aside as old lumber. Our mothers, who danced all their lives to the tune of Lady Coventry's minuet, will scarcely conceive how ephemeral are the triumphs of the successors of that paragon, who had

the

the good fortune to flourish at a period when the empire of beauty and taste dreaded no other enemies than the small-pox and old age. The *minuet de la cour* and the *cotillon* were afterwards thought better calculated to display the female figure to advantage, and these lasted in fashion long enough for one generation of dancers; but reels, strathspeys, and waltzes now succeed each other with such rapidity, that only the most flexile form and fixed attention can rise to the praise of having learned the figure, before they must assume different contortions, and wind into another meander. The like observation extends to all other accomplishments: there is even a fashion in language; the accent must retreat, or advance, according as ton, not syntax, has ordained; and the word of the year must hold a prominent place in our conversation. Our passions and sensations must be subject to like control; we must either be immoderately happy, monstrously delighted, intensely charmed, or amazingly interested. But as expressions of extreme suffering are best adapted to the joyless career of a fine lady, we must allow that her task of learning will be chiefly bounded by the compound epithets of immensely dull, horribly fatiguing, and insufferably vapid. A few mornings' observation will show her what *misfortune* is most in vogue, and give the proper tinge to her *dolours* for the ensuing winter.

If the quackery of education only extended to the formation of vain and frivolous beings, we should have far less reason to complain of its prevalence. Many strong minds would resist these shackles, and disappointment

ment would divert ill-directed understandings to some nobler pursuit. But, as we have before observed, a system of morals is formed still more dangerous than this system of manners. The popularity of either mode of education seems to depend more on the situation than on the intellects of their respective partisans; yet it appears as if the frivolous system was most in repute among second-rate gentility; while the bold theory of human perfectibility seeks its converts among those who, feeling themselves to be above the immediate influence of the temporal considerations which restrain their fellow-creatures, would fain get released from the eternal consequences of indulging their guilty passions. A morality, therefore, which rejects the basis of religion, is admirably suited to people who, while they seem to

make

make the opinions of others their standard of right and wrong in affairs of vanity and fancy, really bow to no other idol than selfishness, and, amidst a life of real privation, are secretly pursuing self-enjoyment. To banish from the mind the ideas of an omniscient God, and a retributive hereafter, gives an amazing release to the appetites; but this liberty will not satisfy these new organizers of the human soul. The passions must be made tyrants; and for this end the most suitable means are provided. The habitual indulgence of violent desires, is by them called exerting the noblest energies; and discarding the restraints of virtue, is misnamed ingenuousness and obedience to the honest dictates of nature. These iniquitous principles frequently preserve those external pretences of decorum, which are judged

judged expedient to forward their universal adoption in this country; and those very systems which inculcate vice profess the greatest regard for virtue. To confine our observations to what we are now discussing; volumes have been written on the subject of education, which profess to form a most amiable and intelligent being, infinitely superior to the present inhabitants of this world, and which, but for the studied omission of revealed truths and religious motives, might pass for the effects of real philanthropy. The disappointment of those parents who attempt to form their children upon these models cannot be pitied, unless they really are ignorant that human wisdom never discovered a perfect system of ethics, without borrowing the aid of revelation; nor can she even then devise barriers

barriers sufficiently strong to prevent our frail natures from deviating into bye paths of error, unless she renounce the guidance of her own pale fires, and submit to be led by the clear radiance of the gospel*.

The deficiency of this new system of self-dependent virtue, is not more apparent in the weakness of its restraints, and the feebleness of its motives, than in the very limited circle to which it even *pretends* to direct its improvements. Many Christian graces are excluded from its good deeds; and the cardinal virtue of our ancestors, the very bond of social intercourse, is now little inculcated in education, or enforced by fashionable practice; I speak of moral honesty, and the simple but energetic principle of paying every

* The subject of education is resumed in Letters Vth and XIIIth.

one his just debts. The difficulty which I find in treating this point in such à manner as to render it palatable to polite readers, is a sufficient proof that the duty is *quite gone out*. Yet honour and honesty were once thought to have a reciprocal relation; and the alliance was so congenial, that I think the former quality has appeared to be in a hectic state ever since it has been separated from its co-relative. A person of strict honour and independent principles, in debt to every tradesman he deals with, and actually living, if not by shuffling and evasion, at least by the forbearance of people whom he despises, seems a contradiction in nature; for generosity, pride, and dignity of sentiment, are supposed to be blended with meanness, servility, and cruelty of conduct. To live, to breathe at the mercy of another, nay to feel that you are really injuring those on whose forbearance you depend, and introducing anxiety and distress into a rank of life of which you were born the guardians: how does this accord with the magnificent nobleman, or high-spirited commoner, who know themselves to be parts of the legislature of their country? Yet even in those important branches of the state, the art not only of ruining themselves, but of living after they are ruined, is practised by many adepts in (must I say) the mystery of swindling. Living within the bounds of your income is so far from being considered as the test of a gentleman, that in the world of high fashion it conveys the oblique insinuation, that you are a narrow soul, destitute of taste, or at best merely a good sort of *spiritless* creature.

ture. This propensity to squander the bounty of Providence with careless profusion, has unhappily descended from the high to the lowly scenes of life. Its effects upon the middle and inferior orders have been already considered; in the higher it may be lamented, not only on account of the individual distress that it occasions, but as tending to make the humble classes think still more meanly of their superiors. I have ever been of opinion that the influence of birth and rank was more beneficial to the community at large, than that of wealth, and that the faults of the former were less prejudicial. To instance in pride; which, when it proceeds from hereditary superiority, is generally polished by education, and softened by habitual restraint; whereas the pride of mere wealth mostly seizes an unimproved mind,

mind, at a period of life in which habits have been formed on vulgar models, and of course it must become more odious to those whom it affects. Whether it is ingrafted on native servility or rudeness, or on the lately-acquired consequence arising from the possession of money, ostentation and self-indulgence will be the result, unless checked by extraordinary goodness of disposition. The man of rank, on the other hand, knows his own title to the respect of his neighbourhood to be indefeasible, nor does he feel the necessity of continually defending the dignity which was handed down to him by his ancestors. He has been accustomed to the luxuries of life from his infancy, and his relish for them is too much palled by long indulgence to allow him to attach importance to such distinctions. This appears

appears to be the natural bias of these two characters, unless they are diverted out of their course by any accidental impulse. Let it be remembered too, that attachment to hereditary patrons, and respect for the old manor house, (the antient possessors of which are deposited in the family vault under the parish church), are feelings congenial to the minds of the common people, and such as our constitution wisely cherishes. The influence which an ancient and respectable family possessed over its tenantry and neighbourhood, cannot be soon acquired by the nabob, or manufacturer, who purchases the estate, however estimable his character, or conciliatory his conduct. A series of years must elapse before they can form any tie but what interest creates; and till the generation which served the old family

family has passed away, the new will be considered as interlopers, who have risen on the ruins of a race that was far more deserving. I must observe, that in these times every thing which tends to weaken the tie that connects the poorest man in the kingdom with the highest, is to be deprecated; and I regret the degradation which rank and station suffer in the eyes of the community, not only by the contagious influence of unbounded expense, but by transferring its power to other hands, which, even if as well-disposed, will be less able to exert it beneficially.

Shall we not then, my dear Miss M——, reprobate that false candour, which induces us to give soft names to such a vice as extravagance? Heaven forbid that we should here withhold that pity from *undeserved* distress to which

which it is ever entitled! I am not speaking of those who, by unforeseen, unavoidable misfortunes, by the pressure of domestic calamity, by the treachery of enemies, the uproar of the elements, or even by misplaced confidence, are involved in pecuniary difficulties. The sorrows of such are sacred; let the world compassionate, and, if it can, assuage them. I confine my censures to those who voluntarily offer their fair possessions, their extensive influence, and every other blessing of which God has made them the guardian, at the shrine of vanity. These I charge with contributing to the ruin of their country, as well as of themselves. I accuse them of perverting their highly responsible station to the corrupting of national habits, and to the subverting of the interests of the order to which they belong. These offences

offences must not pass off with the slight censure, that they were very generous people, and no one's enemies but their own; and every eulogy on their taste, spirit, and hospitality, is a severe charge against them, for not bounding these propensities by their lawful ability of indulging them.

It is indeed allowed, that people eminently gifted with genius are apt to fall into these pecuniary embarrassments; and perhaps it is just, that a more lenient censure should attach to errors which seem rather to proceed from the limited faculties of our nature, than from intentional injustice to others, or overweening attachment to ourselves. The intenseness of thought which accompanies any extraordinary effort of intellect, whether it be engaged in " bodying forth the forms of things unseen," in developing

ing the abstruse mazes of science, or in conducting the intricate and cumbersome machine of public business, necessarily withdraws the attention from what seem comparatively petty considerations; and the harassed mind, fatigued by the painful stretch of its faculties, finds the hours of relaxation insufficient to recruit its exhausted powers. When such an excuse can be fairly urged for embarrassments, let us abstain from reproach; sufficient to such a culprit, is the punishment which the consequences of indiscretion must inflict; especially as people of this stamp are generally rather dupes than knaves, and suffer more from misplaced confidence, and the extravagance of their connexions, than from the ungoverned importunity of their own desires.

Few, however, are lighted to ruin by

by the starry lamp of genius.; and fewer yet can plead, that close attention to the welfare of the many compelled them to neglect their own. It is vanity which generally misleads the unthrifty; and the seductions of amusement, not the calls of business, deliver the careless spendthrift to the iron gripe of insolvency.

But let me recollect that it is my own sex I am now addressing; and as we cannot be called to such high responsible stations as preclude the possibility of those domestic attentions which form a principal part of our bounden duty, we can never plead the excuse that might shelter the improvident legislator, general, statesman, or magistrate, from severe censure. And though genius does not deny her visitations to women, she seldom pours such full influence upon

our

our souls as to absorb the sense of other duties. I will not permit the fabricator of a novel, the composer of a poem, or even the writer of *moral essays*, to claim those privileges of abstraction, which I would grant to a Burke and a Bacon. Literature is with us an ornament, or an amusement, not a duty or profession; and when it is pursued with such avidity, as to withdraw us from the especial purposes of our creation, it becomes a crime.

So far are rank and station from excusing us from this obligation to pecuniary exactness, that they seem rather to bind it upon us the closer; for in the higher walks of life, the attention of the husband is often engrossed by what he owes his country; while the wife cannot show her patriotism better than by relieving her partner from the weight of domestic incum-

incumbrance, and acting as a faithful steward and intelligent agent in every affair which can be submitted to her management. Punctuality and regularity in money transactions are still acknowledged to be counting-house requisites. May they long continue to distinguish and give respectability to the commercial world! but why should they be discarded from being supporters to the shield of ancestry and the coronet of nobility. I have heard it remarked (and the observation was judicious), that arithmetic has been of more real service to the world, than all other remains of classical learning or science; and in what respect does considerate expenditure (we are now addressing a class to which the term frugality may seem unappropriate) imply the absence of any noble quality? Can generosity,

can

can benevolence subsist upon funds which are not your own? When you bestowed what belonged to your children or your creditor, you did not *give*, but *surreptitiously apply the possessions of another*. The character of Charles Surface, in that very superior comedy "The School for Scandal," if not the hasty sketch of inconsiderate genius unconscious of its dangerous tendency, must be deemed a marked attack on the probity which is our national distinction. In either point of view, his celebrated animadversions on the old proverb, "Be just "before you are generous," ought to be received with groans and hisses, not thunders of applause*. They are, indeed, characteristic of a dishonest spendthrift; but they bear no mark of

* See the scene between Charles and Rowley, in the fourth Act of the School for Scandal.

integ-

integrity hurried away by the violence of ill-regulated passions; for they do not result from the strong impression made by a recent tale of distress, but from a mind *resolved* to be unjust, and enamoured of its own baseness. The sentiment which restrains him from selling the picture of his friend and benefactor, ought to have taught him that the necessities of Old Stanley might be supplied, by discharging his four valets with their bags and bouquets; from whose attendance only a consummate coxcomb could derive satisfaction, and not from a misappropriation of what he owns belonged to his tailor and hosier. How can the audience in the last scene acquiesce in Maria's destiny? Charles indeed tells us, that he never more *can* err, because he shall now have a monitor and guide; but has he not already told us,
that

that he does an imprudent action precipitately, lest he should be checked by the *monitor* within him? To such a character the sober paces of justice will ever appear "lame and hobbling;" but the misfortune is, it is not "Generosity," but dishonesty, which outstrips her. The insolvent must relinquish the sublime pleasure of relieving indigence, from an absolute *impossibility* of enjoying it. He may be *base*, he cannot be *benevolent* in any thing but desire. If he truly valued the ability of giving, he should have reserved some little remnant of his possessions from the gulph of dissipation, and saved his tender heart from the exquisite anguish of finding himself incapable of relieving misery.

Compassion is one of those inherent qualities of the female mind, which seem to defy the influence of situation.
Even

Even fashion dares not utter a decree against the sovereignty of benevolence; and though a fine lady must be too frigid to *feel*, she thinks herself bound to *affect* tenderness. She is indeed allowed to be a little whimsical in the objects of her bounty, as all must be who renounce the dictates of nature, and resign themselves to the caprices of art; yet, as it is necessary to have her name down in charitable subscriptions, though it be only to relieve

" A fiddler of note, who, for lace on his coat,
" To his tailor stands much in arrears;"

we may observe, that without some attention to pecuniary concerns, she cannot be (I will not be so uncouth as to say honest, but) *genteelly* benevolent. And yet, after all the abuse that can be bestowed upon the impertinence of tradesmen, they are necessary

y appendages to the votaries of va-
y, without whose assistance every
empt to propitiate the idol they
re, or to outshine a rival, would be
ossible. The aspect of a decora-
1 painter, when he sets out an
rtment in a style of elegance, is so
y engaging, that if the obligations
ich are due to him were but height-
d by passing through the alembic
German sentiment, they might be-
ne native alcohol; and no longer
ding the feeble shoulders of the old
dame *Justice*, they would even in-
ase the speed of Charles Surface's
nired equestrian nymph *Generosity*.
perusing the items which form the
ts of a genteel bankrupt, we might
cover what portion should be as-
ned to honour, and what to hones-

I hope no well-bred person will
ny, that expensive furniture, elegant

Even fashion dares̸ ⟋⟋ ses, and
against the sover⟋⟋ ⟋re as ne-
and though a⟋⟋ ⟋nal bursts
frigid to *feel*⟋⟋ spirited ma-
to *affect* t⟋⟋ ⟋ng-table; every
allowed t⟋⟋ re, who lent his aid
objects⟋⟋ ⟋ne Herculean labour of
who⟋ ⟋ng a large fortune with ra-
and⟋, presents a claim upon *honour*,
o⟋ich, if people are faithful to the
⟋inciples they profess, will be readily
admitted in a reversed proportion to
the real value of the service, or the
moderation of the demanded recompense.

One word more upon an evil which, on account of its destructive tendency, should be hunted out of the world, by the heavy club of argument, and the piercing shaft of ridicule: does not this inattention to the distresses which arise from extravagance, result

from

from the want of more enlarged views in those who form the principles of youth? Education, whether it proceed upon the showy or the philosophical plan, is now directed to the formation of a selfish character. Even the minute attention which is bestowed upon children induces them to over-rate their own importance, and to undervalue others. The love of praise, or of distinction, to which they are taught to make so many sacrifices, unquestionably seeks its own gratification; and when the exercise of benevolence is recommended as a means of enjoying pleasant and escaping painful emotions, self is still held forth as the predominant feature. But beside those whom we may wish to gain as admirers, or as pensioners, there is a very numerous body of our fellow-creatures to whom people of rank ought to extend their views; I mean those whose good opinion they do not think worth courting, and whose services they cannot command. Those who are conversant with the great, know well that they are apt to consider their own domestic servants as superior in situation to respectable tradesmen, or professional people not decidedly in the line of gentlemen. A contempt for every thing city, or bourgeois, forms a part of the instruction of young people of fashion: this is certainly very blameable, however it may be extenuated by the citizen or bourgeois deserting their own characters, and assuming the cast airs of quality.

It seems doubtful, whether manners really have improved by breaking the connexion that subsisted in feudal times between the chieftain and his vassals.

vassals. It might, now that the sword of civil discord sleeps, and the rage of family animosity has ceased, be converted into a most powerful means of improving the habits of every order, and correcting the faults of all. But then the nobleman and his dependants must not meet on terms of equality. The yeoman's wife must not affront the baroness, by adopting her paraphernalia, or aping her table; nor must the baroness invite her rustic neighbours to laugh at the simplicity which it is her interest to cherish *. I am indulging an Utopian idea, that a spot in this island can still be found, in which affectation and false refinement has not corrupted the manners of the inhabitants; who therefore look up to their superiors as to their bene-

* See Letter the XIVth.

factors and friends, without envy, and without any ridiculous intention of imitating a style unsuitable to their station, and derogatory to their characters. Could such beings be found, surely occasional intercourse between respectful gratitude and generous affability, might afford superior pleasure to what the best-conducted masquerade ever bestowed; as the mistress of the feast would enjoy the certainty of giving delight, and the partakers of it would not find it *difficult* to express gratification. Such meetings would also prove a noble school of instruction to the rising branches of a gentleman's family, who would thus contemplate characters with whom they had no other means of becoming acquainted, and practise duties for which the ordinary routine of high life, as divided into London, Bath, and

and summer excursions, leaves no opening. By learning the pursuits, resources, and difficulties of classes not remotely separated from their own, they would imbibe a strong attachment to the obligations of justice, and would correct that criminal thoughtlessness which impedes the fulfilment of the divine precept, "Whatsoever "ye would that others should do to "you, do ye even so to them." They would see (and surely to see is to admire) that blunt intelligence which forms a predominant feature in the true Englishman. They would observe boldness of remark, originality of idea, and all those peculiar traits of character which courtly refinement melts into one mass. A morning spent in unmeaning shopping, would then afford less retrospective pleasure to indolent beauty; and the foreseen perplexities of a disappointed tradesman would arrest the profusion of the prodigal. Patronage, too, would be thus assisted in discharging its highly-responsible trust; and merit would have some hope of obtaining that attention which would divert the smiles of greatness from parasites and mercenaries, whom sickly vanity or capricious folly (confined to the partial sphere of domestic observation) selected as proper objects of reward. But, however the middle orders may suffer from the cold haughtiness, the contracted views, or the careless disregard of greatness, they should remember, that till they substitute modesty, humility, and simplicity of manner, in the room of that dashing air of equality which they esteem so genteel, mutual disgust must increase that distance which it is the interest of both parties to diminish

by

by mutual kindness. Such conduct our holy faith inculcates; and the consideration of what this country now is, leads us to consider what it would become, supposing we were Christians in practice as well as in name.

The lukewarm religion of the fashionable world is the last topic that I mean to discuss in this letter. I am told, that the aspect of the times improves in externals; and that, except a few professed infidels and notorious demireps, ladies think themselves bound to consecrate one hour of the Sabbath by appearing at some place of public worship. But the claims of another world are not to be commuted by such a slight penance; the offering of prayer and praise must not be immediately succeeded by the sacrifice of fools. The denunciations of the law, and the promises of the gospel,

must

must be meditated upon in private, and the preacher's exhortations must produce other effects than a compliment to the elegance of his manner, the perspicuity of his language, and the happiness of his allusions. The Christian mother, too, like pious Hannah, should take care to bring her young offspring to God as soon as they can be taught habits of attention; and the mistress of a family should resolve with Joshua, that she " and her " household would serve the Lord." It must also be remembered, that our church has two services, corresponding with the divinely-instituted morning and evening worship of the tabernacle. Nor is this all; religion has her private as well as her public duties; meditation, prayer, and reading the holy scriptures, require retirement. She who passes the day in a crowd,

crowd, cannot abstract her thoughts from temporal objects; similar scenes must excite similar ideas, and the pursuits of vanity will be accompanied by their usual round of agitations and cares. The lady who thus attempts to divide her Sabbath between God and Mammon, feels indeed the servitude of both, but loses the reward affixed to the spiritual duty; I mean the serenity, the renewed strength, and the refreshment which a Sunday spent in the bosom of domestic enjoyment and cheerful piety never fails to bestow.

I fear, my dear young friend, I have wearied you by this long review of abandoned, frivolous, or capricious characters; who, by intruding upon public attention, call themselves the world, and in the clamour of their vices and follies drown the mild voice of retired goodness. I am convinced, that even in the highest circle of fashion the number of really excellent women far exceed the profligate and thoughtless; but as they are not "ravished by the "whistling of a name," they choose to let their modest worth pass silently along, content with domestic affection, friendship, and cordial esteem. Do not misconstrue those observations into a general satire on birth and affluence, which proceed from a conviction that vice owes her most dangerous allurements to a false idea of her being universal, and that she affords exquisite though temporary enjoyments. In speaking of the fashionable world, I adopt a well-known phrase, which implies unity and populousness; but I know that it contains many inhabitants who are discontented with its laws, and many who, though they are ranked among its citizens,

tizens, yet never bowed down to its idols. It is my wish to prevent that which is in itself detestable, from being adopted as fashionable; being aware that the unguarded are often cheated out of those principles by the magic of a name, which they would not sacrifice to passion, or yield to criminal importunity.

Your lenient temper may probably think that I have treated the mere fine lady, the pretty butterfly of vanity, with too much severity; but if I could awaken these triflers from their dangerous torpor, surely severity would be mercy. They are probably responsible for many misemployed talents, at least they are sporting with that important trust, existence. While they falsely conceive themselves sent into the world to display their beauty, their accomplishments, and their taste, life glides

other sex, our minds were less enabled by nature and education to resist these sophists, who never could endure the Ithuriel spear of learning and deep investigation.

Religious knowledge will enable us to avoid this snare; and from my zeal to recommend this defensive armour to the youth of both sexes, I have been accused of enforcing theological erudition at the expense of religious practice. I can only say, that such was not my design; the most guarded language, however, cannot prevent *intentional* misconstruction. Many of our first divines, in the arguments which they oppose to the opinions of certain schismatics, affirm, that though our Lord improved morality to its highest possible perfection, by removing it from external behaviour to the heart, his design, in coming into the world, which has been denied to genius enriched by learning, and enforced by those strong powers of argument which result from the united bounty of nature and education. A recollection of the candid treatment which I have formerly experienced from the public encourages me to hope that my motives for this undertaking will apologize for its deficiencies. Works on religion and morals, in this country, can rarely pretend to any novelty, beside the title and the arrangement; but the mere name of something new bestows a momentary celebrity on even *jejune* productions; while the sterling compositions which they modernize sleep in the library. But if, while employed in reading a recent appeal to their consciences, one profligate should be converted, one prejudiced mind illuminated, one wavering understanding fixed, or one thoughtless being awakened from the dream of vanity, I may hope for more than an *earthly* reward, provided my admonitions are dictated by *singleness* of heart and *uprightness* of intention.

That you approve the instructions which you so little need, makes that a pleasure which would otherwise be a laborious task. Adieu, my dear Miss M——; may we never waste the rich legacy of friendship which was so tenderly bequeathed to us, prays your sincerely affectionate friend, &c.

LETTER V.

On Religious Knowledge, and the peculiar Notions of Calvin.

MY DEAR MISS M——,

We have considered what our sex was intended to be by nature, and what criminal or ridiculous compliances with the caprices of vanity and affectation would make us. We have examined the inroads that luxury and wealth have made in our manners and comforts, and the temptations to which we are exposed from the celebrity that fashion often attaches to folly, and sometimes to vice. We have also seen the necessity of consideration; but consideration is of no avail, unless the mind is prepared by previous instruction,

struction, to render its own reflections valuable. If criminal desires, vain pursuits, and irritable passions, follow us to our closets, they will never become the school of wisdom.

The mistakes into which the most superior understanding is apt to fall, when hurried on by an overweening confidence in its own powers, must strike every observer of human nature. Genius, indeed, often absurdly affects singularity, and diminishes both its respectability and its happiness by a *settled* determination to differ from other people. The dangerous mistakes to which this self-dependance betrays those who are so unhappy as to cherish it, should make us rejoice that custom has *immemorially* considered humility of judgment to be requisite to women. The general docility of our understandings disposes us rather to receive dogmas,

dogmas, than to build systems; and the liveliness of our sensibilities rather fits us for the exercise of ardent devotion, than for the indulgence of chilling doubts and perplexing discussions. We pity the weakness of our sex, when we see a sister deviate into enthusiasm or superstition; but when she turns a declaiming deist or contentious sceptic, we look upon her as an unnatural monster or frightful prodigy.

From the time that pure religion emerged from the corruptions of papal imposition, to the middle of the last century, no one doubted that the best method of arming an inexperienced girl for the perilous conflict which she would be called to sustain against the world, the flesh, and the devil, would be by intrusting her with "the shield of faith," and teaching
"her

" her to wield the sword of the spirit, " even the word of God." Our ancestors knew that these were the weapons with which the Captain of our salvation defeated the prince of darkness, when he made that memorable and instructive assault upon him in the wilderness, and vainly hoped that ambition, presumption, or the infirmities incident to his assumed nature, might induce him to defeat the ends of his incarnation. Our ancestors, poor indeed in *philosophistical* illuminism, but rich in heavenly wisdom, did not suspect that by imprinting the Christian doctrines deeply on the minds of their daughters, they fettered them with prejudices; nor did they suppose that they would make better women, by being kept in profound ignorance of the gospel terms of salvation, till their understandings were
arrived

arrived at maturity, and enabled to meet their spiritual pastor with the bold objections of an expert caviller. They reverenced the book of God, they sincerely reverenced it; but they never thought that from motives of respect they ought to withhold it from childhood, much less from youth. They never suspected, that the awful simplicity of its narratives could *contaminate* the innocent ignorance of juvenile modesty; and though the sacred volume contained many abstruse doctrines, they ever found it easy to repress the inquiries of awakened intelligence when they verged on indecorous curiosity, by remarking that in time they would have clearer notions than what their tender age now permitted them to entertain, though the full developement of mystery was reserved for another state of existence.

The

The indefatigable assiduity of infidel philosophers has given popularity to other principles of instruction; and, under the pretence of avoiding superstitious prepossessions, the minds of young women are now often subjected to every impression that will prevent them from making revealed religion their future choice.; for, will a rational being ever submit to a code of laws of which it neither sees the utility nor the obligation? Assured that morality will make her good, that science will enrich her with wisdom, and that accomplishments create elegance, what is there in the precepts of the gospel, or in the lives of its professors, to induce her to make it a voluntary choice, especially when she is told that she is free to reject it, and to choose the laws by which she shall be judged.
Liberality

Liberality looks as well as charity; conscious merit has a more imposing air than humility; a Sunday rout seems more pleasant than family devotion; and if faith and holiness are not necessary passports to a better state of existence, the woman of the world is for the most part a more desirable companion than the pious Christian. If the task of religious instruction be not begun while learning is a duty, I know not at what period of life the mind will feel its own deficiencies, and set about acquiring what it perceives that it can do very well without. The seeds of science are sown in childhood, and left to ripen with our years; and yet we do not hear of *prejudiced* geographers, astronomers, or mathematicians. As the understanding unfolds, clearer views are obtained; the rudiments by which we gained our

first

first ideas are neglected, the easy but perhaps indirect terms by which we were enabled to conceive objects far removed from our observation are disused, and one comprehensive word conveys to us the meaning which we first learnt by a long sentence. The first principles of religion are not more difficult to be conveyed to the mind of a child, than the rules of grammar; and they who affirm that they have a tendency to cloud the understanding, and limit the bounds of ingenuous research, must urge their false tenets to hearers alike destitute of historical knowledge and personal observation.

But we will suppose a young woman, hitherto uninstructed in the precepts and doctrines of revelation, possessed of sufficient humility of mind to think all her literary and polite attainments insufficient. We will fancy her

her so ingenuously disposed, as not to start at several mysterious passages in the scripture, which bear hard upon the pride of reason, when it has been previously nurtured in the school of deism; and that she does not shrink from many positive injunctions inimical to the opinions and habits that she has long been accustomed to adopt. We will imagine, (contrary to the experience of all who have, in latter times, attempted to make *adult* converts among those who are totally destitute of religious knowledge) that she will find her new studies easy; and we will even grant that their difficulties will not be increased by the intended disciples having ever resided in a Christian country, against the creed of which (since she has not adopted it) she must certainly have conceived either contempt or dislike.

We

We must suppose, that her early instructors have been able to give some satisfactory reason (which we cannot divine) why this knowledge has been so long withheld, and also have convinced her that there is *now* an imperious necessity for her being acquainted with her title to eternity, though if she had died younger she need not have known it. We must believe her willing to renounce what appears like *safe* ignorance, and desirous to incur the *fearful* responsibility which arises from knowing her duty. After all these allowances, we must still ask how will she have time to become a Christian? A young woman of fashion has not an hour to spare, scarcely one disengaged moment, in which she can pursue reflection and strengthen conviction; and young women in humbler life are almost as fully occupied for they must improve their school-accomplishments, and make those ornaments in the morning which their evening engagements will call upon them to display. And yet, if they become Christians from conviction at this period of their lives, they must encounter the labours of a philosopher with the courage of a hero. They must be *argued* out of the deism in which they have been tutored, and *persuaded* to renounce the motives and habits which they have been taught to adopt. "It is one thing," says Dr. Waterland, "to understand the "doctrine, and quite another to be "master of the controversy." A girl with a common capacity, who has received an ordinary education on Christian principles, knows enough to entertain notions that are sufficiently clear to her own judgment, though she may not be able to answer every objection that may be urged against her belief; but adult converts must examine step by step the evidences on which our faith is built, and must be able to confute all gainsaying, before their new opinions can be said to be confirmed. And after they have done all this, they will still have their church to choose; and the pretensions of every denomination of Christians must be examined before they can properly determine. This is requiring more labours from every *private* member of our congregation, than our ecclesiastical constitutions impose upon those who are to be masters in our Israel. The longest life (allowing for those interruptions which our new instructors cannot pretend to exclude) would not be sufficient to complete these *converts of reason*, who are supposed to be

so

so much preferable to what are scornfully called *hereditary believers*. And when they are completed, what would they do to promote their own happiness, or that of others? The labour of acquiring the theory of duty, would occupy that season of life which ought to be devoted to the practice; there would be much scholastic discussion, and few Christian graces. Yet those who recommend this method of disciplining the world, are the loudest in declaiming against the effects that theological controversy has upon the heart and understanding. The dry disquisitions of schoolmen and divines (for these disputants are always coupled, though nothing can be more dissimilar) is the favourite topic of abuse and ridicule among those who seek to form a nation of controversialists, and to forbid even a woman from clinging to the mercies of her Saviour, unless she can refute all the gainsaying of infidels; nay, she must herself have been reclaimed from deism by the power of argument. I by no means insinuate, that such a conversion is impossible. I only maintain, that it will be attended with so many difficulties that it must be too rare to be depended upon as a certain consequence.

We might now appeal to statesmen and legislators, who know the political importance of religious restraints, whether it be safe to run such a risk of national infidelity. Our laws are founded on, or at least adapted to, our religion; our habits grow out of both; our well-being as a people is intimately bound and connected with the sincerity and universality of our Christian profession. I introduce this motive, because,

cause, though a free-thinker may renounce his God, his creed obliges him to call himself a patriot, and consequently he must affect to love his country. It is acknowledged too, that in his individual capacity no husband desires to have his wife destitute of principle, nor his daughters atheists; however convenient it may be to his passions, that other women should not be influenced by those restrictions.

We may safely lay it down as a position, that *religion must be taught in youth,* lest it should not be taught at all, or lest we should see the doughty disputant forget devotion, humility, and charity; the times also require that it should be *thoroughly* taught. Let the young Christian be well versed in the principles of her faith, and the ground on which it stands; she will often hear those principles ridiculed, and she will see that foundation sapped. You will not accuse me of contradicting my assertions concerning the bad effects of controversial studies; for it is very different, to *learn* doctrines while assisted by the simplicity, humility, and, docility of childhood; and to be *reasoned* into their verity, when you have long been under the influence of confirmed habits and pertinacious opinions. A much wider range of learning must be gone over in the latter case, than when our instructions are limited by the design of enabling our pupils to give " a reason " for the hope that is in them." We may understand the Copernican system of the heavens, without being able to refute Tycho Brahe's; and we may adopt Sir Isaac Newton's theory of gravitation, without knowing how to disprove the absurdity of Descartes's vortices.

vortices. Hereditary belief and blind acquiescence have been exposed to much censure; and yet I trust, in times when religious disputation was unknown, and in situations to which it has never penetrated, many a sincere and humble soul has found them passports to the kingdom of God; and I fear too many individuals have reason to lament their natural tendency to doubt and scrutiny in matters of faith. We, however, admit, that in a general point of view religion has been benefited by the violence of her assailants. Her evidences have been examined; her mysteries cleared of many adventitious incumbrances; the errors which had been surreptitiously introduced into her doctrines have been exploded; and her pure precepts have been more clearly enforced, and more beautifully developed.

We now live in times peculiarly dangerous to our faith; yet it seems as if the good providence of God had proportionably multiplied our protections. Hosts of learned, intelligent, and liberal divines, have rallied around the insulted cross of their blessed master. A woman in humble circumstances, with common abilities and moderate information, may now know more of the religion she professes, than any but the most studious could acquire three hundred years ago. As satanical zeal has increased in violence, so the pious champions of our faith have roused with fresh vigour to the combat. Pernicious doctrines have been multiplied and familiarised in every form; and the most eminent scholars of the age have also, by popular treatises, and even by addresses to the lowest vulgar, repelled their assail-

assailants. The subscribers to a market-town circulating library, when they choose their novel or their play, may truly say, " my bane and anti-" dote are both before me." This is certainly consolatory; but the assurance that our principles will be assaulted, either by books or conversation, renders it no longer safe for us to rest in that limited information which was once thought sufficient for our sex; and since we may become enlightened Christians, without such expense of time, and hazard of our peculiar character, as makes it unadvisable for us to be in general deep readers, it most strictly behoves us to profit by the judicious instructions which have been adapted to our capacity and leisure; not in order that we may become disputants, but to prevent our being " tossed about by every
" wind

"wind of doctrine," or seduced by the evil spirits who are sure to attempt our destruction.

The above observations, my dear Miss M——, lead us to conclude, that we must not rest in what our parents do for us; but that we should in our riper years build upon the foundation which they laid in childhood, in order that our religious knowledge may keep pace with our other improvements. I remarked in my last letter, that the work of education is as endless a labour, so far as relates to accomplishments, as the task of Sisyphus; for grown ladies and gentlemen learning to dance, sing, draw, or even walk, is now too frequent to excite ridicule. But it would be a serious misfortune, if, while the hoary head must bend and the stiffened joints relax, to acquire the graces, and to excel in the
amuse-

amusements of youth, the studies most proper for mature and declining life should be laid aside the moment the girl is emancipated from the sway of the governess. If, to encourage industry and gratify opulence, we permit the order of the seasons to be reversed, and suffer the fruits and flowers of summer to adorn winter, who in return gives his ices to the fervid hours of July, let the products of *reason* be still restrained to their *natural* periods. The aim of modern education is, to make children prematurely wise; but as the forced plant wastes its vigour by its early redundance; so the human mind seldom fulfils that promise of future excellence, which an extraordinary degree of early cultivation deceitfully cherishes; it generally stops at a certain point of improvement; and when we expected our assiduity to produce a genius, the labouring mountain brings forth a coxcomb *. This must be the consequence of a system, which stops too soon in essentials, and goes on too long in mere appendages; which supposes a girl of fifteen sufficiently taught in what relates to her *eternal* interests; and that a woman of fifty must receive lessons from a fashionable music master, that she may execute a new tune with all its scientifical flourishes.

Religious instruction, therefore, is of a twofold nature. It should be commenced early, not to instil prejudices, but to guard against prepossessions, and to impress the learner's mind with a proper conviction of the importance of the work. This instruction must be ever suited to the age and understanding of the pupil, both in matter and degree; but when the girl writes woman, let the mother deeply

---

* See Letter XIII.

impress upon her daughter's mind this solemn consideration, that as religion discloses to us another world, in which the employment of the blessed, during the circling years of eternity, will be to know and to adore God, if we would enjoy the promised heaven, we must in this life cultivate those habits. For the soul carries with it the propensities that it acquired below; and how shall we become meet for the society of angels, if we neither understand nor delight in their occupations?

The scientifical turn which education has lately taken, increases the necessity for early impressing on the juvenile mind a sense of the divine authority of scripture, and of the insufficiency of human reason to discover the origin and end of man. Women are seldom very deeply versed in any branch of philosophy; and a smattering of

science

science is extremely apt to produce that dependence upon second causes, which is one of the strong holds of deism in weak minds. A half-informed young woman, when she has found out the *immediate* reason of vegetation, congelation, or any elementary process, is too apt to think that she has discovered *all*, without extending her views to the great God who at first endowed matter with those wonderful properties which it has possessed for many thousand years, and without whose continual influence every movement in the stupendous machine of nature would become confused and disordered. The danger of the young student's views being thus limited, is increased by the prevalent use of terms, adopted, perhaps, from a persuasion that they are comprehensive, but which an eminent scholar and

and divine* proves to be unphilosophical; such as "the power of attrac-
" tion, the law of vegetation, the order
" of the seasons," and the like. "In-
" ert matter," he observes, "has no
" power; a law pre-supposes a law-
" giver; and a propelling impetus
" must originate in something foreign
" to the thing thus over-ruled." Were
we sure that these studies would be
extended till the mind obtained that
link in the chain of science, which
proves the necessary dependance of
material nature on intellectual existence, we should be certain of gaining
a sincere, though a late convert to revealed truth; but when we consider
how soon the progress of learning will
be arrested by the frivolous pursuits
or business of life, let us at least take
care to run no hazard of unfitting the

* Dr. Paley. See Natural Theology. Dr. Hey makes the same remark.

" manner of ceremonies, but also in
" matters of faith *."

It cannot be denied, that even in the age of the apostles, and especially from the period when Christianity received the sanction of the civil power, heresies, schisms, and furious disputes, have disturbed the peace of the Christian world. Part of these troubles must doubtless be ascribed to the unremitting zeal with which the archapostate (figuratively styled the dragon) opposes the mystical spouse of God. She is sometimes driven into the wilderness, harassed by persecution, and denied repose. At other times, she is attempted to be lulled by a fatal security into that lukewarmness and indifference, which is still more dangerous to her well-being. Her afflictions are often from without, but yet

* Article 19th.

more

rable books for the education of youth which have deluged the nation. In this design of fitting the rising hope of Britain for a Pandæmonium of philosophists, no branch of information has been suffered to escape untainted. If the young lady read history, she will find it questioned whether the propagation of the gospel really was accomplished by miracles or by human ingenuity; whether the early Christians were martyrs or fanatics; and whether much good has resulted from the extension of the religion of Jesus? In biographical sketches, she will find piety, or at least attachment to any peculiar mode of worship, coupled with a weak understanding, or a contracted heart; while heathen persecutors, deists, and libertines, are adorned with the freshest flowers of eulogy. If she read geography, or travels, she will
perceive

lieves the Creator of the world to be a God of order and unity, would blush to assert, that physical and moral confusion and discord, were parts of his design. The Christian, who traces the attributes of the author of nature through the course of two successive revelations, must be absurdly impious, if he seriously affirm, that God "made " men to differ on such an important " point as religious belief, on which " he enjoined unity by precept, and " enforced it by miracle."

" It must needs be that offences " will come," said the Saviour of the world. It is necessary to the constitution of a probationary state, that there should be trials to afflict and punish vice, and to purify and exercise virtue. " But," he continues, " woe to that man by whom such " offence cometh." It was determined

perties, can produce; and she will be reminded, that when natural preparations can assume appearances seemingly miraculous, we should scruple to call in an invisible agent. Some instances will be given of successful cheats; and it will then be asked, with much apparent modesty, if the flowering rod of Aaron might not have been a slight-of-hand illusion, and the cures of Christ have proceeded from a degree of medicinal knowledge unknown in a barbarous country? Astronomy also supplies a very powerful engine for shaking the faith of those who expected scripture to develope the secrets of nature, instead of the mysteries of grace; and think that the inspired narrator of the creation should have prematurely disclosed the laws of planetary motion, to gratify the curious; though his mission was intended to preserve,

preserve, in one nation, a sense of their obligation to worship the " Lord " God, who fashioned the earth and " all things that are therein," who made the heavens and all their host, who sanctified the closing day of creation, and who suspended the punishment of disobedient man, and again set life and death before him.

When a young woman has been duly informed that scripture narration is designed to illustrate moral and theological truths, she will not reject it because its language is accommodated to the prevailing ideas of the times in which it was written. She well knows that " the pillars of the round world," must be metaphorically understood, and that the rotation of the sun round the earth is a condescension to popular opinion. She will confess that the existence of deceit is no argument against

the

assumes over weak, ill-regulated, or ill-informed minds, we hope that folly may excuse the faults of many; let us ourselves beware of leaving the true fold, to hearken to irregular or unskilful shepherds. Of their inward illuminations, assurances, and experiences, we can form no notion, and may only hope that they seem so far convincing to their bewildered minds, as to excuse them on the score of sincere ignorance; but their actions prove them to be amenable to the church of God, whose peace they disturb by verbose declamations, and contumacious disputes, concerning matters, either in themselves unimportant, or appertaining to those councils of God into which we dare not pretend to penetrate. It is considered as a fundamental principle in politics, that it is better to endure a small evil, than to attempt to remove it with the hazard of inter-are resolutely bent to mis-state and mislead. Their futile spleen will only serve to confirm her faith; for she must recollect her Lord's prediction, "that the world would say all manner "of evil, *falsely*, of his disciples, for "his name's sake."

After this certainly *faint* specimen of the liberal care with which our pretended perfectionists guard the ductile mind of youth from *prejudices* and *misconception*, will they have the effrontery to complain of unfair prepossession, if we endeavour to pre-occupy the vacant soil? Had these or similar objections to the verity of Scripture any weight, had they never been refuted, or, like the dispossessed demoniacs, been even forced to bear testimony to the God whom they resisted, we might for a moment hesitate. But every objection which deists now raise
against

against the gospel has been refuted numberless times. Our modern unbelievers must feel the pangs of wounded pride, at knowing that they can only throw the broken lances of vanquished cavillers against the invulnerable bulwark of religion. These pigmy opponents have so often been foiled in the field of controversy, that nothing is left them but to lurk in bye-paths, with the cowardly hope of ensnaring silly women and kidnapping unsuspecting children, under the common pretence of extraordinary kindness. We have historical testimony, that the nefarious Illuminati gave it in charge to their propagandists, to use every possible method to make *female converts*; well knowing that, though our dispositions and propensities did not so strongly stimulate us to throw off moral restrictions as the

other

other sex, our minds were less enabled by nature and education to resist these sophists, who never could endure the Ithuriel spear of learning and deep investigation.

Religious knowledge will enable us to avoid this snare; and from my zeal to recommend this defensive armour to the youth of both sexes, I have been accused of enforcing theological erudition at the expense of religious practice. I can only say, that such was not my design; the most guarded language, however, cannot prevent *intentional* misconstruction. Many of our first divines, in the arguments which they oppose to the opinions of certain schismatics, affirm, that though our Lord improved morality to its highest possible perfection, by removing it from external behaviour to the heart, his design, in coming into the world,

world, was *not* to teach a pure system of morality, though this system is one of the consequences appertaining to his mission. They extend this observation to the Mosaical law, which they affirm was built upon, or rather took for granted, those notices of right and wrong, of the immortality of the soul, and the being of a God, which are often called natural religion; but which ought to be referred to the traditionary remains of that first revelation which God made to Adam in Paradise. When morality is taught upon merely worldly motives, however refined and exalted by light derived from the gospel dispensation, it is confined to exterior deportment; let us superadd the inducements which Christianity presents, and it then becomes that perfection of virtue to which we are all commanded to aspire;

being assured, that though it is unattainable as a whole, yet if pursued with singleness of heart, and with a sincere desire of progressive improvement, the weakness of our nature will be pardoned by a God who knows our infirmities, in consideration of the all-sufficient merit of a sacrifice ordained by himself, to prove his abhorrence of sin, and his mercy to repentant offenders.

The foundation on which Christianity is built, and its superiority to mere moral obligations, should be understood by every Christian; but to separate faith from morals is the work of an enemy. It is only "through "faith, working by love," that we are made meet for the inheritance of the saints in light. The degree of our respective duties, of knowing and acting, depends upon our opportunity of exerting

exerting either faculty. Those whose limited understandings, or humble stations, prevent them from acquiring much information, may be truly sincere in the practice of Christian virtue; but where abilities are granted, and leisure allowed, a more ample stock of Christian knowledge is indispensable; and for this reason, because such persons are more exposed to those temptations from which it is the best human preservative. The readers whom I particularly address require this salutary aid. General opinion (except in those points wherein it is partially misled by fashion) prescribes those outward decorums of conduct which are necessary to pass well in the world; but those who are thus circumstanced require to be taught, that unless they found this decorum on inward purity of heart, and a desire

rupting the public peace; the church militant is a society of human beings, and, as such, fallible; she must, therefore, be governed by coercive laws, similar to those which regulate other communities; and, provided her errors do not affect important points of faith, which might justify her members in renouncing their allegiance, she may claim their obedience in things indifferent, even on the sole ground of her own authority, without positive warranty of scripture. If scruples of conscience are really felt, on account of some of her institutions, a candid discovery of them to some judicious and religious friend, (let us say, to the parochial minister,) might enlighten the dubious judgment, and confirm the wavering mind. If after these measures are taken, apprehensions still remain, we must hope that in such a case, dissent is not sinful.

dium between gross ignorance and inquisitive research, and should be as much proportioned to the capacity and station of the student, as liberality should be adapted to the fortune of the giver. A thirst for what is called religious edification has transformed many an industrious simple mechanic into a vagabond fanatic, empty of every valuable quality suited to his rank and education, but swollen by conceit and spiritual pride into a false belief of supernatural endowments. A desire to penetrate into inscrutable mysteries has overset many a weak understanding, and perverted many an excellent housewife into the useless character of an enthusiastical devotee. These misfortunes, however, generally proceed from the *quality*, not the *quantity* of knowledge which is imbibed. Here, as in the groves of Paradise,

Paradise, the tree produces both good and evil; and it unfortunately happens, that what is most suitable to our palates is often most pernicious to our constitutions. By some unaccountable propensity, weak minds are always most anxious to dive into unfathomable depths; their very incapacity to acquire what others know, stimulates their eagerness to discover what cannot be known.

As right principles are the best human means of procuring right conduct, I would earnestly solicit the young student to consult such guides *, as
will

---

* Could the recommendation of an obscure partially-informed woman add celebrity to the names of Gilbert West, Sherlock, Paley, Hey, and Bryant, she would mention these authors as instances of that close investigation, and full view of the subjects on which they treat, which conveys perspicuous

will assist her in founding her faith, rather on the convictions of her understanding, than on the impulses of fancy, or the warmth of devotional feeling; though this last will be superadded, in proportion as the certainty of faith increases, and as habit confirms piety. I would peculiarly recommend to my own sex such writers as aim at communicating *clear* ideas. When our understanding is thoroughly informed by these, we may with more safety consult florid and rhetorical authors, if our relish for their manner have not been aba-

---

ous information to the mind of the reader. The name of Dr. Rogers may be added to the list, not only on account of his sermons, but of his valuable tract on the visible and invisible church of Christ; in which he enforces a duty now too much disregarded, I mean submission to our ecclesiastical superiors, in a clear and convincing manner.

ted

ted by a more improving course of study. We are charged with being " of imagination all compact ;" and one reason that is suggested against the expediency of our becoming deep theological readers, is our natural turn to enthusiasm. As the enthusiast is generally unhappy in herself, and certainly very unamiable to others, the utmost care should be taken to avoid this dangerous substitute for true piety; by not suffering *fancy* to interfere in so momentous a point, as that of *examining our title to salvation*. That modesty of knowledge, which is alike anxious to avoid being ignorant of what it ought to know, and of penetrating into " those secret things " which belong to the Most High," should be especially recommended to women. This would be our best preservative against the fallacious representations

sentations of a party, who now dreadfully disturb the peace of the church, and (I hope *undesignedly*) assault the foundation of the edifice which they affect to reverence. By recommending clear distinct ideas to the young members of our establishment, I also wish to discredit the assertions of another set of enemies to our Sion, who represent our creeds as formed on confused notions, and blind credulity; and our hierarchy, as one of the impositions which priest-craft and spiritual ambition forced upon the servile mind of half-awakened ignorance.

It is evident, however, that while we are encompassed by this wall of flesh, our perception of spiritual objects must be faint and indistinct. Of the personality and ubiquity of the Deity, for instance, the most learned men confess that no distinct notion can be formed. One of the reasons given by our philosophistical perfectionists, why children should not know that there is a God, proceeds from the impossibility of their forming just notions of Him. This overstrained respect is affected; for the most exalted human intellect labours under the same defect. May we not inquire, in what respect the doctrine of the unity of the triune Godhead is less conceivable by the capacity of his finite creatures, than that God exists through all time and space?

"Thus far shalt thou go and no far- "ther, and here shall thy proud waves "be stayed," said the creative word, when the foaming ocean first poured into its prepared abyss. The limits of human knowledge, though various as our understandings, have a similar curb affixed, beyond which they cannot pass. The first business, therefore, of tuition is, to draw this boundary line, and to inform the pupil what learning and attention can do, and what it must leave undone; how far reason may develope mystery, and where she must bow her head, and confess her human fallibility. When an ambassador assures us that he comes from heaven, we may call upon reason to inquire into the nature of his message, and the validity of his credentials. When he preaches " righteousness, "temperance, and judgment to come," she must confess that he speaks the language of his native country; and when he appeals to miracle and prophecy, she allows that, according to her own pre-conceived ideas, the sovereign who employs him would thus accredit his messenger. He may, indeed, discover something of the *internal* affairs of those regions different from what reason imagined was the case; and he may propose such *terms*

of peace as she did not expect; or enjoin such *confirmatory* ceremonies as she did not conceive to be absolutely necessary. If the ambassador only came from an unknown country, he might justly answer the inquiries of reason, by saying, " Such are the cus-
" toms of the nation to which I be-
" long. With us, they are of great
" utility; though, as they are found-
" ed on usages materially different
" from yours, I cannot fully explain
" them to you." But if he be also the agent of our lawful king, against whom we have rebelled, and with whom we seek reconciliation, unless reason exceed her trust she can only ascertain the absolute verity of the envoy, and advise us to accept the offered mercy on the terms proposed. These may seem to us not so honourable to the nature of our prince, as some that we could have suggested;

but as we have never seen him, and do not know the precise rules of his internal government, our own presumption, in judging when we have not sufficient ground to form an opinion, deserves the severest censure. All that we know of him indeed, either by his visible acts, or by the discoveries made by his ambassador, bespeaks him holy, wise, just, and merciful; but as we cannot discover how these attributes blend with each other, so that none should preponderate, we are incapacitated from prescribing bounds to any of them. It cannot be said, that this ambassador may have misrepresented his master; for he has silenced this objection, by shewing what we all know to be the royal signet; a visible unequivocal interruption of the course of nature; which is, unquestionably, the method by which God would speak to man.

Reason, if faithful to her office, will also acknowledge, that a direct revelation is such a solemn interposition of Heaven, as cannot be lightly and casually afforded. It must not only be absolutely necessary to those to whom it is made; but it must discover truths which could not otherwise be known *. Had the law and the gospel

---

* The necessity of a divine revelation may be gathered from what the celebrated deistical writer, Lord Herbert of Cherbury, says of what he calls five short notices imprinted by God on the minds of all men 1st, That there is one supreme God. 2dly, That he is chiefly to be worshipped. 3dly, That piety and virtue are the principal parts of his worship. 4thly, That we must repent of our sins; and if we do, God will pardon them 5thly, That there are rewards for good, and punishments for bad men, in a future state.—Our divines, in answer to these allegations against the necessity of revelation, justly observe, that we must not judge of natural religion, or deism, from what we *now* know, since even those who reject Christianity partake of the light that it has diffused; but from what the world was previous to the coming of

-pel taught us nothing but what human reason could have discovered, we must then have allowed that sceptics are right in affirming that belief in revelation supposes a needless interposition of the Almighty. Every mysterious doctrine that scripture con-

Christ. They propose the learned age of Augustus as a fair specimen. The first and second notices were then disregarded; for no nation, but the Jews, acknowledged or worshipped one supreme God. The most enlightened men of that period sacrificed to sensual and numerous deities. Nor would the third be more regarded; for the mode of propitiating false gods was by absurd and brutish rites. In respect to the fourth notice, the heathens reproached the Christians for declaring that God would pardon sinners; and as to the 5th, it was hoped by some sects of philosophers, denied by others, and doubted by all. See Hey's Lectures, vol. i. p. 342.

The mere belief of the immortality of the soul, is very different from a persuasion that this future state will be retributive. Modern heathens proceed no further than, in the words of Pope, to expect " an equal heaven, in which their faithful dog will bear them company."

"because of the house of the Lord our
" God, we shall seek to do her good."

The church of England is that branch of the universal church, under whose shadow we are invited to take shelter. However lightly it may be esteemed by various fanatics who have sprouted forth under its mild protection, it is esteemed, by foreign protestants, as the pre-eminent sanctuary of the reformed religion. I will refer you to the decision of an eminent divine, who was highly celebrated all over the Continent for his learning and moderation, and was himself a member of the Presbyterian ministry. The name of Le Clerc sanctions his opinions with theological readers. Speaking of episcopacy, he observes, "I
" have always professed to believe,
" that episcopacy is of *apostolical* in-
" stitution, and consequently very
" good

certain, that the promises of supernatural assistance, which Christ made to his followers, were given to that collective body, or (to refer to our ecclesiastical declaration of faith) to " that congregation of faithful men, " where the pure word of God is " preached, and the sacraments duly " administered *," which we call a church. By thus consecrating community to the purpose of sanctity, the author of our religion has not departed from the method which he follows in the ordinary providential government of the world; where we see good of various kinds, comfort, security, strength, pleasure, wealth, and prosperity, all flowing from men combining together; and misery, weakness, and poverty, ensuing from their acting separately or in opposition to

* Article 19th.

each other. That it was the design of our blessed Lord, that all his followers should be knit together in the closest bond of concord and amity, cannot be doubted by any who carefully examine the sacred records of his life and conversation. I will point out one instance, the solemn commendatory prayer preserved in the seventeenth chapter of St. John's gospel, which is particularly in point. Remember, Christ offered it not only for his immediate apostles, but "for "all who should, through their "preaching, believe in him in all the "world;" and that it was an act immediately preceding his bitter passion. How urgent is the motive, how impressive are the requests that are contained in these awful words, "That "they also may be one, even as thou, "Father, art in me, and I in thee;
"that

"that they also may be one in us, that the world may believe that thou hast sent me." Are they indeed sincere, who attempt to diffuse the light of the gospel among heathen nations, and connect their missionary zeal with restless solicitude to increase the schisms and dissentions, which our Lord deprecates, as preventives of the universal reception of his faith? I fear, my dear Miss M——, the world will never know that *Jesus was sent by God*, while regard for truth is sacrificed to a blind zeal for mastery, and the very name of *evangelical* is assumed as a mark of distinctive pre-eminence, and a taunting proverb of reproach.

The texts of scripture that enjoin this duty of unity and Christian communion, are so numerous in the gospels, the acts, the epistles, and even in the

the revelations, that it is difficult to imagine how this vast body of evidence can be evaded, or rather braved. The primitive church acted upon this principle; and, with equal firmness, dealt her ecclesiastical censures on all who disturbed the peace of the community with new and strange doctrines, or disgraced it by their scandalous lives. Different formularies were indeed adopted in national, and even in provincial churches; but "one "Lord, one faith, and one baptism," were universally preserved. Among the numerous dispersed and persecuted members of our holy religion, the leading principles of all churches were the same; the members of all joined in communion. The obligation to this unity and fellowship appeared so strong to the founders of the Reformation, that it was with the utmost reluc-

reluctance, and in consequence not only of the scandalous corruptions, but the invincible obstinacy of the church of Rome, that they at length ventured to apply to themselves the angelic summons recorded in the apocalypse, and esteemed it to be their duty to " come out of the corrupted " Babylon." Many wise and temperate men have *lamented* while they *acknowledged* the necessity for this secession, which doubtless opened the door to numerous dissenters, who have pleaded for a license and freedom of choosing to which that precedent gives no countenance. The hazardous expedient of separation should never be resorted to, unless the seceders can prove, that the church, from which they disjoin themselves, has, like that of " Rome, " erred not only in their living and
" manner

"manner of ceremonies, but also in matters of faith *."

It cannot be denied, that even in the age of the apostles, and especially from the period when Christianity received the sanction of the civil power, heresies, schisms, and furious disputes, have disturbed the peace of the Christian world. Part of these troubles must doubtless be ascribed to the unremitting zeal with which the arch-apostate (figuratively styled the dragon) opposes the mystical spouse of God. She is sometimes driven into the wilderness, harassed by persecution, and denied repose. At other times, she is attempted to be lulled by a fatal security into that lukewarmness and indifference, which is still more dangerous to her well-being. Her afflictions are often from without, but yet

* Article 19th.

more frequently from false brethren. That the Almighty *suffers* these trials of his people as a community, on the same principles as he *permits* individual correction, was ever acknowledged; but to affirm, that he *made men to differ* in religious matters, is quite a modern discovery. He suffers evil, but he cannot be said to be the original author of it. He permits calamity; this world could not else be a probationary state; nor could virtue be perfected without suffering. Patience is prescribed as the softener of pain; pain is necessary to prepare us to resign this too much valued life; but will any one thence assert that the Almighty made his creatures on purpose to suffer*? The deist, who be-

---

* See Natural Theology, on the Goodness of the Deity.

lieves the Creator of the world to be a God of order and unity, would blush to assert, that physical and moral confusion and discord, were parts of his design. The Christian, who traces the attributes of the author of nature through the course of two successive revelations, must be absurdly impious, if he seriously affirm, that God "made " men to differ on such an important " point as religious belief, on which " he enjoined unity by precept, and " enforced it by miracle."

" It must needs be that offences " will come," said the Saviour of the world. It is necessary to the constitution of a probationary state, that there should be trials to afflict and punish vice, and to purify and exercise virtue. " But," he continues, " woe to that man by whom such " offence cometh." It was determined

mined by the foreknowledge and wisdom of God, before the foundation of the world, that, in the fulness of time, Christ should be offered up as a sacrifice for the sins of the world; but woe to the treacherous, avaricious Judas, who betrayed his meek and holy master! All ages and nations of the Christian world have joined in execrating the perfidious disciple, who was the immediate means of binding his Lord upon the cross, at the same time that they have clung to the benefits of the atonement. Woe also to him who, through the pride of reason, spiritual self-sufficiency, contempt of subordination, or ambition of pre-eminence, unnecessarily dissents from the church of Christ, or attempts to shake the faith of others, and to alienate their obedience! His vanity may, indeed, be gratified by the applauses of those who adopt his tenets; but what recompence

vidence of God, who at that time enlightened our Sion with luminaries of surprising splendour, the founders of our church, as well at its first establishment under King Edward the VIth, as at its re-edification under Queen Elizabeth, were guided by the most admirable moderation. Nothing was rejected merely because it was the usage of popery, unless it was also tainted with the errors of that ambitious hierarchy. Nothing new was adopted, unless the utter unfitness of former customs rendered the introduction of novelty unavoidable. Hence we retain not only the constitution of the primitive church, but also many of its usages. Nay more, our liturgy was *compiled*, rather than composed; with a respectful reference to venerable rituals, their doxologies and creeds were adopted; several prayers of our service were entirely translated from

assumes over weak, ill-regulated, or ill-informed minds, we hope that folly may excuse the faults of many; let us ourselves beware of leaving the true fold, to hearken to irregular or unskilful shepherds. Of their inward illuminations, assurances, and experiences, we can form no notion, and may only hope that they seem so far convincing to their bewildered minds, as to excuse them on the score of sincere ignorance; but their actions prove them to be amenable to the church of God, whose peace they disturb by verbose declamations, and contumacious disputes, concerning matters, either in themselves unimportant, or appertaining to those councils of God into which we dare not pretend to penetrate. It is considered as a fundamental principle in politics, that it is better to endure a small evil, than to attempt to remove it with the hazard of interrupting the public peace; the church militant is a society of human beings, and, as such, fallible; she must, therefore, be governed by coercive laws, similar to those which regulate other communities; and, provided her errors do not affect important points of faith, which might justify her members in renouncing their allegiance, she may claim their obedience in things indifferent, even on the sole ground of her own authority, without positive warranty of scripture. If scruples of conscience are really felt, on account of some of her institutions, a candid discovery of them to some judicious and religious friend, (let us say, to the parochial minister,) might enlighten the dubious judgment, and confirm the wavering mind. If after these measures are taken, apprehensions still remain, we must hope that in such a case, dissent is not sinful.

But let it be remembered, that an ingenuous and sincere mind is more apt to veil its disagreement in modest silence, and to *lament* it as a misfortune, than, by *blazoning* its non-conformity to the world, to communicate its scruples to others, and thus to make a merit of disobedience. When converts to any new opinions accompany this change by marks of hostility to the party which they have deserted, somewhat very different from gospel sincerity, it is to be feared, lurks in their ostensibly regenerated hearts.

You will ask me, if I have not acknowledged, that good has resulted to the church from these internal struggles? Most unquestionably, the assailing weapons of false brethren have, like the censers of Korah and his rebellious partisans, been converted into "broad " plates for a covering for the altar."

But though thus appropriated by that Providence who brings good out of evil, they were still "the censers of "sinners against their own souls*." That the defence and security of the church should grow out of the means that were concerted for her destruction, is analogous to the sensible operations of nature. Those violent gusts of wind, which wreck our stately vessels, and cover the earth with the ruins of her proudest structures, or fairest products, are deemed salubrious to the health of its inhabitants, by scattering the seeds of pestilence, and restoring the vital purity of the atmosphere; yet, notwithstanding this happy effect, the tempest is still a sore calamity. Why natural evil should subsist, has perplexed the minds of many philosophers; and perhaps the

* See Numbers, 16th chap. verse 38.

best

best answer that has been given is, that the scale of being is so extended, and its ramifications (especially if we extend our views to other worlds, and other orders of rational and dependant beings) are so complicated, that a great general advantage necessarily involves a particular calamity*; which calamity, in a probationary state of existence, is no impeachment of the justice of God. How moral evil came into this world, we learn from Holy Scripture; and when the Almighty makes good to issue from it, he gives, I may say, a visible proof, not only that he is "Lord of the Evil "One," but that he does not "wil- "lingly afflict the children of men." The advantage, therefore, which has resulted to the church, from being thus continually forced to defend and

* This is the opinion of Dr. Paley.

examine her doctrines, cannot be urged in proof that God made men to differ in religion; or that it is his pleasure there should be a diversity of worship among Christians. He enjoins concord and unity. That he suffers men to disobey this command, is no more a proof that it did not proceed from him, than that the existence of murder, adultery, and theft, *rescind* the obligation, and *disannul* the authority of the commandments.

When I speak of the church in general, I keep our nineteenth article in my eye. This church, we are informed, is scattered over all the Christian world; various modes of worship, and particular tenets, belong to its disjointed parts; yet I trust, in spite of the efforts of ill-disposed men, some bond of union, some token of intercommunity, still subsists between its members;

members; sufficient to allow us to speak of it as a whole, though certainly not as that closely-cemented, well-compacted building which its blessed Founder and his apostles laboured to form; and in point of purity, as well as doctrine, very different from that glorious church, which (in the language of eastern metaphor) is denominated the spouse of the Lamb, and is to be presented to her Lord without spot or wrinkle, holy, undefiled, and glorious in majesty and beauty; while myriads of myriads join in singing one spousal song. Such is the promised state of the triumphal church: if we would partake of it, we must adhere to her during her militant probation; and, in the spirit of the royal psalmist, "we shall be solicitous to heal her breaches;" we shall rejoice in her prosperity; and "because

"because of the house of the Lord our God, we shall seek to do her good."

The church of England is that branch of the universal church, under whose shadow we are invited to take shelter. However lightly it may be esteemed by various fanatics who have sprouted forth under its mild protection, it is esteemed, by foreign protestants, as the pre-eminent sanctuary of the reformed religion. I will refer you to the decision of an eminent divine, who was highly celebrated all over the Continent for his learning and moderation, and was himself a member of the Presbyterian ministry. The name of Le Clerc sanctions his opinions with theological readers. Speaking of episcopacy, he observes, "I "have always professed to believe, "that episcopacy is of *apostolical* institution, and consequently very "good

"good and very lawful; that man
"has no right to change it in any
"place, unless it was impossible other-
"wise to reform the abuses that crept
"into Christianity; that it was justly
"preserved in England, where the
"reformation was practicable without
"altering it; and that therefore the
"protestants in England, and other
"places where there are bishops, do
"*very wrong* to separate from that
"discipline; that they would do still
"worse in attempting to destroy it,
"in order to set up presbytery, fana-
"ticism, and anarchy. Things ought
"not to be turned into a chaos, nor
"people seen every where without a
"call, and without learning, pretend-
"ing to inspiration. Nothing is more
"proper to prevent them than the
"episcopal discipline, as by law esta-
"blished in England; especially when
"those who preside in church govern-
"ment

"ment are persons of penetration, sobriety, and discretion." He afterwards acknowledges that it has been so clearly proved, that the truth of it cannot be denied, that Christ and his apostles instituted the episcopal form of government; and that the church never had any other for one thousand five hundred years, from our Saviour's days downward *.

The testimony of an adversary has great weight. From motives of political expediency, Mr. Le Clerc exercised the functions of a minister in a society of Christians who had rejected the episcopal form which he so highly commends.

Notwithstanding the grateful obligations which we owe to the fathers of the Reformation, we cannot deny that they partook of the passions and infirmities of human nature. The

* Biblioth. tom. ix, page 159.

cruel and perfidious treatment which they had experienced from the Romish church stimulated the protestants to an unwarrantable degree of fury, hatred, and revenge. The aim of many of these seems to have been, to make the separation and distinction between themselves and the apocalyptical Babylon as marked as possible. Thus, instead of taking the scriptures for their guide, and the primitive churches for their model, it was sufficient for them to reject many ancient and beneficial customs, merely because they had been adopted by their opponents, whose touch was esteemed to be contamination. Protestantism was not without severe provocations in England, as the reigns of Henry the VIIIth and Mary the Ist amply testify; but whether it was owing to the more enlightened sobriety of the nation, or, as I believe, to the good providence of God, who at that time enlightened our Sion with luminaries of surprising splendour, the founders of our church, as well at its first establishment under King Edward the VIth, as at its re-edification under Queen Elizabeth, were guided by the most admirable moderation. Nothing was rejected merely because it was the usage of popery, unless it was also tainted with the errors of that ambitious hierarchy. Nothing new was adopted, unless the utter unfitness of former customs rendered the introduction of novelty unavoidable. Hence we retain not only the constitution of the primitive church, but also many of its usages. Nay more, our liturgy was *compiled*, rather than composed; with a respectful reference to venerable rituals, their doxologies and creeds were adopted; several prayers of our service were entirely translated from the formularies of early times, or from the writings of the fathers; and in others the sense has been condensed, and suited to our customs, modes of thinking, and the alteration of manners and situation.

Nor is it merely on account of her constitution, and liturgical service, that the church of England claims such high consideration; the same wise moderation which determined her to preserve what was valuable and important in these points, kept her also in a happy medium between those opposite errors which at that time distracted the peace of the world, and which, I grieve to say, still subsist. Perhaps our best way of gaining a clear notion of the doctrines of our national church will be, to examine the notions of those who dissent from her; and though the antipodes are

not

did not subscribe to the still more reprehensible parts of a system that has caused such a long, and, it is to be feared, incurable schism among the reformed churches. But these evangelical teachers affirm that she did; and it is these very doctrines, which in their opinion constitute that purity of the gospel, and those original principles of our church, which they are anxious to restore.

To repel this charge, not only from our present hierarchy, but from its venerable founders, many learned divines have stood forward, and manfully encountered a torrent of, not only professional but personal obloquy. In this contest, the names of Kipling, Daubeny, and Pearson, are especially celebrated. The first gentleman, in a small but irresistible pamphlet, plainly shows, by extracts from Calvin's works,

that her existence is the firmest bulwark against the ambition of either party? Unless they are mutually insincere in their own religious professions, it is evident that they believe they would mutually prove but weak opponents to each other, supposing this formidable rival could be overthrown. This is a strong argument, to persuade every lover of temperate opinions to support what is such an object of terror to those of violent and extreme notions.

But before we proceed to the proposed investigation, I will mention one other claim which the national church has to our obedience. It is the established form of worship. I do not propose to found spiritual belief on political expediency; but I assert, that the religion of our country has a prior right to our attention, so far as to to induce us to give it a serious investigation; and if her doctrines are found to be evangelical, and her usages, as far as change of manners will allow, apostolical; if in that human mixture which must always be admitted into ecclesiastical institutions, there be nothing contrary to scripture; if she affect no wanton exercise of authority, and assume no high pretensions to infallibility, nor absolute control over the consciences of men; it seems as if no reason can be urged for renouncing her communion, except it be the strong predilection which arises from our having been educated in some other religious society. Had we only non-conformists of this latter description to lament, the aspect of the present times would not be so alarming to the friends of our venerable establishment, because such opponents are

the

the most moderate, steady, and respectable; but the dreadful opinions that arise out of the abuse of religious toleration, namely, that in this land of liberty every one has a right to choose his religion, gains ground; and the pride of exercising a supposed privilege, joined to the desire of being distinguished by superior intelligence and discrimination, and, I fear I must add, the arts and allurements of the enemies of all religion, seduce many unstable minds, especially in the lower ranks of life, who renounce the communion of the church from which they have received baptism, with the same inconsideration and indifference as they assimilate their garments to the prevailing fashion*.

As

---

* That schism is not considered as a light and trivial offence by the regular ministers of the presbyterian form of worship, may be perceived in the following

As women are most disposed to think seriously, and to be sincere in their

following extract from the works of an eminent Scotch divine, who indeed does but echo the sentiments of all well-constituted churches antient and modern, not excepting those founded by Calvin, or his *immediate* disciples. Dr. Hill, in his Theological Institutes, observes, " The name of
" schism, therefore, is reserved for separation pro-
" ceeding upon some frivolous reason, which is
" often merely a pretext for gratifying the pas-
" sions of ambition, avarice, resentment, and envy.
" When attachments to particular teachers form
" Christians into parties, they fall under the cen-
" sure which Paul addressed to the Corinthians,
—" I hear that there are contentions and schisms
" among you. Every one of you saith, ' I am of
" Paul, I of Apollos, and I of Cephas, and I of
" Christ.' Is Christ divided?" When the separa-
" tion proceeds from the idea of forming a more
" perfect establishment, it is seldom duly consi-
" dered that no human institution con be faultless,
" and that the evils which necessarily arise from
" schism far counterbalance any advantages which
" may be expected from improvements not essen-
" tial to the constitution of the church. When
" Christians separate, because the discipline of the
" church

their religious professions, hence arises the necessity of their not only being well

" church does not appear to them sufficiently
" strict, they act as if the comfort and benefits
" derived from the ordinances of religion depend-
" ed upon the character of those who partake with
" us; or as if the purity which the anabaptists
" require in the church of Christ could be attain-
" ed on this side the grave. And when their only
" complaint is with some regulations of the
" church concerning matters acknowledged to be
" in themselves indifferent, they forget that it is
" impossible to frame any regulations of such mat-
" ters which will meet the prejudices and opinions
" of all; that obedience to competent authority
" enjoining what is not unlawful for the sake of
" order does not imply a sacrifice of Christian li-
" berty; and that the new congregation cannot
" exist, and attain the purposes of its institution,
" without some exercise of the same authority.

" Whatever be the nature of the frivolous or
" corrupt motives which give to separation the
" character of schism, the conduct of all who at-
" tain the name of schismatics is blameworthy. It
" does not correspond to the description of the
" catholic church, which is said in scripture to
" be ' one body, in which there ought to be no
" schism;'

"*life**, they cannot fail of being finally
"saved, being under an immutable
"decree, and guarded by Omnipo-
"tence. The reprobates, how much
"*soever they may exert themselves for
"the purpose**, cannot attain ever-
"lasting salvation, being *hindered*
"therefrom, and repelled by Almighty
"God. As the final salvation of the
"elect is in no degree doubtful, from
"their first entrance into this world
"to their departure out of it, but is
"all that time fixed and certain; so
"neither is the eternal damnation of
"a reprobate ever uncertain during
"his passage through this world, but
"is, even before he is born, unaltera-
"bly fixed and sure. That he should

* The advocates of Calvin deny that the words
in italics are in his writings. They are, however,
fair inferences from what precedes them.

"perish,

" perish, is the very purpose for which
" he was created.

8thly, " Neither the best purposes,
" nor the best endeavours, nor the
" best acts of an elect, even after re-
" generation, are in any way prepara-
" tory to eternal salvation. On the
" contrary, as the elect people of God,
" under the Mosaical dispensation,
" were commanded to desist from
" their worldly occupations; so, in
" respect of all spiritual concerns, the
" elect under the gospel-dispensation
" are enjoined to bid adieu to all wills,
" works, and endeavours of their own,
" and to keep most religiously a per-
" petual Sabbath; that there may be
" free and ample scope within them
" for the operations of God's spirit.

9thly, "God, who of his own will
" and pleasure predestinated the elect
" to eternal salvation, *himself prepares*
" and

clusively, in which the names of about one hundred and fifty chapels, churches, and meeting houses, are enumerated, where the ministers whose names are subjoined are said *to preach the gospel.* The inference fairly is, that the gospel can only be heard in those specified places. The most learned, impressive, enlightened, and, I may add, valuable clergy of the establishment are not in this number; it is therefore obliquely denied that the gospel is preached by them.

If we ask these pretenders to superior light, what their gospel is, they will perhaps answer, in the language of a charming poet and worthy man, whose mind was unhappily warped by this prejudice, " It is the divinity of the " glorious reformation; I mean in con- " tradiction to Arminianism, and all " the isms that ever were broached in this

" this world of error and ignorance.
" The divinity of the reformation is
" called Calvinism, but injuriously; it
" has been that of the church of
" Christ in all ages. It is the divinity
" of Paul, and of Paul's master, who
" appeared to him in his way to Da-
" mascus *." According to this account,

---

* See Mr. Cowper's Life, vol. i. page 374.—
Does the letter from which this extract is taken
deserve praise, either for liberal ideas, enlarged information, or correct expression? When were the
peculiar doctrines of Calvin the religion of the
church, unless we bound the church to his *immediate partisans?* and to his *singular* tenets only can
the term Calvinism be justly applied. Calvin indeed pretended to shield them behind some mis-
constructed texts in St. Paul's epistles; but where
are they taught by Paul's master? Surely not when
he met him in the road to Damascus; for if this
great apostle was predestinated to be saved, that
astonishing vision was unnecessary. "Saul, Saul,
" why persecutest thou me?" is not a favourable
text for those who hold unconditional election, and
the impeccability of the elect. I should conceive
that

count, Luther, Melancthon, Erasmus, and Cranmer, were *not* reformers.

If we again inquire what are the tenets of Calvin, they will answer, (at least, they thus answer in books held out to ensnare the multitude), they are the doctrine of original sin, of the benefit and necessity of the atonement, of the Trinity, and of the assistances of the Holy Spirit. But these are the acknowledged doctrines of the church of England, for which she has been long assailed by her other opponents, who, with a degree of unfounded self-flattery similar to the evangelical, call themselves unitarian Christians; forgetting that the first article of our

that Mr. Cowper had only read one side of the controversy between the Arminians and Calvinists, and, like many others, confounded Calvin's very dangerous and distinguishing tenets, with those which he held in common with the other reformers.

church

church is a solemn profession of her belief in *one* God. But to return: to discover the reason for the controversy that we are now considering, we must search deeper, and we shall then find that, beside the particulars in which Calvin joined other protestants, the sombrous hue of his imagination, and his impatience of superiority, induced him to adopt singularities in doctrine and discipline. In the former, by reviving the exploded notions of the necessitarians; and in the latter, by establishing the presbyterian form of church-government, which, according to the concession of Mr. Le Clerc, was an anomaly in the Christian church. As the church of England preserved that form of ecclesiastical government which had been universal for fifteen hundred years, we might, without going further, infer that she

did

did not subscribe to the still more reprehensible parts of a system that has caused such a long, and, it is to be feared, incurable schism among the reformed churches. But these evangelical teachers affirm that she did; and it is these very doctrines, which in their opinion constitute that purity of the gospel, and those original principles of our church, which they are anxious to restore.

To repel this charge, not only from our present hierarchy, but from its venerable founders, many learned divines have stood forward, and manfully encountered a torrent of, not only professional but personal obloquy. In this contest, the names of Kipling, Daubeny, and Pearson, are especially celebrated. The first gentleman, in a small but irresistible pamphlet, plainly shows, by extracts from Calvin's works,

works, what these much-debated doctrines really are. A translation is subjoined *, which enables even the unlearned reader to determine how far they are supported by the authority of scripture, or corroborated by the public acts of our church. I hope the reverend author will pardon me, if, from a wish to introduce his valuable remarks to those to whom they may prove impenetrably defensive armour against the assaults of very vigilant adversaries, I take the liberty of making a large extract from this work. The knowledge of what strict Calvinism really is, must precede our attempt to justify our church from the charge of having apostatized. The

* They are given in Latin, with references to the works from which they are taken. Many evasory replies have been made to this pamphlet; but, the author believes, no clear refutation.

opinions of Calvin, which the Dean of Peterborough has translated, are,

First, "That omnipotent Being, "who has existed from all eternity, "after he had decreed to create man "in his own image, foreordained his "fall from original righteousness, by "which fall Adam's own nature would "be corrupted and depraved; and "viewed with the eye of prescience "the whole of Adam's offspring as a "mass of corruption and perdition.

2dly, "Among the vast multitude "of human beings composing this "mass of corruption and perdition, "Almighty God decreed, before the "foundation of the world, to bring "some to everlasting salvation, and "to damn all the rest eternally. This "decree or purpose of God is termed "by Calvin *predestination*; one being "thereby predestined to everlasting happi-

"happiness, and others condemned
" by it to everlasting misery.

3dly, "The objects of this decree
" are, not collective bodies of men, as
" Jews, Gentiles, Greeks, Romans;
" but individuals, as John, Matthew,
" Thomas, Peter, every one of whose
" fate after death is fixed by it, be-
" fore he is born, immutably and ever-
" lastingly.

4thly, "Adam, agreeably to the
" pre-ordinance of God (for we are
" now coming to the execution of his
" decrees), fell from innocence; and
" in consequence of this lapse, the
" whole of man's nature, as the Deity
" had foreseen and foreordained, un-
" derwent a complete change; it be-
" came corrupt, depraved, vicious;
" and every descendant of Adam,
" through his first parents' trans-
" gression, became a lost, a damned,
"and

" and accursed creature, and fuel for
" the flame of divine vengeance.

5thly, " From the birth of Abraham
" (if not from an earlier period) to
" this present time, the Deity, agree-
" ably to his eternal purpose and im-
" mutable decree, hath constantly
" been taking, and will continue daily
" to take, those individuals, whom he
" predestinated before the world be-
" gan to everlasting salvation, out of
" this mass of corruption and perdi-
" tion. All the rest, every one, whom
" he passeth by, and leaves in this state
" of corruption and perdition, he
" reprobates; *i. e.* abandons to wick-
" edness in this life, and will torture
" eternally in the next. Those, whom
" he makes choice of, selects, and
" segregates for salvation, are called
" *elect*. Those whom he leaves in
" their original pollution, abandons,
" and

" and will eternally torment, are called
" sometimes preterites, but most com-
" monly reprobates. By election and
" reprobation, is executed the immu-
" table decree of predestination.

6thly, "This discrimination made
" by the Deity between the elect and
" the reprobates is arbitrary; in no
" degree owing to any superior excel-
" lence, worth, or merit in the former,
" either present and actual, or future
" and foreseen, but wholly and solely
" to God's will and pleasure. He ex-
" tricates the elect from destruction
" for a demonstration of his goodness.
" He leaves the reprobates in their
" original state of perdition for a dis-
" play of his power and glory.

7thly, " After the elect are put
" under the custody and protection of
" Christ Jesus, *do what they will in this*
" life.

" *life**, they cannot fail of being finally
" saved, being under an immutable
" decree, and guarded by Omnipo-
" tence. The reprobates, how much
" *soever they may exert themselves for*
" *the purpose* *, cannot attain ever-
" lasting salvation, being *hindered*
" therefrom, and repelled by Almighty
" God. As the final salvation of the
" elect is in no degree doubtful, from
" their first entrance into this world
" to their departure out of it, but is
" all that time fixed and certain; so
" neither is the eternal damnation of
" a reprobate ever uncertain during
" his passage through this world, but
" is, even before he is born, unaltera-
" bly fixed and sure. That he should

* The advocates of Calvin deny that the words in italics are in his writings. They are, however, fair inferences from what precedes them.

" perish,

" perish, is the very purpose for which
" he was created.

8thly, " Neither the best purposes,
" nor the best endeavours, nor the
" best acts of an elect, even after re-
" generation, are in any way prepara-
" tory to eternal salvation. On the
" contrary, as the elect people of God,
" under the Mosaical dispensation,
" were commanded to desist from
" their worldly occupations; so, in
" respect of all spiritual concerns, the
" elect under the gospel-dispensation
" are enjoined to bid adieu to all wills,
" works, and endeavours of their own,
" and to keep most religiously a per-
" petual Sabbath; that there may be
" free and ample scope within them
" for the operations of God's spirit.

9thly, "God, who of his own will
" and pleasure predestinated the elect
" to eternal salvation, *himself prepares*

" and

"and fits them for it. The means
"used by him for this purpose are the
"preaching of his word and the ope-
"rations of his Spirit; both which
"together constitute what is denomi-
"nated special calling.

10thly, "The operations of God's
"Spirit are manifold. 1st, He forms
"in the elect a new understanding.
"2dly, He destroys their natural, and
"creates in them a new will. 3dly,
"Every propensity they may have,
"and every effort they may make, to
"do works pleasing and acceptable to
"God, is his. 4thly, He also it is,
"who begins, continues, and finishes
"every good work done by them, and
"who makes them persevere to the
"end in well doing. In each of
"these operations, he does not con-
"cur or co-operate with the elect,
"but is *sole and entire operator*;
"and

"and they are his instruments or
"organs.

11thly, "Though the elect may
"for a time resist the grace of God,
"they cannot finally overcome it.
"This grace is sovereign and invin-
"cible in its operation.

12thly, "God, who arbitrarily pre-
"destinated the reprobates to eternal
"destruction, himself also prepares
"and fits them for it. He does this
"by blinding their minds, hardening
"their hearts, stupifying their intel-
"lects, depriving them of the know-
"ledge of himself, withholding from
"them the influence of his Spirit,
"and delivering them over to the
"devil.

13thly, "The number of the elect
"is very small; the reprobates, of
"course, must be numerous.

Lastly, "The reprobates, those num-
"berless

"berless rational beings, whom Almighty God hath raised up for the illustration of his glory, are hateful to him. He also hates in proportion to their naughtiness the chosen few *."

I think, my dear Miss M——, I see you start at hearing such abominable tenets ascribed to the church of which you are an affectionate member; and perhaps for a moment you may wonder how you overlooked their absurdity and impiety, when you gave your hearty assent to the compendium of her doctrines. But be not alarmed; I hope these blasphemous dogmas do not constitute the gospel of *all* the one hundred and fifty meeting-houses, chapels, and churches, where *evangelical* ministers deliver their numer-

* Other reformers held the doctrine of absolute predestination, particularly Zuinglius.

ous lectures. I am certain, that such are not, nor ever were, the tenets of the church of England. Many who call themselves Calvinists do not go to these lengths; that is to say, though they adopt the name of calvinistic, as a rallying point for their party, they really are not disciples of Calvin; and among his professed followers, it is extremely difficult to persuade them to state their sentiments ingenuously when engaged in controversy; though in their extemporary addresses to their flock, they insist upon the absolute depravity and inertness of man; on the superiority of preaching, as a means of grace, over the written word of God or the sacraments; on sensible and immediate conversion, or regeneration; and on the impeccability, or, as I believe it is oftener called, assurance of the elect. On the 8th, 9th, 10th,

10th, and 11th dogmas, expounded by spiritual pride and enthusiasm, depend all the rhapsodies relating to the pangs of the new birth, wrestling with God, full conviction of future salvation, and entire change of affections and dispositions: this they suppose is contained in the scriptural expression regeneration; which, with them, is to turn from complete wickedness to sinless purity, though the early Christians confined this term to the sacrament of baptism, and the inward grace therein conveyed*. These opinions are founded chiefly on some detached texts of St. Paul's controversial epistles; in which he was debating a subject very different from that of the arbitrary election and reprobation of individual Christians, namely, the rejection of the Jewish nation, and the

* See Hey's Lectures, vol. iv. p. 292.

call

call of the gentile world. By separating these texts from their contexts, and by disdaining to attend to the general analogy of scripture, a saturnine imagination composed that extraordinary system which Dr. Jortin defines to consist of " human beings " without liberty, doctrines without " sense, faith without reason, and a " God without mercy."

I purpose, in a subsequent letter, to solicit your attention to a few instances of misquotation; to show that, by the method just alluded to, scripture may be made to prove whatever an artful polemic shall think fit. I must first rescue the church of England from the charge thus brought against her; and, happily, we are enabled to repel it by those articles, and liturgical formularies, which it has been so long the aim of our unitarian

adver-

adversaries to wrest from us. Had we been destitute of those authoritative standards of consistency and verity, and had we had nothing to appeal to but the writings of individuals, or the loose unweighed prayers and exhortations of private preachers, we could not have stood upon our defence with so much boldness. For, though the main body of our clergy have always resisted Calvin's doctrines, a few have leaned to his errors; and, it is melancholy to own, men of profound learning, as well as piety and goodness. This, however, is only a proof of human infirmity, and no more affects the general agreement, of our church, than St. Peter's temporizing opinions, respecting the necessity of Jewish observances, impeached the validity of the sentence pronounced in that case by the apostolical college.
A slight

A slight review of our articles and liturgy will be sufficient; in which I shall closely follow the steps of the venerable guide to whom I have just referred you *. It must be observed, that our liturgy is addressed to the people, our articles to the learned. In the latter, it was necessary to mention the opinions which were at that time much agitated; and as it was the wish of the founders of our church to enlarge its pale as widely as possible, many of those articles were couched in terms, to which all who were not absolute bigots might subscribe; if, therefore, in this mitigated and prudential confession of national faith, Calvinism be abjured †, what shall we say of the principles of our opponents,

* Dr. Kipling.

† By Calvinism, nothing can be meant but the the peculiar tenets which Calvin held. They who disown these are not Calvinists.

who

who endeavour to fix this stigma upon us?

I will first observe, that our articles uniformly assert the *universal possibility of salvation*; which is directly contrary to Calvin's declaration, that much the greater part of the human race are absolutely and unconditionally excluded from mercy. The 31st article affirms, "That the death of "Christ is a perfect redemption, pro-"pitiation, and satisfaction for *all* the "sins of the whole world, both ori-"ginal and actual;" which implies, not only that all Christions are offered eternal salvation; but that the heathen world are delivered from the imputation of the original guilt of Adam, and also from the eternal consequences of actual transgression, provided they frame their lives according to the imperfect knowledge which they possess.
Unless,

Unless, therefore, universal redemption can be reconciled with the utter reprobation of a vast majority of mankind, this article might decide the controversy. You well know, universal redemption does not mean that all men *will*, but that all men *may*, be saved.

On the doctrine of original sin, our church, in her 9th article, acknowledges that in every one born into the world, even in the regenerated (or baptized and obedient Christians), a propensity to evil still remains (the conscience of every one must attest this truth), which partakes so much of the nature of sin as to deserve damnation. Between *deserving* damnation from the justice of God, and being damned without the interposition of mercy, the difference is immense.

Calvin terms good works the fruits of

of grace; that is to say, he ascribes them solely to the over-ruling power of God. Our 12th article determines them to be " the fruits of faith;" that is, as being produced by our co-operation with our divine Assistant. This is farther specified in the 10th article, where the grace of God " is said to " work *with* us."

The 15th and 16th articles decide so pointedly against Calvin's idea of the impeccability of the elect, that to refer to them is sufficient to show that our church never held tenets so contrary to scripture, and so apt to engender the deadly sin of spiritual pride. I call it deadly, because there is so little hope that they who have fallen into it should ever experience a real conversion and true repentance.

The 17th article, which the Calvinists chiefly build upon, uses the term election,

election, indeed; but not as confined to particular persons. It speaks of the deliverance of the whole Christian world, not only from curse and damnation, but also God's intention to bring them to everlasting salvation, as vessels made for honour. While it encourages godly persons to rejoice, and to meditate on the high promises to which, as Christians, they are entitled; it dissuades curious and carnal persons from attempting to penetrate into those mysteries of God's secret counsels, by which the "devil doth "either thrust them into desperation "or into wretchlessness of unclean "living, no less perilous than despe-"ration." The word reprobation is not mentioned in this article; in Calvin's system, it ever stands opposed to election; the election therefore here meant cannot be Calvin's election. And that a conference was held between them and their opponents; in which the Calvinists attempted to establish several new articles, that had been agitated during the latter part of the reign of Queen Elizabeth. As a proof that the absolute predestinarians in those days were more ingenuous than their offspring, by confessing that our thirty-nine articles would not suit their purpose in their present form, I will subjoin a copy of the celebrated Lambeth articles, proposed by the Calvinists in the time of Queen Elizabeth, and brought forward at the Hampton-court conference, in the reign of her successor.

1st, God from eternity hath predestinated certain men to life; certain men he hath reprobated.

2d, The moving or efficient cause of predestination unto life, is not the foresight

its various offices. I will again take Dr. Kipling's pamphlet for my guide. Our absolution cannot accord with Calvinism; for would its compiler dare to affront the Deity, by ascribing to him attributes directly contrary to what he believed him to possess? Calvin's God *desires and ordains* the death of myriads of sinners, to whom he denies all power " of turning from their " wickedness." The prayer of St. Chrysostom, the collect for the 4th Sunday after Trinity, the petition to be delivered from eternal damnation in the litany, the blessing which concludes it, every sentence which testifies that at the last judgment all men shall give an account of their works, the first prayer in the office of baptism, the exhortation which succeeds the gospel in that office, the prayer which consecrates the water, and the request that *whoever* is dedicated to God by the priestly office and ministry, may be everlastingly *rewarded*, are anti-calvinistic; and, not to multiply examples without bound, every prayer which entreats an increase of virtue, or preservation from guilt, is decidedly hostile to these terrible ideas.

The Calvinists, when hard pressed for reasons to justify God's justice in thus arbitrarily fore-dooming his creatures to perdition, reply, we cannot say what effect this may have on probationary beings in other worlds. In answer, it is acknowledged the effect may be powerful; and the argument would be valid, if those beings at the same time perceived that the wicked man perishes on *account* of his wickedness, and not by an *over-ruling* decree which he cannot withstand.

To

To those who objected to this system, that it renders prayer not only useless but absurd, Calvin was accustomed to answer, that as no individual knows whether he is elect or reprobate, therefore supplication must be permissible. It should seem as if he had not then risen to that degree of enthusiasm to which his followers have since attained; for, to know this, comes under those terms of experience and illumination, to which they now so generally pretend. But whatever he might urge on this head in respect to private prayer, it cannot reconcile the propriety of such general addresses as the confession, in which God is implored to forgive all sinners, or the entreaty that he would "have mercy "upon *all* men, Jews, Turks, Infidels, "and Heretics;" or that the sins of dying men, which, if pardoned at all, have already been pardoned by an eternal and irreversible decree, " may be " done away by his mercy in Christ " Jesus, and their pardon sealed in " heaven before they go hence, and " be no more seen."

Thus refuted, our adversaries ought, in propriety, to have confessed their mistake, and renounced the charge; but another subterfuge remains: they insist, that our first reformers were Calvinists. If the assurance of their own words can avail, Cranmer, Hooper, Latimer, and Ridley, were decidedly anti-calvinists*. History confirms their testimony, by recording their conduct. It is known, that the venerable archbishop, to whom we look up as the builder of our Sion, *rejected* the assistance of Calvin, and *solicited* the advice

* See Anti-Jacobin Review for September, 1803.

the scaffold; the house of lords was abolished, its members massacred, or exiled; the gentry ruined; the clergy sequestered; and the country became the seat of civil war, the sport of contending factions, the scene of fraud and oppression, where God was insulted with hypocritical worship, and man preyed on man. The prime mover of this vast machine of mischief closed his guilty career unrepentant for the numberless murders and perjuries which his ambition had prompted him to commit; true, to the last, to the dreadful tenets of his faith, and in full persuasion that he was an elect and chosen vessel, so entitled to eternal glory, that no crimes could forfeit his claim.

Allow me to relieve your fatigued attention, by directing it to the death of a gentleman, who, I think, was the

that a conference was held between them and their opponents; in which the Calvinists attempted to establish several new articles, that had been agitated during the latter part of the reign of Queen Elizabeth. As a proof that the absolute predestinarians in those days were more ingenuous than their offspring, by confessing that our thirty-nine articles would not suit their purpose in their present form, I will subjoin a copy of the celebrated Lambeth articles, proposed by the Calvinists in the time of Queen Elizabeth, and brought forward at the Hampton-court conference, in the reign of her successor.

1st, God from eternity hath predestinated certain men to life; certain men he hath reprobated.

2d, The moving or efficient cause of predestination unto life, is not the foresight

despair, which at last swallowed up all his literary and social talents, and almost petrified his benevolent heart. The idea of his utter rejection by God, was attended by a belief that every attempt to counteract it would but aggravate the severity of his doom. He did not, therefore, dare to go to any place of worship, nor even to pray. The last of his posthumous compositions, published by Mr. Hayley, entitled the Cast-away, when read with this clue, appears to me the most affecting lines that ever flowed from the pen of genius; and it pleads more strongly than a thousand arguments against permitting such unworthy ideas of the Almighty to enter into our minds. May the example of a Cowper's despair not plead in vain! then shall we cease to lament the years which the amiable, but, in this point, bewildered sufferer spent

not communicated, to all men, by which they may be saved if they will.

What horrid blasphemy!

8th, No man can come unto Christ, unless it shall be given unto him, and unless the Father draw him; *and all men are not drawn by the Father.*

9th, It is not in the will or power of every man to be saved.

The difference of these articles from those of our church need not be pointed out, nor will I expatiate on their unscriptural absurdity and dreadful tendency. There is a degree of clumsy management in the 8th; which, considering the care with which they were framed, is surprising. It begins with a text of scripture, which is made to speak as they would have it, by an *absolute addition* of their own, for which there is not the least authority. But to return to historical testimony: though

urged in proof of the prevalence of Calvinism in his reign; for this ostensible countenance was merely a vizard to cover that monarch's design of introducing popery, under the fraudulent pretence of universal toleration. The subsequent reign is accused of patronizing errors of a different sort; and the style of merely moral exhortation, adopted by some of our clergy, has been urged, as a reason for the revival of Calvinism, under the name of Methodism, about the middle of the last century. During the period in which our church is charged with having kept the great doctrines of our religion too much out of sight, she still, by her articles and liturgy, retained her original tenets and integral constitution. It is remarkable, that those eminent divines* whose vindications

---

* Tillotson, Sherlock, Seed, Warburton, Rogers, Waterland, Jones, &c.

King Charles the First's reign, Calvinism indeed triumphed; but the victory was not gained by reason; the sword was the terrible arbitrator; the king and the primate bled upon

the decrees of God are conditional, in consequence of foreseen faith and virtue, or foreseen infidelity and wickedness. On universal redemption, he says, that though Christ made atonement for all mankind, none but those who believe in him can claim that benefit. On the corruption of man, it is his opinion, that we are incapable of doing or saying any thing good, without the regenerating power of the Holy Ghost; yet divine grace may be resisted, and rendered ineffectual, by the perverse will of the impenitent sinner. That it is the grace of God which preserves us in a regenerate state; but that the righteous may lose their justifying faith and die in their sins.

At the synod of Dort, summoned in 1618, on account of this controversy, our divines bore public and decided testimony to the doctrines of universal redemption and free agency; and the king, with the greatest part of our clergy, disapproved the proceedings of that synod, and preferred Arminius to Calvin.

the

shop's Bible, published in the year 1572, just after the ratification of our articles. These were both acts of authority; and, as such, may be properly appealed to, in testimony of the real doctrine of our church. With a few miscellaneous remarks we will dismiss the subject of strict Calvinism,—I wish I could say to the oblivion that it deserves.

We will first observe, that preaching Calvinism, as Christianity, must lessen the influence of pure religion, except in weak and depraved minds. One of the offices of reason, as we have before remarked, is, to judge by the tenor of the message, whether it comes from God. Now, whatever diminishes our sense of moral obligation, is contrary to those preconceived notions of the justice and goodness of the Deity which revelation is intended to confirm.

only *eminent* instance of a person's taking the dark side of Calvinism, by believing himself to be a reprobate, and incapable of the mercy of God; I mean the humble, melancholy, and too keenly susceptible Cowper. In early life, when he had just recovered from a dreadful mental disease, he fell into the society of some well-meaning people who had adopted those unfortunate notions. The grateful bard, attached by their kindness, united himself to them by the strongest ties of affection, and suffered his enlarged understanding to be warped by their system. His biographer does not state at what period of his life the fatal notion of his own reprobation was imprinted on his mind; but knowing that this was the case, we cannot wonder at his frequent fits of despondency, nor at that frightful lapse into intense despair,

despair, which at last swallowed up all his literary and social talents, and almost petrified his benevolent heart. The idea of his utter rejection by God, was attended by a belief that every attempt to counteract it would but aggravate the severity of his doom. He did not, therefore, dare to go to any place of worship, nor even to pray. The last of his posthumous compositions, published by Mr. Hayley, entitled the Cast-away, when read with this clue, appears to me the most affecting lines that ever flowed from the pen of genius; and it pleads more strongly than a thousand arguments against permitting such unworthy ideas of the Almighty to enter into our minds. May the example of a Cowper's despair not plead in vain! then shall we cease to lament the years which the amiable, but, in this point, bewildered sufferer spent in agonizing woe; the innocence of his life, and the amiable tenor of his writings, seem to justify the resplendent vision of hope, which depictures him as awakening from his long night of wretchedness, at the rapturous sound of " Well done, good and faith-" ful servant, enter thou into the joy " of thy Lord !"

To return to our historical detail. It is not even pretended, that Calvinism predominated during the reign of Charles the IId. The resignation of the non-conformist clergy during that period proceeded no less from their abhorrence of episcopacy, than from their dissatisfaction at the *doctrines* of the restored church, whose funds they had appropriated to themselves during the suspension of her lawful ministers. I believe the temporary favour which King James the IId showed to the dissenters was never urged in proof of the prevalence of Calvinism in his reign; for this ostensible countenance was merely a vizard to cover that monarch's design of introducing popery, under the fraudulent pretence of universal toleration. The subsequent reign is accused of patronizing errors of a different sort; and the style of merely moral exhortation, adopted by some of our clergy, has been urged, as a reason for the revival of Calvinism, under the name of Methodism, about the middle of the last century. During the period in which our church is charged with having kept the great doctrines of our religion too much out of sight, she still, by her articles and liturgy, retained her original tenets and integral constitution. It is remarkable, that those eminent divines* whose vindications

* Tillotson, Sherlock, Seed, Warburton, Rogers, Waterland, Jones, &c.

of the mysteries of our holy faith, have immort ized their own names, and that of their country, flourished at this very period, when, according to the representations of our enemies, nothing but the oratory of a Whitfield, or the labours of a Wesley, could have saved us from the total loss of Christian principles and vital religion.

It is not necessary to subjoin any additional proo s to th above justification of our church from the charge of Calvinism; but as partial election is the key-stone on which that system is built, I will just mention, as a corroborative testimony, that our church always held the contrary doctrine of universal redemption, or that every man has it in his power to be saved. I will refer you to the homilies, and especially to the preface to them, and to Archbishop Parker's preface to that translation of scripture called the Bishop's Bible, published in the year 1572, just after the ratification of our articles. These were both acts of authority; and, as such, may be properly appealed to, in testimony of the real doctrine of our church. With a few miscellaneous remarks we will dismiss the subject of strict Calvinism,—I wish I could say to the oblivion that it deserves.

We will first observe, that preaching Calvinism, as Christianity, must lessen the influence of pure religion, except in weak and depraved minds. One of the offices of reason, as we have before remarked, is, to judge by the tenor of the message, whether it comes from God. Now, whatever diminishes our sense of moral obligation, is contrary to those preconceived notions of the justice and goodness of the Deity which revelation is intended to confirm.

firm. To say, therefore, that the elect cannot sin, or, what is nearly the same, that their sins will not make them *forfeit* divine favour, or, that the reprobate, do what they will, cannot *attain* it, impeaches the attributes of God, and weakens the moral feeling in man. A confused understanding may blunder upon this notion, and really believe it to be tenable; but a depraved heart will cling to it as a defence of its own enormities.

On the other hand, no good can arise from maintaining these doctrines. If an *irreversible* decree save the elect and condemn the reprobate, faith and virtue are no ways necessary to the future blessedness or misery of either; and if belief in the great doctrines of redemption are not requisite, such acquiescence in the opinions of Calvin cannot be indispensible. A Soci-

Socinian, a Papist, a Jew, a Turk, or an Infidel, if previously *ordained* to bliss, has the same title to glory as the most determined propagator of unconditional election.

All controversies on points which are mutually allowed to be not essential to salvation are much to be deprecated, as they engender violent animosities, instead of that spirit of brotherly love which was intended to be the distinguishing token of Christianity. They unsettle the faith of weak minds, who in a variety of opinions know not which to prefer; and they weaken the influence of our faith among infidels, who may justly reproach us with not suffering our principles of unity to influence our practice. The seventeenth chapter of St. John, which I before quoted, seems also to justify me in observing, that

that these dissentions retard the extension of our faith among heathen nations.

Some may here ask, is the blame of controversy then all on one side? Why does not the church give up these disputed points, and adopt what her adversaries require? It may be answered, that in these realms she is the constituted guardian of the national religion, and is therefore legally *empowered* to execute the divine command of " contending earnestly for " the faith once delivered to the " saints." The forcible arguments by which she proves these tenets to be founded on a misinterpretation of holy writ, and particularly on a misconception of St. Paul's design in his epistles to the Romans and Galatians, which seem by St. Peter's account to have given rise to early controversies in the church, would take more space than I can allow to this subject. The authors to which I have referred you will supply them. I have only endeavoured to recapitulate that part of their labours which vindicates our establishment from having *renounced* her original doctrines.

Before I conclude this letter, two circumstances more must be observed. Even if we sacrificed truth to peace, unity could not be obtained. The nearer we advance to Calvinism, the further we retreat from Socinianism. The total annihilation of our church, (may God, in his mercy, avert that evil!) would not promote the universal accord for which all parties affect to wish. Indeed, from the moderation of her tenets, she is considered by impartial foreigners to be the rallying point at which it may be hoped

her

her contrarious opponents will one day meet. By extending her influence, we cement the bond of union; by lessening the number of her members, we recruit the armies of contention.

An established church never *begins* controversy. Having gained the desired ascendancy, she rests secure. Her errors proceed from supineness, not from activity. They who wish to obtain the eminence that she occupies, recommend themselves to those who are impatient of controul, or desirous of change, by complaints against her tyranny or apostacy. To the first of these clamours it may be answered, that no society of Christians can assemble without adopting various rules and forms that are not enjoined in scripture; that the majority here, as in other cases, must have power to bind the minority; and that the decisions

cisions of the former, when sanctioned by the civil power, possess the obligation of law, to which every member of the community is bound to yield obedience; unless the required terms of communion are evidently contrary to the law of God. A change of spiritual masters would only produce a change in the manner of government, not in the measure of submission; and I quote from a known enemy to our church, when I ask, " Would not the "loins of an imposing Independent, " or Anabaptist, be as heavy as the " loins of an imposing Prelate or " Presbyter*?

With a sentiment so much in favour of acquiescence in the present order of things, from one who was so little to be suspected of partiality to epis-

* Henry Cromwell's letter to Fleetwood. See Elegant Epistles, page 261.

copal supremacy, I conclude this letter. In my next, I must notice symptoms of hostility from a quarter, whence, according to their professions, we should look for the most cordial co-operation in the great work of promoting the eternal salvation of our fellow-creatures. The task in which we are engaged is irksome; but the prospect of the times announces its sad necessity. In the hope that my labours are welcome to you, and may be useful to others,

     I remain, &c.

END OF VOL. I.

T. Bensley, Printer,
Bolt Court, Fleet Street, London.

Lightning Source UK Ltd.
Milton Keynes UK
UKHW020808220119
335989UK00010B/777/P